The Children's Film Foundation
History and Legacy

Robert Shail

BFI palgrave

A BFI book published by Palgrave

For the kids of Lawrence Weston School, Bristol (Class of 1979)

First published in 2016 by
PALGRAVE

on behalf of the

BRITISH FILM INSTITUTE
21 Stephen Street, London W1T 1LN
www.bfi.org.uk

There's more to discover about film and television through the BFI. Our world-renowned archive, cinemas, festivals, films, publications and learning resources are here to inspire you.

PALGRAVE in the UK is an imprint of Macmillan Publishers Limited, registered in England, company number 785998, of 4 Crinan Street, London N1 9XW. Palgrave Macmillan in the US is a division of St Martin's Press LLC, 175 Fifth Avenue, New York, NY 10010. Palgrave is a global imprint of the above companies and is represented throughout the world. Palgrave® and Macmillan® are registered trademarks in the United States, the United Kingdom, Europe and other countries.

Cover image: *Johnny on the Run* (Lewis Gilbert, 1953), International Realist
Images courtesy BFI National Archive

Designed and set by couch
Printed in the UK

This book is printed on paper suitable for recycling and made from fully managed and sustained forest sources. Logging, pulping and manufacturing processes are expected to conform to the environmental regulations of the country of origin.

British Library Cataloguing-in-Publication Data
A catalogue record for this book is available from the British Library
A catalog record for this book is available from the Library of Congress

ISBN 978–1–84457–858–0

Contents

Acknowledgments

I would like to acknowledge the individuals and institutions who helped make this book possible. For their assistance in the principal archive work, my thanks go to the British Library, the British Film Institute, the National Library of Wales, the British Board of Film Classification and the library of the University of Wales, Trinity St David. For invaluable assistance in researching the films, my thanks go to Doug Weir and Marianthi Makra of the BFI and to the staff of the National Screen and Sound Archive of Wales. Also to Sonia Mullett, formerly with the BFI.

I would like to thank the following who were kind enough to provide me with interviews: Gerry O'Hara; Bernard Ashley; John Krish; John Tully; Harley Cokeliss; Pam Poll; Monica Sims; Claude Gresset; Iain Smith; Greg Childs; and Anna Home.

A huge debt of gratitude is owed to all the people who agreed to take part in the interviews and questionnaires which form the basis of Chapter 4; it was a joy to hear all the wonderful memories of time spent in darkened auditoriums on a Saturday morning. Special thanks to Alex Jones and James Taylor-Godard for their extended interviews.

Further thanks go to Dr Matt Briggs for his help in getting this project off the ground, along with the three professors: James Chapman; Duncan Petrie; and Andrew Spicer.

My personal thanks go to Steve Gerrard for his support, to my daughter, Gwen, for her invaluable assessment of the films, and to my matchless wife, Cerri, for far too many things to list here.

This book was supported by the Leverhulme Trust who have my gratitude.

Introduction

At approximately 10am on every Saturday morning across the UK, thousands of children made their eager way to their nearest cinema. After paying a few pennies, they would enter the dark arena with their friends or siblings and wait for the show to start. With the curtain up, they would find themselves in a world of cowboys and indians, of spaceships and laser guns, and of crazy cartoon antics. Sometimes, however, they were also confronted by the sight of children of their own age, looking and speaking remarkably like they did. These kids were often involved in adventures that took them on a hunt for buried treasure, or put them up against a gang of desperate bank robbers. These stories always began in the same way, with the sound of church bells and the sight of pigeons rising into the air in Trafalgar Square.

The latter image was the logo of a unique organisation: the Children's Film Foundation (CFF). From its creation in 1951 until the early 1980s, the CFF produced feature films, comedy shorts, cliff-hanger serials and assorted other items for showing at Saturday film clubs. Its work introduced film-going to generations of British children. Later it became the Children's Film and Television Foundation (CFTF) and its productions were also seen on the small screen. In its final years it moved from film-making into script development and then took on an advisory role as it struggled to find funding. More recently it changed name again and is now the campaigning organisation known as the Children's Media Foundation (CMF), which champions the interests of young media users in the UK. Apart from making a huge impact on the cultural and social lives of children in Britain, the Foundation was an experiment which sought to demonstrate the power of film to positively influence the citizens of tomorrow. It also served as a training ground for technicians, as well as young actors (many of whom went on to have successful careers as adults).

This book sets out to describe the activities, impact and legacy of the Foundation. Chapter 1 outlines its history, drawing on primary documentation to deliver a breakdown of its historical development, including the context in which it was established. Chapter 2 presents a chronological assessment of a representative example of the films which it produced across that history, enabling that development to be seen through its material products. The films also provide a remarkable visual record of wider social change in Britain. Chapter 3 gathers together a number of interviews with personnel who worked for the CFF behind the camera, including writers, directors and producers, as well as key staff from the Foundation's offices. The stars of the CFF films have not been interviewed here as these have been the subject of a good deal of media coverage elsewhere. Chapter 4 is drawn from a series of interviews and questionnaires carried out with former audience members, along with one or two individuals who helped to run the Saturday clubs. Their memories afford a vivid snapshot of what it was like to take part in an important cultural phenomenon of postwar Britain. The final chapter brings the story up to date by looking at the activities of the CMF, which has inherited the mantle of the Foundation. Its campaigning work raises a number of issues that were central to the original ethos of the Foundation and these are discussed in this chapter. Appendices at the rear of the book supply a chronology of the Foundation's output, a selection of further reading materials and a list of the cinemas mentioned by those who took part in the audience survey.

The intention of this book is principally to provide a detailed chronicle of the Foundation's work throughout its lifespan. In doing so a number of key themes and questions emerged. What were the achievements of the Foundation, and the Saturday clubs which it supported? Can cinema really influence the moral development of young people as they become the adult citizens of a future Britain? Can a case be made for maintaining the legacy of the Foundation today? And following on from that question, is it important to protect media production for children that is distinctively British? By the book's conclusion some of these themes will be reconsidered in light of the media context of today. Public interest in the cinematic depiction of children and childhood remains high with many books on the subject,[1] a recent retrospective in *Sight & Sound* magazine,[2] and the release of Mark Cousins's documentary *A Story of Children and Film* (2014), but this volume offers something different, a study of an organisation that made films for children, not just about them. Above all else, this book is a celebration, albeit a sometimes critical one, of a special institution.

Notes

1. See, for example, Neil Sinyard, *Children in the Movies* (London: B. T. Batsford, 1992).
2. See *Sight & Sound* vol. 24 no. 4 (April 2014).

1 The Story of the Foundation

The story of the Children's Film Foundation spans four decades and provides a fascinating snapshot of social and cultural change in Britain, particularly in relation to evolving attitudes towards children and childhood. In their films, those at the CFF tried to address children in their own terms and at eye level, but often ended up reflecting their own conceptions of childhood as much as they responded to the children's viewpoint. Along the way issues such as class, gender roles and ethnic diversity were reflected in the Foundation's output, albeit largely unconsciously, with the CFF sometimes lagging behind the wider society and then rushing to catch up in its later years. The Foundation's story also reveals much about the changing nature of film production in Britain as the organisation drew on personnel from the industry both behind and in front of the camera. Changes in the financial structure of the industry and the vagaries of various governments in their attitude to cinema are reflected in its history. The rapidly growing impact of television was another key factor, with the Foundation initially keeping its distance but eventually being forced to acknowledge the altered environment in which it worked, a fact finally reflected in its metamorphosis into the Children's Film and Television Foundation in the early 1980s. Just as it needed to update its storytelling methods over the course of thirty-five years, the images it created mirrored a nation's changing fortunes, seen at first in the 1950s still recovering from the deprivations of war and then experiencing successive economic fluctuations. The comparatively empty streets of the postwar era are soon filled with parked cars, as high-rise blocks appear on former bombsites and are then demolished themselves to make way for newer developments. Short back-and-sides is replaced by long hair for both sexes, and shirts and ties disappear as flared jeans become de rigueur. A whole history of everyday life is played out for us in the grain of these films.

This is the story of a unique institution, much imitated subsequently around the world, but pioneering in its own way. The stories it chose to tell reached succeeding generations of British children and those beyond the UK, leaving a mark into adulthood. The following account draws on archival materials and press coverage of the Foundation held by the British Film Institute. Some of the Foundation's records still remain unexamined and awaiting full access but the materials currently available yield more than sufficient sources to construct a detailed account of its work.

Children's cinema before the CFF

In order to understand how the Children's Film Foundation came into being we need to briefly trace the development of children's film-going in Britain through to the 1940s. In doing so we can see how pressures grew on the industry to regulate the way it catered to a young audience and provided a context for the creation of the CFF. According to Terry Staples, whose book *All Pals Together: The Story of Children's Cinema* (1997) remains an invaluable guide to the history of children's film-going in the UK, the first screenings specifically devoted to children can be traced back to at least 1900.[1] As he puts it, 'the showmen's approach was straightforwardly commercial and exploitative', with marketing specifically directed at the target audience. Children's screenings began to proliferate as cinema managers realised that this was an advantageous way of making use of an auditorium in timeslots that would otherwise be empty. This explains in part the tendency to screen films for children on Saturday mornings, generally an idle time for most cinemas. The other reason was that it was a time when most children were free to attend; screenings on a Sunday morning would have been likely to provoke disapproval from church groups. School holidays could provide further screening opportunities. The more formal organisation of a regular Saturday morning screening specifically for children, rather than an ad hoc arrangement, is usually credited to the Granada chain and began in 1927.

An early aspect of these screenings, which was to become crucial for the creation of the CFF, was the insufficient care taken by some cinema managers regarding both the content of the screenings and, on occasions, the actual organisation of them. Failures in the latter led to a series of appalling accidents, including one during a touring cinema show at the Harvey Institute in Barnsley on Saturday, 11 January 1908, where sixteen children suffocated to death in a mêlée on a stairwell. The problem persisted unabated right through the 1920s until the worst cinema disaster involving children took place on 31 December 1929 at the Glen, Paisley when seventy-five children died in a panic following a minor fire in the projection booth; only one member of staff was supervising the screening at the time. These disasters brought public attention to the unregulated nature of children's screenings. As the 1930s progressed, and such incidents fortunately ceased, these understandable anxieties were overtaken by concerns about the content of the shows.

Staples meticulously charts the increasing furore over what was being screened to children from 1909 through to the early 1940s. This concern was initially voiced via local authorities using the Cinematograph Act of 1909, which had actually been designed to improve physical safety in cinema buildings, to refuse licences on issues of programme content, thereby widening the remit of the Act to include the moral health of patrons. An attempt by the industry to challenge this was defeated in the High Court with the consequence that the floodgates were opened to a range of individuals and pressure groups who besieged their local licensing authorities with complaints over the screening of material they saw as inappropriate.[2] Many of the organisations pushing for reform had a specific religious agenda and focused on what they saw as the untoward effects of cinema on the behaviour of children. They were particularly alarmed at what they perceived as the increasing lack of respect shown by youngsters towards traditional values and those in authority. It is certainly the case that there were cinema managers who paid little attention to what was screened at the children's shows, often simply shifting films over from their general screenings without much thought. The 'U' certificate issued by the British Board of Film Censors (BBFC),[3] now often associated specifically with children's films, was then widely used for any film which did not fall into the only other available category, the 'A' certificate, which served to indicate content more suitable for adults. The result was that the content of 'U' films could be very varied. However, the objections raised often reveal more about the anxieties of the adult groups making them than the actual nature of the films. A common target, for example, was the increasingly large number of films coming into the UK from the US whose only sin appears to have been that they weren't British.[4]

A series of public inquiries into the content of children's screenings followed and continued throughout the interwar era. One of the first was undertaken by the National Council for Public Morality in 1917 and focused on children in London. Its report actually came down on the side of the industry, making only gentle recommendations that more films be made with children specifically in mind. The arrival of sound at the end of the 1920s seemed to intensify concern and no fewer than five different inquiries were mounted in London, Birmingham, Sheffield, Birkenhead and Edinburgh. These inquiries were largely inconclusive, resulting in often contradictory recommendations but, as Terry Staples shows, critics of children's screenings could select from the different reports the elements which seemed to support their case and use them judiciously to further their cause.[5] This included some Conservative MPs who kept the controversy rumbling on across the decade. However, the only two concrete regulatory changes to take place were a Home Office circular in 1933, which urged cinemas in England and Wales to display film classifications more prominently and a recommendation to the BBFC to introduce a new category for horror films, the 'H' certificate, which it duly instigated.

Nonetheless, by the late 1930s some producers and exhibitors had started to respond to the general climate of approbation by making and/or showing films aimed exclusively at children. A good number of these were sponsored or organised by religious groups but they also included the Granada chain run by Sidney Bernstein. This scheme only ran for just over a year between 1928 and 1929 across a handful of cinemas in London – it seems to have petered out due to the unpopularity of the selected films – but it was effectively a model for the system which would be supported by the CFF from 1951 onwards. Ironically, the most influential model for the development of children's screenings in the UK actually came from the US in the form of the Mickey Mouse Club. The particular innovation of the Club, which was subsequently franchised in Britain, was the inclusion in its programmes of a mix of short and feature items, along with competitions and other entertainments often overseen by a compere. Care was taken to select films designed to appeal to the intended audience and potential criticism was offset by such conceits as beginning every screening with the singing of the national anthem. Crucially, the Mickey Mouse Club both appeased the moral campaigners and provided a new stream of revenue for cinemas.

A number of British cinema chains began to ape this format, including the Union circuit. This was then taken over by the ABC cinema chain, which developed Union's clubs into the ABC Minors from 1937 onwards. Many of the respondents to the audience survey which I carried out for this study (see Chapter 4) could still recite word for word the song of the ABC Minors club:

> We are the boys and girls well known as
> Minors of the ABC,
> And every Saturday all line up
> To see the films we like and shout aloud with glee,
> We like to laugh and have our sing-song
> Just a happy crowd are we-e
> We're all pals together
> We're Minors of the ABC!

The success of the ABC Minors, with its membership cards, sing-alongs, prizes and well-selected programmes, soon led to imitations from other chains such as Gaumont. The Odeon chain tried its own version but then took the expedient step of simply licensing the American Mickey Mouse Clubs for the UK market. It was during this period, and through the years of World War II, that the basic format for the Saturday morning clubs solidified into a formula. The elements which made this up will be discussed later in this chapter.

The development of an organised system of children's film screenings during the 1930s indicated the commercial viability of such a model but did little to stop the flow of criticism or the plethora of public inquiries, which ran on well into the 1940s.[6] Characteristic of these is an article published in *The Times* in 1946 written by the sociologist J. P. Mayer. Many of Mayer's criticisms were the same as had been voiced for the previous twenty years, but a key one was his assertion that simply not enough films were being made with a specific audience of children in mind.[7] Further regionally based reports followed, along with more letters to *The Times*, and a conference organised in part by the British Film Institute. Concerns were intensified by the more general focus of the press in the immediate postwar period on the problem of juvenile delinquency. The debate eventually reached the House of Commons in the winter of 1946, although there remained no consensus over what action, if any, should actually be taken. There appears to have been little desire within government for any form of legislative intervention.

The industry itself, however, was increasingly keen to forestall such an eventuality and therefore took steps to respond to the public criticism. Central to this response was J. Arthur Rank who, by the early war period, had acquired ownership of the Gaumont chain to put alongside his Odeons, giving him a national network of cinemas totalling 600, most of which had Saturday children's clubs. In 1943 he established the unified Odeon National Cinema Club with its motto of 'Uplift with a smile' and Mickey Mouse was banished. With his background as a Methodist and a Sunday School teacher, it is perhaps unsurprising that he recognised the clubs' potential as a moral beacon, as well as the commercial possibilities. As Geoffrey Macnab puts it, Rank 'wanted to entertain the youngsters, lure them to the cinema at a tender age so that the habit stuck ... thereby helping to bolster his box-office receipts', while also being keen 'to inculcate youth with "good Christian values"'[8]. The new clubs the Rank Organisation created had their own song and a creed printed on the back of membership cards which included telling the truth, obeying your parents, being kind to animals, and helping to 'make this great country of ours a better place to live in'.

Initially the programme content of Rank's wartime clubs doesn't appear to have changed much, hence the continued criticism, but in 1943 he began the first tentative steps to remedy this. Working from an initial script by Mary Cathcart Borer (who would go on to work for the Foundation) called *The Bicycle*, one of Rank's network of companies, Gaumont-British Instructional (GBI), was given the task of producing a worthy ten-minute film for children extolling the virtues of honesty. The film itself, now entitled *Tom's Ride*, was released to the clubs in 1944 and, in its own modest way, laid the foundation for what eventually became the CFF. It told the story of how young Tom finds a mislaid notecase containing £5 and, having resisted the temptation to keep the money himself, returns it to its rightful owner (after an exciting bicycle pursuit) with the help of the police. Even if *Tom's Ride* 'bemused and excited its young audience, combining a riveting chase sequence with a pious homily',[9] Rank deemed the film a success and consequently called in Mary Field to head up the new Children's Film Department (CFD) within GBI; Field was to become probably the single most influential person in the history of the CFF. She had trained as a teacher and historian but in the early 1920s had entered the film industry as an advisor on historical subjects for British Instructional, before being appointed education manager. She made her name on the pioneering natural history series *Secrets of Nature* (1922–33) and went on to make the *Secrets of Life* (1934–50) series for GBI, along with a number of other educational documentaries aimed at schools. During the war Field worked on government information films. Her background couldn't have been more appropriate, particularly in terms of her commitment to the educational value of films, although she herself never had children. She remained in charge of the CFD until its closure in 1950. The CFD produced short documentaries, cartoons, a series called *Our Club Magazine* (an idea which the CFF revived later in the 1950s) and one more ten-minute drama, *Sports Day* (1944), intended to warn against cruelty to animals and again scripted by Mary Cathcart Borer.

Unfortunately, the response from interested parties to these early efforts was almost uniformly hostile, the general view being that, in their attempt to be morally uplifting, they had adopted a painfully snobbish and patronising tone. A rethink was required and the desire to foreground entertainment values was immediately evident in the next short drama film, *Jean's Plan* (1946), in which the heroine is mainly concerned with thwarting jewel thieves. This time both critical and audience responses were positive, even if the moral wasn't quite as clear as before. A five-part serial followed, called *Dusty Bates* (1946), which featured a juvenile Anthony Newley and the CFD began to import appropriate films from foreign producers like the National Film Board of Canada (again a strategy later taken up by the CFF). By 1947 the unit had changed its name to Children's Entertainment Films (CEF) and had funded the first full-length feature produced in English specifically for children. *Bush Christmas* (1947) was an Australian-set adventure story which proved to be a considerable success. Written and directed by Ralph Smart, it integrated its message of racial tolerance and understanding into an entertaining narrative. The CEF went on to make several features in the UK and employed a number of personnel who were to work with the CFF, including writers Pat Latham and Mary Cathcart Borer and the directors Don Chaffey and Lewis Gilbert. Despite maintaining a steady production rate right through until 1950, including making films on location in Europe as well as at home, the CEF was never able to produce anywhere near enough product to meet the needs of Rank's own Gaumont-Odeon chain, let alone attract the attention of the ABC Minors or any of the independents, which remained suspicious of its output. The major problem was the cost of production in comparison to the modest returns possible. Despite this, the CEF had provided a potential model for what might be achieved. Over the next eighteen months this was to result in the creation of the CFF.

The birth of the Children's Film Foundation, 1950–2

A crucial step in the creation of the CFF was the publication on 5 May 1950 of Wheare's Departmental Committee Report into children and cinema. To the surprise of many, it came to the broad conclusion that Saturday cinema clubs for children were actually a good thing – 'entertainment of this kind seems to us worthy of all the help that can be given it' – even if some of the content was not to the report's liking. Even more importantly, it held the CEF up as an exemplar for what could be done with appropriate support.[10]

Meanwhile Mary Field had made her own, somewhat idiosyncratic attempt to further the case for public sector investment by undertaking an experimental survey. She was keen to show that the films made especially for children by the CEF had more impact than ones produced commercially. As early as 1947 she had made audio recordings of audience reactions to test this hypothesis and in 1948 she tried to obtain visual evidence by taking still photographs during a live screening with the aid of a flash, something which didn't go down terribly well with the young audience being photographed. In 1951, after a year's sojourn at the BBFC and just prior to becoming the first chief executive of the CFF, she embarked on a similar experiment but this time with an infrared camera. The project was funded by the Carnegie Trust and finally completed in May 1952, by which time the CFF was already up and running, but Field used the results to reinforce her case for the continuing existence of the Foundation. The CEF film used for the test screenings was *The Mysterious Poacher* (1950), one of two films shot on location in Austria. Her findings included some oddities. For instance, she

Mary Field, the most influential person in the early history of the CFF

advised film-makers against showing shots of children eating meals because the young audience would find images of children sitting down less interesting than if the subjects were standing. Despite this, many of her recommendations, such as the need to avoid unexpected frights or the importance of encouraging positive identification with characters, became basic guidelines for the subsequent CFF output.

The most important impetus to the creation of the Foundation came from the Rank Organisation. At this point in its history, Rank was suffering serious financial problems. Needing to make cutbacks but wanting to continue the work of the CEF, it attempted to offload responsibility for implementing the recommendations of the Wheare Report to the wider industry. The four major trade associations representing producers, distributors and exhibitors agreed to step in to create a new production body to be called the Children's Film Foundation. These bodies were the British Film Producers' Association, the Association of Specialised Film Producers, the Cinematograph Exhibitors' Association and the Kinematograph Renters' Society. Funding was to come from the British Film Production Board (BFPB), which would allocate part of the Eady Levy, which it oversaw, to the CFF. The levy, which was the brain child of Harold Wilson, then President of the Board of Trade, had been introduced in September 1950. Essentially a small tax on cinema admissions, it meant that each ticket sold helped provide a small pot of money which could be used to bolster the indigenous film industry. As well as assisting innumerable British film productions, it helped pay for the National Film and Television School. Five per cent of its revenues were set aside for the new Children's Film Foundation for its first six months in operation, producing an estimated initial payment of £60,000; £50,000 was granted immediately on account. In September 1951 it was granted a full year of funding amounting to £100,000. Budgets for each individual film were to be kept as low as possible to make the funding go further. The Foundation was to be a non-profit-making limited company with any income generated put back into the production pot for the following year.

The official launch of CFF Ltd was announced in the trade press on 4 July 1951.[11] The management board was to be chaired by J. Arthur Rank himself, with a membership consisting of three representatives from each of the four trade associations, making thirteen directors in all. Mary Field became its CEO, having initially been appointed as a technical advisor, and immediately began to draw up both short- and longer-term strategy plans. Three subcommittees were established covering production, exhibition and PR. The job of deciding what to include in the production programme was delegated to the production committee, which consisted of four members, one from each of the trade bodies. Films were to be commissioned from anywhere within the UK industry and in August 1951 a meeting was held to invite production companies to submit suitable projects for consideration. The actual office staff of the CFF only numbered five, keeping administration costs low. The production of three features was announced, along with two further projects at script stage, six magazine-style shorts and a slapstick comedy to combine live action and animation. In addition, six two-reel shorts were promised and plans were unveiled for two adventure serials, if funding in its second full year of operation permitted. The industry unions agreed that staff would work for minimum rates to make production funds stretch as far as possible. Mary Field told *Visual Education* (the magazine of the National Committee for Visual Aids in Education): 'the negative attitude towards children and the cinema is ending and a new and positive approach is rapidly gaining ground'[12].

The Foundation moved quickly to win the support of the cinema chains by announcing a neatly democratic distribution policy. This arrangement was the work of a special committee set up within the Foundation and headed by its secretary, W. G. R. Thom; the committee included John Davis from the Rank Organisation. They were particularly at pains to bring on board the circuits outside of Rank and ABC as these had shown little interest in the creation of the CFF. The Foundation divided cinemas into four groupings: Odeon; Gaumont; ABC; and independents (which included chains like Granada and Essoldo, as well as individual family-run cinemas). Each group would take turns in being given the latest CFF releases, while the others would then move their way up through the pecking order from the bottom on a yearly basis, making do with older titles as a back-catalogue developed. Thom announced that the system would ensure equity and that the Independents would receive first choice.[13]

By 1952 the Foundation had begun to release its first productions to the cinema chains. Its work had benefited from the relaxation of laws governing the use of child actors in films but, despite this it still didn't quite meet the initial targets it had set for itself. In 1952 it released two feature films, four shorts, some travelogues and the first editions of *Our Club Magazine.* The features were *John of the Fair*, a period drama set among the fairgrounds of eighteenth-century England and made by Merton Park, and *The Stolen Plans*, a contemporary adventure story produced by Gaumont-British. The latter was to set the pattern for many later CFF films with its story of two children discovering and outwitting a gang of spies intent on stealing the plans for a new aircraft. From the beginning the Foundation aimed to make an international impact by entering its films into competitions and festivals; the two features shared the Silver Gondola award at that year's Venice Film Festival. The four shorts showed a strong preference for animal subjects, which reflected Mary Field's interests. *Rover Makes Good* and *Stable Rivals* were commissioned from small regional producers, Plymouth Films and Anglo-Scottish Pictures respectively, a policy that was pursued throughout the 1950s. Along with *Swift Water*, these were two-reel comedy adventures with strong use of natural settings, *Swift Water* being shot on location in Devon. The final release, *To the Rescue*, was a broad comedy short commissioned from the popular film-maker and actor Richard Massingham, who would have been well known to parents for his wartime public information films. This film again featured animals, this time a poodle, and was entered at Venice in 1953 where it won first prize as best short for children in the twelve-to-fifteen age group. *Our Club Magazine* brought together a number of short news and entertainment items of interest to children. It was to run until 1956, numbering sixteen releases.

The Foundation published its first annual report in July 1952, which painted a rosy picture and unveiled plans for more editions of *Our Club Magazine*, as well as shorts, features and cartoons. In August, the BFPB renewed the Foundation's funding providing another payment of £120,000. It also enshrined the CFF's aims as being 'the production, promotion, organisation, distribution and exhibition of cinematograph films specially suitable for showing at children's matinees'. In an interview that month, Mary Field described its first films as 'exploratory' and suggested that the Foundation would be maintaining a close watch on children's responses.[14] On 20 October 1952 an audience of 300 schoolchildren were invited to a special screening at the Haymarket cinema, London to test their appreciation of the new CFF output. The headmaster of Curwen Primary School, West Ham reported general approval, with particular appreciation for *The Stolen Plans*, although there were complaints about the wooden acting in *Swift Water.*[15] A similar complete programme of CFF items including *Our Club Magazine*, *A Visit to the Farne Islands* and *The Stolen Plans* won first prize at the Festival of Films for Children at Venice in 1952.

Positive responses came from other quarters too. At the third reading in Parliament of the Cinematograph Act on 29 October 1952, Dr B. Stokes (Labour, Stoke-on-Trent) suggested that the CFF was so successful that its grant should be increased by an additional £60,000 per year.[16] The first UK press and trade screenings were organised in October 1952 at the Gaumont, Haymarket and again used *The Stolen Plans* as the lead feature; children were invited to the occasion. Plans were announced for overseas co-productions and a special film screening was arranged for MPs in December that year. The programme consisted of *The Stolen Plans*, *Swift Water* and *Our Club Magazine No.2*. It took place in the Grand Committee Room of Westminster Hall on 3 December and was hosted by Joseph Reeves, MP. Also in December a new partnership with Rank was announced that would enable distribution of the CFF's films internationally. W. G. R. Thom told *Today's Cinema* that it was planning to send films to Europe, Australia and Canada, and the Far and Near East. He said that it had even had requests from Communist Eastern Europe.[17] To add to the general approbation, the President of the BBFC then sanctioned the moral content of the CFF's films.[18] The Foundation certainly showed skill and organisation in promoting its own virtues to a wider world in this early period, a strategy that was crucial to its continuation. It was a modest beginning, but the Foundation was up and running and achieving positive recognition.

Settling into production, 1953–6

Over the next four years the CFF released fifteen features, seven comedy shorts, five educational shorts and two adventure serials, alongside its ongoing production of magazine-style newsreel compilations. It also bought in several features from Eastern Europe which it dubbed into English. Its most unusual production of this period is the short *Bouncer Breaks Up* (1953), which combined live action and animation. The busiest year in the period was 1953, which saw fourteen titles released. This then settled into a more typical rate of five or six per year. The intention was that a complete programme running roughly ninety minutes would be available to each Saturday cinema club, consisting of a feature and two shorts of varied genres. The character of its output at this time, understandably, owes much to the influence of Mary Field. Central to its educational output was a series of four two-reel dramatised documentaries called *A Letter from ...* (1953–4). Each film introduced young viewers to life in a different region or nation of the UK, from Wales to Scotland, East Anglia and the Isle of Wight. The core of the comedy shorts was a series of knockabout misadventures featuring Peter Butterworth, later to become a stalwart of the Carry On films. Produced by Grendon Films, they employed slapstick visual gags with each episode placing Butterworth in a different occupation, from working in a café in *A Good Pull Up* (1953) to assistant in a grocer's shop in *That's an Order* (1956). It was a format that the CFF would then largely abandon until the late 1960s. The first serials, *Raiders of the River* (1955) and *Five Clues to Fortune* (1956), the latter also known as *The Treasure of Woburn Abbey*, used a format of eight fifteen-minute instalments to tell an ongoing narrative. Both serials were produced by Merton Park. The films pitted groups of children against bank robbers or sent them pursuing clues to a hidden treasure. The popularity of these early efforts led to the real heyday of the CFF's cliff-hanger serials in the late 1950s and early 1960s.

The features also show the guiding hand of Mary Field, steeped as she was in the educational value of cinema and in the storytelling formats of children's literature of the 1930s. Animals are again to the fore in *The Dog and the Diamonds* (1953) and *Tim Driscoll's Donkey* (1954), whereas natural settings feature strongly in *The Secret of the Forest* (1955), *Mystery on Bird Island* (1954) and *Adventure in the Hopfields* (1954). The pattern of shooting films in foreign locales for exotic effect began with *The Clue of the Missing Ape* (1953), which was shot on location in Gibraltar. Another CFF staple, the sporting contest, was established with *Heights of Danger* (1953) and *Skid Kids* (1953), which featured motorcar racing and speedway respectively. Here the emphasis was on playing fair at all times. *The Secret Cave* (1953) was adapted from a Thomas Hardy story and would become unique in the CFF canon in being remade in 1985 as *Exploits at West Poley*. *The Stolen Airliner* (1955) championed the Air Cadets, while *The Flying Eye* (1955) and *Peril for the Guy* (1956) introduced another CFF perennial in the eccentric inventor or boffin. Comic adventures with a sympathetic alien appear in *Supersonic Saucer* (1956), another plotline that the Foundation was to repeat, particularly in the 1970s. Perhaps the most ambitious film of this early period is *Johnny on the Run* (1953), the affecting story of a Polish refugee and orphan experiencing prejudice but eventually finding a new home in Scotland. The topic is handled with considerable flair by the young Lewis Gilbert.

The Foundation began to establish a repertory company of film-makers who provided the bedrock of its early output, a pattern it retained for much of its history. Gaumont-British, Merton Park, Rayant Pictures and Associated British-Pathé were its most frequent production partners at this time. Projects were initiated either from outside the CFF by production companies or independent scriptwriters sending in proposals or from within, where ideas were developed by its own small group of creative staff. Original scripts were often developed within the CFF by either Mary Cathcart Borer or Pat Latham, but adaptations of popular children's books also featured regularly. Once a script was approved, a production company would be selected to take it through to completion. Producer-writer Frank Wells (son of the novelist H. G. Wells), like Latham and Cathcart Borer, was to become one of the Foundation's trusted hands in this period. It also began a tradition of recruiting established film-makers from the industry such as director Ralph Thomas (*The Dog and the Diamonds*) and documentarist Basil Wright, who produced *One Wish Too Many* (1956). Along with this, they gave a chance to young talents behind the camera like Don Sharp, Don Chaffey, James Hill and John Guillermin. The first in what would become a long line of young performers destined for stardom appeared, such as Jane Asher, David Hemmings and Frazer Hines. They could be seen alongside useful character actors like Mona Washbourne, John Laurie and George Cole. Michael Balfour, who would go on to appear in numerous CFF productions, usually as an amiable villain, made his first appearance in *The Secret of the Forest*.

The characteristic elements of a CFF feature are much in evidence already at this stage. A gang of assorted kids, or a brother- and sister-team, normally ranging in age from four to fourteen, accidentally uncover the plans of a criminal gang. Unable to go to the police (for some reason provided by the script), they have to catch the villains themselves. Alternatively, they find themselves in a competition, sporting or otherwise, with a rival gang whose underhand methods are resisted by our heroes, who eventually win by fair means. Settings are mainly urban or suburban, usually London, with occasional forays into a rural idyll (more often than not the Home Counties) or to more exotic foreign climes. Boys typically take the lead with girls assigned a supporting role, as are smaller children. Bravery, resourcefulness, loyalty and honesty are prized, whereas villains are often also cheats and bullies. Britain is largely a white country and its children are polite, smartly dressed and show due deference to adults, particularly teachers and policemen. Accents are middle class, even when the settings aren't (Mary Field was keen on overdubbing dialogue and preferred formally trained acting school graduates). There are chases and mild fights but the villains are generally comic and/or incompetent so that there is little real threat. It is for the most part a cosy and reassuring world where virtue wins and is duly rewarded. Not everyone was entirely enthusiastic about some of these tendencies. One reviewer suggested that 'what have so far been mere preferences, to be applied where possible, have now hardened into immovable CFF rules', bemoaning the fact that the children in *The Secret Cave* 'are so excessively well-behaved and nicely spoken that they suggest Kensington Gardens and governesses instead of a Wessex village'[19]. However, the Cinema Exhibitors' Association was more positive, concluding that the CFF was doing 'very useful work ... for the production of films specifically suitable for children'[20].

The Foundation continued to seek international recognition by entering films into festivals. Mary Field attended the Venice Film Festival in 1955 to support the five CFF films in the competition. *Mystery on Bird Island* won the Silver Gondola, following on from *The Stolen Plans* and *Johnny on the Run*, while *Tim Driscoll's Monkey* picked up the first prize for children's entertainment. *The Clue of the Missing Ape* was another Venice prizewinner in 1954, as were *The Dog and the Diamonds* and *A Letter from the Isle of Wight. One Wish Too Many* went on to pick up the Silver Gondola in 1956.

Funding continued through this period at the steady rate of £125,000 per year. The popularity of *Johnny on the Run* led to requests from distributors for wider commercial exhibition, so the Foundation agreed to release it as a B feature, with all profits returning to the Foundation's production pot. It was careful to reassure the BFPB, which had advised against the wider release, that this was a one-off and did not change its need for continuing subsidy from the Eady Levy or alter its not-for-profit status. This minor controversy over the use of tax payers' money to finance a commercial property was to emerge again many years later in relation to the use of National Lottery funds for a similar purpose. It was a difficult balancing act as exhibitors also criticised the Foundation for not allowing more access to its films outside of the Saturday clubs.[21] The problem proved transient as the demand for wider distribution for CFF films never really developed. Nonetheless, W. G. R. Thom felt compelled to write to the trade paper *Today's Cinema* to defend the decision, arguing (rather disingenuously) that some children couldn't get to the Saturday screenings and wider distribution would enable them to see the film.[22] At this time the CFF began the practice of circulating 16mm prints to circulate to non-commercial venues such as children's hospitals, orphanages and other 'closed' circuits. UK distribution moved from Associated

British Film Distributors to British Lion in 1954, with Rank continuing to handle overseas markets. By 1956 nearly twenty countries were taking the films. A request from the US to show CFF films on television was gently rebuffed.

In 1953 the Foundation conducted a survey of 220 cinemas to gauge the success of its releases. Ninety per cent reported that its films were 'very good' and that children preferred them to commercial films. One manager was reported as saying that the films 'dealt in terms which were intelligible to youngsters, with things and situation in which they are naturally interested'[23]. Further positive endorsements included invitations from the Russian, Dutch and West German governments for assistance in setting up their own versions of the CFF; Mary Field made visits to all three countries in 1953 and 1954 with the support of the Foreign Office.

In June 1956 W. G. R. Thom unveiled the plans for 1957 with an air of confidence. There would be two features at £40,000 apiece, two shorts at £10,000 and two eight-part serials costing £60,000. With £15,000 for contingencies, this would account for their usual annual spend of £125,000.

The rise of the Saturday film clubs

By the late 1950s the network of Saturday morning children's film clubs had settled into a well-defined pattern. The clubs can be divided into three groups: those operated by the Rank Organisation and located in Odeon and Gaumont cinemas; those operated by the ABC chain as the ABC Minors; and the rest, which included minor but significant chains like Essoldo, as well as the myriad family-run cinemas around the UK. Rank and ABC each accounted for about 40 per cent of the clubs with the remaining 20 per cent divided between the others. These clubs were not formally organised by the CFF but they signed up to the national system. In effect, this meant that they were able to rent material from the CFF catalogue. They were also sent pamphlets and newsletters advertising the latest batch of releases or reissues. Each cinema manager could decide how much of the package they wanted. This varied greatly, from those who based their entire Saturday morning programme around CFF productions, to those who only used elements. Generations of children started to become familiar with the the Foundation's logo, a shot of Trafalgar Square with the pigeons rising into the air while the bells of St Martin's sound in the background. Oddly, the Foundation was to reshoot this fragment of film over the years, replicating this shot; it's possible on close observation to notice slight differences.

A typical Saturday morning programme was divided into two sections by an interval. The first half consisted of a series of short items which could include cartoons, two-reel comedies, educational and documentary shorts, and an episode from an adventure serial. The second half was a feature film. The interval might simply act as a refreshment break but, depending on the inclinations of the cinema manager, could also be an opportunity to supplement the programme with competitions, sing-alongs, birthday announcements, guest appearances and the like (for a detailed account of the content of screenings, see Chapter 4). The first half of the programme included CFF serials, educational pieces and comedy shorts but sometimes also other, non-Foundation output, ranging widely across silent comedy shorts to various cliff-hanger serials in the Western and science fiction genres. The vast majority of these were American, as were the cartoons. However, the feature in the second half was more often a CFF production. These were deliberately cut to run for about sixty minutes so as to provide a balanced programme of roughly two hours of content in total with a fifteen-minute break.

The popularity of these clubs is hard to overestimate. The CFF's own records suggest that during its peak, from the mid-1950s to the mid-1970s, around 800 cinemas were typically taking part (about half the UK total) with weekly attendance between 320,000 and 500,000, probably averaging at about 400,000; total annual admissions were around 20 million. Each cinema averaged 400 admissions per week, although they could range from 100 to 1,000. Although the films were a key part of the attraction, it would be wrong to suggest that this tells the whole story. As evidenced by the firsthand accounts collated in Chapter 4, the social aspect was at least as important, if not more so. These were communal gatherings that allowed children to escape from the home sphere and the controlling influence of parents or other adults into a place that was still safe, as well as being cheap to access, where they could socialise with friends, exercise their imaginations and indulge in a degree of mild misbehaviour without too much fear of the consequences. As a social institution for children it is one of the most important of the postwar era in the UK and yet also one of the most overlooked by the adult authorities, which may also account for its popularity. A read through the memories gathered later in this book, or in Terry Staples's account, provides clear testimony to the huge impact it had on children. What may have confused, and disappointed, Mary Field is that the educational and 'civilising' influence of the films appears to have been negligible. More fascinating, and concerning, is the degree to which these events evidenced the dissatisfaction of children with their daily round and their intense desire to find at least two hours in the week when they could shake this off. The fact that these feelings have persisted well into adulthood for those audience members, admittedly mingling with nostalgia, also suggests that something in that daily round might still be lacking. Fun, perhaps?

The era of classic serials, 1957–62

During the next six years of production the CFF released twenty-eight titles of its own making along with a sprinkling of imported films (including one from Hungary and one from Australia) at a rate of about five per year. Of these, ten were adventure serials, a far higher proportion than had previously been the case. There is a decisive shift of emphasis in this period onto serials and features, and away from the comedy shorts, educational drama-documentaries and magazine formats, which were abandoned. It has to be assumed that these had not proved especially popular with audiences; the Foundation kept a regular check via cinema managers on audience responses to its work. Mary Field in particular seems to have invested much of her energy during these years into the cliff-hanger serials that characterise the output here.

Five on a Treasure Island (1957) established the characteristic style of the Foundation's cliff-hanger serials

The style was set by the first serial, *Five on a Treasure Island* (1957), which was adapted from one of Enid Blyton's popular Famous Five novels. Across eight episodes, each with a suspenseful finish designed to bring kids back the following week, our gang of four intrepid boys and girls, plus Timmy the dog, succeed in finding the hidden treasure and foiling the villains. The action is gentle and the story has a nostalgic quality even for the time of its release. There is also a clear assumption of audience identification with the overtly middle-class characters. This series was followed in a similar vein by *The Carringford School Mystery* (1958), *The Dawn Killer* (1959) – strong animal interest in this one – and *Mystery in the Mine* (1959), along with the feature *Treasure at the Mill* (1957), which has a similar style. If they might feel dated now, they were certainly popular at the time, and have become indelibly associated with the CFF of the 1950s.

Other genres which had been established earlier continued into this period. There were the semi-comic animal stories which included the feature *Circus Friends* (1957) and the serials *The Adventures of Rex* (1959) and *Ali and the Camel* (1960). *The Monster of Highgate Ponds* (1961), with its fantasy creature, might also fit into this category. The emphasis in all these productions is on the value of companionship and the need to care for others in a responsible way. The films featuring sporting or other contests also continued and include *Soapbox Derby* (1957) and *Blow Your Own Trumpet* (1958). There are a number of films made on foreign locations such as *Toto and the Poachers* (1957), *Hunted in Holland* (1960), *Bungala Boys* (1961) and *The Last Rhino* (1961), as well as the serial *Ali and the Camel*. The message here is often one of international understanding. A car that takes on a life of its own features in *The Adventures of HAL 5* (1957), while *The Cat Gang* (1958) and *Four Winds Island* (1961) have tried-and-tested plots where our gang capture the criminals or uncover the hidden treasure. Familiarity was to be an abiding guideline at the Foundation.

Mary Field's influence can also be felt in the messages contained in some films. *The Kid from Canada* (1957) and *A Film for Maria* (1961) extol the virtues of international cooperation. The latter is also interesting for acting as a kind of advert for the Saturday clubs, being partly created by the audience from one of the clubs. Field's philosophy of telling a strong, compelling story first and making sure that an unambiguous moral stance emerges as a secondary concern remained the CFF's guiding creed, nonetheless. There were less typical entries. *Masters of Venus* (1962) was the only science fiction serial produced by the Foundation, although there were several features, and *Night Cargoes* (1962), *The Piper's Tune* (1961) and *The Young Jacobites* (1959) all involve period settings, a device that was to remain rare in the CFF's output. Perhaps the most striking production of the period was *The Salvage Gang* (1958), featuring beautifully observed London settings and directed with panache by John Krish.

The Foundation continued to work regularly with its preferred production partners from earlier in the 1950s such as Merton Park, Gaumont-British, Wallace, Rayant and Associated British-Pathé. To this roster it added World Wide, which was more usually associated with documentaries, Anvil and World Safari (which specialised in overseas shoots). The last brought producer/writer/director Henry Geddes into the circle of the Foundation; he was to become the most significant figure in its development throughout the next ten years and beyond. The most innovative partnership of this period was with Britain's foremost animation company, Halas and Batchelor, commissioned to produce *The Monster of Highgate Ponds* with its use of stop-motion. Directors Don Sharp and John Hill continued to work on CFF projects and the pattern of bringing in experienced names from the industry grew with Gerald Thomas, later of the Carry Ons, helming *Circus Friends* (for which Peter Rogers, also associated with the Carry Ons, produced and wrote the script). Alberto Cavalcanti, formerly a key figure at Ealing, directed *The Monster of Highgate Ponds* and Muriel Box, one of the few female directors at work in the mainstream industry, delivered *The Piper's Tune*. Mary Cathcart Borer's name still appeared with regularity on the scripts but a new breed of writer was beginning to emerge led by Michael Barnes (later to be credited as Mike Gorell Barnes), who brought a more youthful outlook. Frank Wells continued to act as an overseeing producer for the Foundation on several projects. On the screen itself, the CFF's repertory of character players was supplemented by Wilfrid Brambell, who was about to find fame on television in *Steptoe and Son* (1962–74) and who would continue to appear in Foundation films throughout the 1960s. New stars making their mark and heading for entertainment careers included Michael Crawford, Carol White and Francesca Annis.

The CFF gave a career start for many future stars, including Michael Crawford in *Blow Your Own Trumpet* (1958)

The CFF's funding arrangements were finally enshrined in law with the passing of the Cinematograph Act 1957. The Act provided for 'the imposition of a levy on exhibitors of cinematograph films and for the making from the proceeds thereof payments to, or for the benefit of, makers of British films and to the Children's Film Foundation'. Financial oversight was legally devolved to the Board of Trade, which had been the informal arrangement since 1951, and the Eady funds were to be distributed via the newly formed British Film Fund Agency. The level of grant remained at £125,000 per year until the end of the 1950s and then in 1962 moved to £137,500.

By 1958 the Saturday clubs had reached new heights of popularity with a weekly audience of 800,000 to 900,000. They were never to hit such a high point again. To celebrate the achievements of Mary Field, a special programme of screenings was arranged by the CFF's new secretary Stanley Reed at the National Film Theatre during August 1958. The films chosen to open and close the season, which was called 'The Young Audience', were *Johnny on the Run* and *The Salvage Gang.* A more sobering statistic was that, despite the popularity of the clubs, CFF products still only counted for less than 10 per cent of the material seen by children.[24] With the formal merger of the Odeon and Gaumont chains and a proportionate rise in the number of independents, the Foundation altered its distribution policy in 1962, dividing its films equally between Rank (Odeon-Gaumont), ABC and two divisions of independent cinemas; each had a 25 per cent share of the films on the usual rota basis. The Foundation also took over the job of booking out films directly from its Great Portland Street offices.

In 1960 the Foundation published a comprehensive report to cover its first ten years in operation.[25] It opened with the bold claim that the CFF 'uses the skills and techniques which are at their [sic] industry's command to set a high standard in taste and behaviour before this most rewarding audience'. It set out three main aims, which were to provide 'healthy recreation' for children; to set high standards of taste and behaviour by appealing to children's 'intelligence and love of adventure'; and to aspire to the highest technical standards consistent with 'the telling of a good, clear story'. It was promised that there would be 'no sensationalism or unhealthy excitement or vulgarity'. The language is highly redolent of Mary Field and the Foundation's ethos of the 1950s. The CFF noted the declining popularity of its magazine feature and of the educational shorts, but pointed to the consistent popularity of the sixty-minute features and the serials. It also reiterated its policy of not making work for television.

The financial report showed a total income of £1,185,000 from the Eady Levy to date, with an additional £42,000 from rentals and £4,000 in interest. Running costs totalled £90,000 and all of the remaining capital had been committed back into the production programme. There were 900 shows per week currently taking place and the audience age range was seven to twelve. Of course this figure implied that all these children were seeing was CFF material, which was far from the reality. By this stage Lord Rank had withdrawn and the Board was chaired by John Davis, Managing Director of the Rank Organisation. It had also begun to invite important industry figures to sit on the Board including the animator John Halas. A similar policy had developed on the Production Committee, which then included the director Basil Wright, Peter

Rogers and Richard Attenborough. In 1959 home distribution was moved entirely in-house, having previously relied on Associated British Film Distribution and then British Lion.

In some senses the late 1950s marked a golden age for the CFF, one in which the vision of Mary Field was brought to fruition and achieved international recognition. But this masked two related and inherent problems: first, that the work was not being circulated anywhere near as well as it might have been by distributors and cinema managers who still preferred to screen reruns of American product; and, second, that one particular element of the work was being rejected by the intended audience. This related to the child performers and especially their accents. As Terry Staples reports, 'the audience were put off by the precise elocution of the child actors which led to a degree of derision'[26]. This was a problem that would be addressed in the changed production policy adopted by the CFF in the 1960s. At the end of 1958 Mary Field retired as Executive Officer, becoming head of children's television at ATV the following year, and Frank Wells took over. A new era was beginning.

New realities, 1963–7

The mid-1960s saw the Foundation undergoing a modest but significant change of direction in its approach to production content. In 1964 the *Journal of the Society of Film and Television Arts* issued a special edition on children's films, publishing contrasting short essays by Mary Field and Henry Geddes. Geddes had already made several films for the CFF in the late 1950s and early 1960s as an independent film-maker and had effectively become Frank Wells's righthand man; he was to take over as CEO in 1964. Most of Mary Field's article is spent looking back at the achievements of the old CEF in the 1940s, which she holds up as a model for an effective and moral approach to film-making for children.[27] Henry Geddes's piece, by comparison, looks to the future and is buoyantly optimistic, pointing to the sustained popularity of the Foundation's films. He also puts some distance between himself and the somewhat pious posture of the earlier Foundation; these are 'healthy' films for youngsters, certainly, but the principal job of the CFF is more to supply regular entertainment for children of a kind, provided by no one else. He limits the potential for 'moral' influence to examples such as *Valley of the Kings* (1964), which he suggests encouraged children to take an interest in archaeology. [28]

There seems to have been a sense among the members of the Foundation's Board that, in an age of Beatlemania, independent commercial television and expanding youth culture, the audience was changing. In 1964 a comprehensive survey of its activities was commissioned from the company Group Marketing and Research Ltd, a subsidiary of the Rank Organisation. Some 1,500 interviews with audience members were carried out across forty-two cinemas; the results were published as *Progress Report: The CFF in the Sixties*. The Foundation had always monitored its output by asking cinema managers to complete short questionnaires on a weekly basis, allowing the popularity of each production to be assessed, but this was by far the most systematic investigation it had undertaken.

Go Kart Go (1963) heralded the start of a new era and a more contemporary style for the Foundation

Among the findings was that the average age of club members was now 8.8 years, indicating a downward trend. The Board was immediately concerned that the Foundation was losing about half of its potential audience, those in the nine-to-fourteen age bracket, and needed to take steps to address their needs. The report also noted increasing levels of expectation from children in terms of the technical quality of films. This was seen to be in response to their growing exposure to television productions that were deemed to be more 'sophisticated' than the work offered by the Foundation. In addition, in a turn that would probably have dismayed Mary Field, it was suggested that the high moral tone of the CFF's output should be softened considerably. The report stated that 'the time was ripe for further experiment and research and a setting of different standards'[29]. A tentative programme of 'new look' films was already underway as indication of the CFF's awareness that a change was needed. These included *Go Kart Go* (1963), *Seventy Deadly Pills* (1963) and *Daylight Robbery* (1964). The report also recommended more features and fewer serials, as well as greater use of colour.

Another area covered by the survey was audience preferences. A gender divide was apparently evident, with boys preferring war subjects and Westerns (genres well outside the Foundation's remit), while girls preferred adventure stories. Everyone liked comedies. These findings were taken to validate the gender bias which the Foundation took as self-evident. The children's favourite character type was the villain, which prompted the report's compiler to remind us that this didn't mean that the villain should go unpunished; the moral ambiguities of this finding go unexamined. Henry Geddes responsed to the report's overall results with a new set of guidelines for film-makers. He told them that children wanted stories with lots of vivid action and excitement, clearly drawn characters and a strong sense of right and wrong:

> All children share the same basic likes and dislikes in film entertainment. They are passionately fond of all domestic animals and are visibly upset by any form of animal cruelty. They prefer the maximum amount of screen action and have little patience with unnecessary dialogue or any suggestion of adult romance. They have a strong instinct for fair play and a pronounced sympathy with the underdog.[30]

The films should encourage children to be 'fair, tolerant and responsible' but without preaching. The changing mood is indicated by a specific reference to racial tolerance, alongside valuing common sense and public safety. However, the spirit of Mary Field hovers in the suggestion that the films will help children to 'become responsible adults'. Nonetheless, there was a new view abroad that prioritised entertainment value over traditional moral content and that wished films to address children more on their own terms.

This view was reiterated in another report published from the Foundation's Great Portland Street headquarters in 1967 called *Saturday Morning Cinema*. It opened with a robust defence of the Foundation by Chairman John Davis, entitled 'Films to Be Proud Of'. After boasting of the CFF's unique track record of well-crafted entertainment and high professional standards, he reminded each one of the Foundation's film-makers of

> the important opportunity, in fact responsibility, which he has to influence the young minds in a desirable way ... they must do so without frightening or unbalancing delicate sensitivities; the good and the bad must be obvious but sermons must be avoided.[31]

Some things might change but others remained the same. This is evident from a viewing of *Go Kart Go*, which in many ways is simply an updated remake of the earlier *Soapbox Derby* in terms of its narrative content and its moral position, i.e. cheats never prosper. However, the film does look and feel quite different from its predecessor, with its rougher working-class edge, naturalistic performances and authentic-sounding urban accents, a change typified by the casting of a young Dennis Waterman in the role previously taken by Michael Crawford. There is a more democratic sense of reality here than before, one which seems contemporary in spirit rather than the nostalgic, backwardlooking stance of *Soapbox Derby*.[32] The need to encourage identification with the characters and story from its core audience, who were largely urban and working class themselves, had finally been recognised. In addition, the ethical content is implicit rather than overt.

The Report goes on to record the Foundation's output to date which, as at September 1967, was 113 items, including fifty-five features, twenty-three serials and thirty-five shorts. Its internal structure had undergone some small alterations with the management board being extended from thirteen to sixteen members with the addition of three representatives from the Federation of British Film Makers and its committee structure extended to add finance to the existing production, distribution and PR committees. The practice of co-opting industry professionals onto the management board and the production committee continued with the producer Leon Clore and director Michael Powell appointed to the former, while documentarist Edgar Anstey and writer-producer Frank Godwin were appointed to the latter. The rota distribution system was still in place across Rank, ABC and the two groups of independents but the range of venues for 16mm rental had been extended to include military bases. The demand from exhibitors was still deemed high, with a greater number of supplementary films being brought in from Eastern Europe. The financial statement showed a total income to date of £2,479,000 consisting of £2,245,000 from the Eady Levy, with £61,000 in UK rental revenues and £173,000 from overseas distribution; the Eady Levy annual payment had risen to £192,000 in 1966. All income was being directed back into production (in line with the CFF constitution) with the exception of £202,000 that had been spent on administration. Admissions stood at 17 million per year, with 300,000 attending per week at 800 cinemas, averaging roughly 400 per cinema per week. The number of participating UK cinemas compares well with ten years earlier, although the domestic audience is significantly down by up to 25 per cent. This was more worrying again in face of a rise in the actual size of the potential audience due to population growth, although it was mirrored by a similar decline in the adult audiences for mainstream commercial cinema. Audience loyalty was nonetheless impressive with children attending regularly for around five years on average, and evidence suggested that the proportion of CFF product in Saturday club programmes had increased as American imports had reduced; the rather aged vintage of some of the American material may have been a factor too. Whatever challenges the CFF was facing, a bullish Henry Geddes told *Kine Weekly* in 1967 that it was the biggest producer of children's films in the world.[33]

Looking at the Foundation's output between 1963–7 it is evident that many traditions carried on unaltered. It was still producing a significant number of cliff-hanger serials, with eleven of the twenty-nine releases in this period falling into this category. There was a second Famous Five release, *Five Have a Mystery to Solve* (1964), as well as several more in the same vein such as *The Ghost of Monk's Island* (1967) and *River Rivals* (1967), although some, like *Dead End Creek* (1965) and *The Young Detectives* (1964), had more of the new, contemporary feel. Animal subjects were still much in evidence whether in features such as *Calamity the Cow* (1967) and *Flash the Sheepdog* (1966) or serials like *Beware of the Dog* (1963). Similarly with the use of overseas settings to provide background colour as in the serials *Treasure in Malta* (1964), *Valley of the Kings* and *Son of the Sahara* (1966), as well as the feature *Davey Jones' Locker* (1965) – Malta again. Another friendly visitor from outer space turned up in the serial *Danny the Dragon* (1966) and sporting contests were to the fore in *Wings of Mystery* (1963) and *Eagle Rock* (1964). If there was change, the indications were that it was gradual.

Among the more unusual features were *The Flood* (1963), which set its story against the backdrop of recent flooding in East Anglia, and *Cup Fever* (1965), which featured a guest appearance by most of the then current Manchester United squad, including George Best and Bobby Charlton. The latter kept up the Foundation's record of achievement at Venice by picking up the Silver Gondola. *The Christmas Tree* (1966), one of the Foundation's more deliberately moralistic films of the period, was also recognised at the La Plata Festival in Argentina. An endorsement of the new approach had seen *Go Kart Go* win awards at Venice, La Plata and at the Gijon Children's Film Festival in Spain. A strain of pronounced fantasy and whimsy had started to develop in this period with *Runaway Railway* (1965) and *The Sky Bike* (1967), perhaps in response to the fact that Britain was swinging; the style would come into its own in the early 1970s.

The new attitude was also evident in the shift to a number of new production companies as working partners. From the old guard only Rayant, World Wide and Associated British-Pathé contributed significantly in the mid-1960s; Gaumont-British and Merton Park had vanished from the roster, although this may have been affected by structural changes taking place in the wider industry – the industry as a whole was experiencing a shortlived boom with an influx of American funding, which tended to favour newer and nimbler small outfits. Prominent among the new partner producers were Fanfare and Anvil. The working relationship with producers had also changed. In the 1950s many projects started with ideas generated from within the Foundation by Mary Field and her closest collaborators. Under Henry Geddes, the external producers and independent writers were encouraged to initiate the majority of ideas themselves and then approach the Foundation for support. Familiar names nonetheless continued to appear behind the camera with Frank Wells and Mary Cathcart Borer joined in the scriptwriting credits by the reappearance of Pat Latham (who had married Henry Geddes). However, the new writers were also much in evidence, led by the prolific Michael Barnes, who had a hand in no fewer than nine projects during this period. The list of experienced directors drawn from the industry included former documentary-maker Pat Jackson and Charles Frend from Ealing. Among the newer directors, Jan Darnley-Smith was to become a CFF regular. Henry Geddes's hands-on approach was demonstrated by his personal involvement in creating four of the films. Another innovation of the period was to team a new director with an experienced producer and vice versa, a practice that perisisted into the 1970s.

The output from the mid-1960s is crammed with familiar comedy actors in supporting roles, some of whom appeared several times. The long list includes Wilfrid Brambell, Warren Mitchell, Bernard Cribbins, David Lodge, Norman Rossington, Ronnie Barker and Graham Stark. The register of future stars making early appearances is equally impressive, including Dennis Waterman, Judy Geeson, Susan George, Olivia Hussey, Jack Wild, Sally Thomsett and future music star Phil Collins. Henry Geddes's ambition of shifting away from the middle-class bias of the CFF was helped by the passing of the Children and Young Persons Act 1963, which relaxed the regulations governing the employment of child actors. This made it easier to use performers whose lives were more governed by the need of their parents to earn a daily living. The result was that the Foundation's films started to feature performers from companies like the Anna Scher Children's Theatre whose young actors were often drawn from working-class homes and who attended state schools.

The CFF experienced a rare dispute with the unions during 1963 when members of the Association of Cinematograph, Television and Allied Technicians (ACTT) went on strike while working on a CFF production. The crux of the dispute was the Foundation's informal agreement that all production staff be employed at minimum rates, a situation which helped enable their tight budgets to go further. The dispute was quickly resolved and the agreement remained in place. Production levels were steady throughout the period, averaging five to six films per year. As the end of the swinging sixties approached, the Foundation seemed to be responding to the changing environment with continued confidence. The changes introduced to its work, evidenced by the audience popularity of titles like *Go Kart Go*, *Seventy Deadly Pills* and *Operation Third Form* (1966), boded well for the future and would provide the basis for further alterations to its output into the 1970s.

The last hurrah, 1968–78

The 1970s mark the CFF's last golden era of production before the beginning of a gradual decline in its fortunes. In December 1970 Henry Geddes wrote an article for *Film Finance* explaining the economic strategy of the Foundation.[34] He argued that 'making films for children cannot be a commercial proposition' – a startling statement in light of today's massively lucrative global market in children's media but one intended to make the point to those in authority that the Foundation needed its public subsidy. Each colour CFF feature cost £30,000 and took four weeks to shoot, with a footage ratio of five to one between the filming and the final edit (comparatively low by industry standards). The Foundation's ethos, he said, was to 'provide the best possible entertainment at prices children can afford'. Value for money was paramount, particularly as the CFF continued to insist that participating cinemas keep ticket prices as low as possible. The economic model he had helped create, with its stringently controlled budgets, might serve as a model for others: 'Perhaps if the rest of the industry followed the Foundation's example, the adult public might also rediscover that films can be the best entertainment in the world.' During this period he had also successfully negotiated a further rise in the Foundation's Eady funding to £250,000 per year. The tone of his interview is certainly belligerent, with Geddes insisting that the CFF knows exactly what children want; he makes no acknowledgment of the fact that the Foundation's films were still only playing a partial role in the success of the Saturday clubs, even if they now accounted for an increasing percentage of the material shown. His comments also reflect an increasing awareness that the British film industry was entering a period of steep economic decline, with American funding running out. It was a trend that Geddes was determined the Foundation would not follow.

The Foundation released a booklet in 1969 to celebrate twenty-five years of children's films (encompassing its predecessor, the CEF), which was subtitled 'The CFF Moves into the Seventies'.[35] John Davis's introduction maintained the upbeat tone, claiming the films have 'strong, clear stories and whatever the subject ... they are treated in a way that fully engages the sympathies and interest of the audience'. The booklet also points to the content changes the Foundation had started to make during the 1960s in a section called 'Living with Change', noting its rejection of scripts 'so full of moralising or so outdated in approach that they would never hold a critical audience of children'. A further alteration was announced: the CFF was no longer making children's films – it was producing 'Junior Features'. There were to be more grown-up themes, and no speaking down to children. The Foundation was to become fully contemporary in its outlook, recognising the greater social and cultural awareness of its audience. It even conceded that the 1950s films were dated. On a melancholy note, the death in 1968 of Mary Field was commemorated.

Geddes was certainly in a proactive mood in the early 1970s and put much of his energy into public flag-waving on behalf of the Foundation. Returning from a festival at the American Centre of Films for Children in Los Angeles in late 1973, he told Quentin Falk of *Cinema/TV Today*: 'If there were no children's matinees children would not go to the cinema.'[36] He stated that 65–85 per cent of matinee audiences also go regularly to conventional cinema as opposed to only 37 per cent of those who didn't attend on Saturdays. This was obviously intended as a reminder to the industry at large of the value of the Foundation in creating an audience for mainstream films. Some 60 per cent of the content of the matinees was now produced by the CFF. A quarter of CFF films employed new talent behind the camera and, he said, it was so overwhelmed with scripts that it could only shoot 10 per cent of them. He held the Foundation up as bucking the overall downwards trend of the British film industry. He gave similar interviews to a range of trade journals throughout the period.[37]

His confidence was reflected in the sheer scale of the Foundation output between 1968 and 1978. Seventy-four productions were released at an average of six to seven per year, although the production rate did swing alarmingly, sometimes dropping to just three and then shooting up the following year to ten or eleven. One thing immediately noticeable was that the promised demise of the adventure serials did largely come about. Only four were released: *Project Z* (1968) and *Rangi's Catch* (1972), which were both set abroad; *The Boy with Two Heads* (1974), which has a strong element of fantasy; and *The Unbroken Arrow* (1976), a direct spin-off from the period feature *Robin Hood Junior* (1975). Instead there was a marked return to broad slapstick comedy shorts, a style that had previously been abandoned in the mid-1950s. The most popular of these was *The Magnificent 6½* (1968–71) which ran to three series. The format was for fifteen to twenty minutes of knockabout and comic accidents involving a gang of likeable kids covering an age range of roughly five (the ½ of the title) to fourteen. After two series, the Foundation's reluctance to develop the series for television (still deemed to be the enemy) led to its production company, Century Films, revamping it for the small screen as *Here Come the Double Deckers* (1970) with the backing of Twentieth Century-Fox. This version went on to considerable success while the Foundation's original, now saddled with a different cast, faded away. More CFF work in the same vein followed with two series of *The Chiffy Kids* (1976–8) and three of *Chimpmates* (1976–8), which added in the attraction of misbehaving primates in a manner likely to be seen now as politically incorrect. There was a similar tone to *The Trouble with 2B* (1972) – another spin-off series, this time from the feature *Junket 89* (1970) – and *Professor Popper's Problems* (1974) featuring Charlie Drake. Although the humour was in the main unsubtle, the settings around council estates and comprehensive schools were often realistically observed and facilitated audience identification. Authentic working-class accents were also much in evidence.

Another new trend was towards science fantasy, or just out-and-out fantasy, frequently with the emphasis on laughs again. In this category are *Egghead's Robot* (1970), *Junket 89*, *Mr Horatio Knibbles* (1970), *Blinker's Spy Spotter* (1971), *The Troublesome Double* (1971) and *A Hitch in Time* (1978). Two of the most popular releases of the period came in this mode: *The Glitterball* (1977), featuring another friendly alien and some charming stop-motion effects; and *Sammy's Super T-Shirt* (1978), a candidate for the Foundation's funniest release with its parodies of contemporary film and television hits. Escapism was seemingly a major crowd-pleaser in the 1970s, perhaps as a result of endlessly gloomy news of strikes and economic decline, as well as the eruption of violence in Northern Ireland.

Some old favourites did persist, such as animal subjects, though they often involved a new liberal, environmentalist agenda as in *Seal Island* (1977) and *The Peregrine Hunters* (1978). An environmental theme was also apparent in one of the best films of the period, *The Battle of Billy's Pond* (1976). Exotic foreign locales still appeared in the likes of *Avalanche* (1975), albeit much less often; budgets in the 1970s were even more constrained than before. Competitions and sporting contests were still there in *The Hoverbug* and *Scramble!* (both 1970) but, again, with less regularity. Another old device dusted off was to set a film around a Saturday morning film club, in this case combined with added animal interest in *Raising the Roof* (1971) in which local children take part in a competition to bring in the most unusual pet. One curiosity is the number of films set at sea with *Hijack!* (1975) being the pick of half a dozen. Another popular theme is kidnapping, with nearly as many titles led by the gritty *Black Island* (1978); this may have been influenced by another contemporary major news story, the abduction of heiress Patty Hearst. A proliferation of gentle thrillers appeared, often involving hordes of kids foiling gangs of bank robbers or jewel thieves. A number of them bore a distinct degree of rough-edged realism, in settings, characters and action. Most striking among these was *Hide and Seek* (1972).

The Foundation's ability to call upon renowned directors produced two of the most memorable films of this, or any, period of its operation. James Hill's *The Man from Nowhere* (1976) was a beautifully crafted Victorian mystery with moments of real shock, while *The Boy Who Turned Yellow* (1972) pulled off a remarkable coup in securing the services of Michael Powell and Emeric Pressburger, who delivered one of the most idiosyncratic and original of all CFF films. This era probably boasts a wider range of film subjects than any other. Other notable directors recruited included Philip Leacock and Gerry O'Hara.

Special mention should be made here of the contribution of one Henry MacLeod Robertson. Robertson, who was also known as Harry Robertson and Harry Robinson, was a composer and conductor whose prolific credits include the themes for television shows such as *Six-Five Special* (1957–8) and *Oh Boy!* (1959), various stage musicals, commercials, scores for Hammer horror films and the novelty hit record 'Hoots Mon' recorded under the pseudonym Lord Rockingham's XI. He probably holds more CFF credits than any other single person, having supplied the scores for over thirty of the Foundation's films from *Valley of the Kings* to *Terry on the Fence* (1985). Many were characterised by knowing references to well-known melodies or by their comic cadences. He even contributed to a couple of scripts as H. MacLeod Robertson.

There was certainly no shortage of praise and public recognition for the Foundation at this time. In 1969 the CFF featured heavily in the BFI's 'Silver Jubilee of Children's Films', which toured over 300 cinemas across the UK. In 1970 the CFF started its own annual Oscars-style competition with the Chiffy Awards, capped by an event staged at the ABC Kingston upon Thames in front of an audience of 1,800. The proceedings were filmed by the BBC for its primetime evening news magazine *Nationwide* (1969–83) and by the Central Office of Information for overseas distribution. *Go Kart Go* won the top prize at the inaugural contest. The Foundation's twenty-fifth anniversary was celebrated in April 1976 with a special matinee event at the Odeon, Leicester Square, attended by the Duchess of Kent. The screening included premieres of *The Man from Nowhere* and *The Battle of Billy's Pond.* It was followed by Children's Film Month across more than 600 UK cinemas and a season of CFF films at the National Film Theatre and at BAFTA in London. Clips from CFF films were also a regular feature on the popular BBC children's quiz show *Screen Test* (1970–84) hosted initially by Michael Rodd. Much of the credit for this increased level of profile-raising activity has to go to the ever energetic Henry Geddes.

The films of the 1970s also provide an invaluable record of changing styles, habits and environments. The children here are startlingly informal in comparison with their predecessors in the world of the CFF. The smart shirts, skirts and ties of the 1950s have been replaced by a relaxed outfit of jeans, trainers, t-shirts and tank-tops. Hair is long for boys and girls. Adults are addressed with a degree of sardonic irreverence rather than the formal politeness of old; there is little use of the term 'sir' to address adult males outside of the classroom. The once empty streets are now full of cars and the bombsites have finally disappeared, to be replaced by blocks of flats, some of which have aged alarmingly quickly. Most adults are much less formal too, including the schoolteachers who often have a weary, careworn air but are also invariably fair, kindly and well intentioned. The villains are a good deal more realistic and can generate a proper sense of menace. The influence of popular crime shows from television like *The Sweeney* (1975–8) is palpable. Britain is a more racially diverse place and gender differences are less pronounced, although the narratives are still largely dominated by male characters and interests. Class barriers seem to have broken down somewhat and there is much greater emphasis on the working class as the socially dominant group, as opposed to the middle class of the past. The cultural revolution of the 1960s was for the most part ignored in terms of direct content in the stories told by the CFF, but its consequences are everywhere to be seen.

The strong track record of the CFF in producing the stars of tomorrow was being increasingly recognised by the wider media, with actors like David Hemmings, Susan George, Michael Crawford and Francesca Annis featuring in magazine photo spreads.[38] The pattern continued into the 1970s with Linda Robson, Pauline Quirke, Brinsley Forde, Gary Kemp, Phil Daniels, Leslie Ash and Sophie Ward making early career appearances. Among the innumerable guest performers (they seemed to be obligatory in the slapstick shorts) were Roy Kinnear, Harry H. Corbett, Alfie Bass, Robin Askwith, Richard Wilson, Michael Elphick and even the cricketer Gary Sobers. The Foundation continued to garner international awards. *The Battle of Billy's Pond* was recognised for its environmental message at Belgrade, while the second series of *Chimpmates* shared the highly prestigious Ruby Slipper at the Los Angeles Film Festival in 1977 along with *The Glitterball.* Other award winners were *The Johnstown Monster* (1971), *Robin Hood Junior, What Next?* (1974) and *Mauro the Gypsy* (1972), the latter being commended at the Moscow Film Festival for its contribution to racial understanding.

The new breed of small independent production companies working for the Foundation was much in evidence in the 1970s with Fanfare and Anvil joined by Pacesetter, Interfilm, Michael Forlong, Mark Forstater and the prolific Eyeline. Writer Michael Barnes joined forces with director David Eady to set up Eady-Barnes Productions, which was responsible for five films during the decade. Longstanding scriptwriters Frank Wells and Pat Latham were still much in demand, as was director Jan Darnley-Smith. Frank Godwin became an increasingly influential figure as producer and director alongside scriptwriting partner C. M. Pennington-Richards. Newer faces behind the camera included the husband-and-wife film-making team of Peter and Carole Smith at Kingsgate, the versatile Harold Orton,

Frank Godwin, one of the CFF's stalwarts behind the camera throughout the 1970s and 80s

who was employed in a number of roles and the talented, American-born Harley Cokeliss, creator of both *The Battle of Billy's Pond* and *The Glitterball.* The structural shifts in the wider industry, which saw the decline of major integrated companies like Rank and ABPC and a move towards smaller independents benefited the Foundation by enlarging its pool of potentially suitable collaborators, especially as these companies were often accustomed to working with low budgets and short shooting schedules.

By the mid-1970s the popularity of the Saturday clubs was holding up remarkably well, with 800 cinemas still taking part and the audience remaining steady at between 350,000 to 500,000 per week. It was an achievement all the more remarkable in the face of an overall decline in cinema attendance in the UK. Entry fees remained very low at between five and fifteen new pence. By 1974 the deteriorating supply of material from the US had resulted in the CFF supplying 80 per cent of what was shown. In order to meet this demand, the Foundation had taken to reissuing its earliest features, although often with abridged running times; the perceived wisdom appears to have been that the pace of its early work was too slow for a 1970s audience. This continued success was recognised in a piece for *Films Illustrated* in 1977, which celebrated the Saturday clubs and pointed to the lack of recognition afforded the CFF in fostering talent and promoting film-going in the UK.[39]

However, by the late 1970s the picture was changing markedly. A report in *Screen International* in 1978 showed a dramatic drop in the number of cinemas running clubs with the figure down to just 350, less than half the number at the start of the decade.[40] Increasing heating costs had made it less economically viable to open screens on a Saturday morning and the widespread conversion of old single-screen picture palaces into multiscreen 'studio' operations resulted in auditorium spaces that were less appropriate for hosting the clubs. Apathy was reported among the major circuits with some cinema staff no longer wanting to work on Saturday mornings. Labour Party backbench MP Gwyneth Dunwoody petitioned the then Education Secretary, Shirley Williams (also Labour), to investigate showing CFF films in colleges of education, with the hope that trainee teachers would then take them into schools, thereby boosting the potential audience. The request wasn't followed up. Fortunately the Foundation's overseas export markets were still buoyant. The CFF further stepped up its own advertising campaigns with short compilations of clips, often introduced by popular television presenters like Ed Stewart, which began to form an integral part of the Saturday club programmes in an effort to retain the audience with the promise of good things to come. EMI, which had taken over the ABC chain in 1969, began to produce trailers to advertise the Saturday clubs, which were screened during mainstream evening programmes. These were aimed squarely at parents and sought to reassure them that their treasured offspring would be in safe hands while alone in the cinema. A battle for audiences was clearly underway.

A major factor in the dwindling of club attendance was undoubtedly the developments in Saturday morning children's television at this time. This was normally a neglected area but on 2 October 1976 the BBC launched *Multi-Coloured Swap Shop*

(1976–81), hosted by Noel Edmonds. In a number of respects the programme replicated the Saturday clubs. It ran for the best part of three hours covering the whole of Saturday morning. Its magazine format showcased a variety of material, including cartoons and short drama serials, as well as educational, sports and news pieces, plus quizzes and competitions. The whole thing was held together by a group of energetic presenters which, ironically, featured Keith Chegwin, star of several CFF films. The programme was instantly popular and set a trend for Saturday morning viewing that led to *Saturday Superstore* (1982–7) and *Going Live!* (1987–93). ITV had its own rival with *Tiswas* (1974–82), which became even more popular and was considerably more anarchic. This approach to Saturday morning television persisted well into the next century such was its success. In a cruel contradiction, the very thing that contributed most to the decline of the clubs was, in its own way, proof of the appeal of their format.

By 1974 the annual grant to the CFF had risen to £300,000 in line with sharply increased inflation rates in the wider national economy and by 1977 it was £350,000. Features were now costing £35,000 and serials £58,000. However, by 1978 the grant was being squeezed as the Eady Levy was redistributed to favour the BFI, the National Film School and the Script Development Fund; falling Saturday club attendances were blamed. The Foundation had continued to import the occasional children's film from Eastern Europe for dubbing and had re-edited two early CEF films, *The Lone Climber* (1949) and *The Mysterious Poacher*, for reissue. They even put a call out via the trade press to any companies who had old children's films that might be suitable for reissue. A problem with supply had begun to develop due to the rather parlous state of some CFF prints which, by this time, had been circulating around the Saturday clubs for years. In 1977 the Foundation admitted that it was finding it difficult to come up with new subjects.[41] Although it still vehemently opposed the release of its films to TV in the UK (it had been approached by both the BBC and ITV), the CFF had opened access to overseas markets. This began in the late 1960s with the US, where CBS had launched its *Children's Film Festival* slot, which ran until 1978 and prominently featured CFF productions. By 1977 the Foundation had distribution deals in more than forty countries for television broadcasting. The pressure to change its stance on domestic distribution was growing.

The 1970s is in many respects a decade of considerable success for the CFF, with its films receiving wide recognition. It was acting vigorously to broaden its reach and increase vital income against a background of industry collapse and economic constraint. It's also a period in which it produced some of its most popular and well-regarded work, branching out on the one side into broad humour and fantasy, and on the other into greater realism and social relevance. At the same time, declining audiences and growing financial pressures were creating major challenges by the end of the decade, a situation that came to crisis point in the next.

The curtain falls, 1979–86

In May 1979 a Conservative government was elected and Margaret Thatcher became Prime Minister. A new era was dawning and that applied to the CFF as much as anyone else in Britain. The consensus politics of the postwar era, which had helped support the Foundation whether Labour or Tories were in office, was about to end. Later that year the Cinematograph Films Council (CFC), which advised the Board of Trade on film policy, recommended that the Eady Levy payments to the Foundation should be reduced by half. The funds produced by the Levy were already dwindling as UK audience levels fell away. The new government was bent on a policy of cutting taxation and spending, thereby reducing the size of the public sector. Crucially, the move to reduce the CFF's funding was supported by the ACTT (Association of Cinematograph, Television and Allied Technicians), the largest and most influential industry union, which argued that the CFF needed to restructure or risk closure.[42] The whole film industry was feeling the pinch and the Foundation was a relatively easy sacrificial lamb to offer up when government funds were under threat. Rather disingenuously, ACTT and the other trade associations continued to voice their support in principle for the CFF but seemed to expect it to find its funding elsewhere. This was a difficult ask for an institution whose entire ethos had been based on the premise that only a subsidised body could produce the kind of work in which it specialised.

The amount eventually awarded to the Foundation in 1980 was £330,000 rather than the £660,000 it had been hoping for, a figure that had leapt up with inflation over the course of the previous three years. It was a drastic cut from £550,000 in 1979–80. The Foundation claimed it needed £660,000 just to maintain production at present levels due to the increased costs related to film-making. Even more alarmingly, the CFC had brought up the possibility that this might be the last payment the Foundation would ever receive. The main reason given was the precipitous decline in attendance at the Saturday clubs. In its newsletter in February of that year, the Cinematograph Exhibitors' Association, which remained the key group on the Foundation's management board, mourned:

> It is of course a very sad matter that the CFF will, if the CEA view prevails, cease to produce children's films. But every other source of revenue open to them has been explored and there is nothing that will produce anything like the amount of money required to finance film production, unless they sold their backlog to television, which CEA would certainly not countenance.[43]

The position of the CEA, which essentially represented cinema managers and owners, reflected a growing awareness that the Saturday clubs were failing and that the task of trying to continue with them was becoming irksome. It was suggested that the remaining clubs could be supported through the existing CFF back-catalogue until their eventual demise, which presumably wouldn't take long. With support fading on all sides, the Foundation was facing a grim prospect as the new decade began.

The most important factor providing fuel for those in government and the industry who favoured the closure of the CFF was the decline in the Saturday clubs. By 1979 Rank was only operating sixty-eight clubs nationally and EMI's ABC chain had just eighty-six. Rank had already ceased to operate a formalised club system as such, simply designating the screenings as being principally for children. ABC followed suit in 1980 but went further, leaving it to individual cinema managers to decide whether or not to run special Saturday morning shows at all, a move that would entail managers dealing directly with the CFF themselves. In addition, each ABC cinema that continued screenings now had to show a profit on them if they were to continue. National weekly attendance figures across all cinemas had fallen to 50,000 from 350,000 just three years earlier and the annual total was around 2.5 million, down from 25–30 million in the 1960s. By the autumn of 1981 both EMI and Rank had wound up their Saturday clubs completely. This only left the remaining independents, which numbered about 100 and generated roughly 10,000 admissions per week.

Despite the dire warnings from the CFC and the Exhibitors' Association, the Foundation limped on. The increased costs in film production were already having an impact, which was then worsened by the drastic cuts in CFF funding from 1980 on. The number of new releases in 1979 was four and in 1980 this fell to three. The reduced funding meant only one film was made for release in each of the following three years, totalling just ten films in five years. Some titles indicated that old habits die hard in terms of content. There were still animal films like *A Horse Called Jester* (1979) and *High Rise Donkey* (1980), more kidnappings in *The Boy Who Never Was* (1979), and science fantasy in *Electric Eskimo* (1979). A gang of kids foiled the crooks in both *The Mine and the Minotaur* (1980) and *4D Special Agents* (1981), the latter designed to support a kids' campaign by the police. Realism was to the fore again, particularly in the lorry-driving adventure *Big Wheels and Sailor* (1979) and in the suspenseful *Danger on Dartmoor* (1980). Much of the output is decidedly unexciting, with the exception of John Krish's *Friend or Foe* (1982), a remarkably adult and richly textured World War II drama adapted from a Michael Morpurgo novel. It showed the quality the CFF was still capable of, as well as demonstrating a growing maturity of approach and ambition. It won three international prizes, including the prestigious Ruby Slipper in Los Angeles. The final release under the CFF banner, *Tightrope to Terror*, written and directed by Bob Kellett and shot on location in the Alps, was released early in 1983. The output for the year was bolstered slightly by the release of a ninety-minute feature called *Professor Potter's Magic Potions*, which was in fact a re-edit of the 1972 six-part series *The Trouble with 2B*. In the midst of this struggle, the Foundation received the highest recognition in its history when it won the Michael Balcon Award from BAFTA in 1980, acknowledging its outstanding contribution to cinema.

In these final years the CFF was still working with Frank Godwin at Monument Productions, as well as Eyeline, Eady-Barnes and Anvil, although its last two projects, *Friend or Foe* and *Tightrope to Terror*, were made in-house. It still managed to draw in some distinguished names with ex-Ealing writer T. E. B. Clarke penning *High Rise Donkey* and actor Barry Foster, as well as old hand Wilfrid Brambell, taking guest roles. Ironically, considering his involvement in *Swap Shop*, Keith Chegwin even appeared as himself in *High Rise Donkey*. Further international awards arrived, with *Big Wheels and Sailor* voted Best Feature at the 1980 Los Angeles Film Festival, *4D Special Agents* winning in Gijon and *Electric Eskimo* garnering two awards.

Having reached the edge of extinction, the Foundation was thrown a lifeline. In 1982 a possible new deal was announced, just as its Eady Levy grant was about to be withdrawn completely.[44] The plan was dependent on an agreement that had been anathema to the Foundation for the whole of its existence: permitting its films to be shown on British television. In exchange for releasing films from its back-catalogue for TV, Rank would supply funding of £400,000 per year for three years, with three new feature films to be made each year. These new titles might obtain a limited cinema run, but would ultimately also end up being broadcast on TV. Ten films were to be released for broadcasting each year from the catalogue, plus the new productions, with the BBC to be the recipients for the first two years and then ITV for the final year. Rank's thinking seems to have been that this three-year period would enable the Foundation to establish itself as a provider of children's filmed dramas for television broadcasters like the BBC, perhaps on a semi-commercial basis. This strategy might secure it a longer-term future.

By this time a new managerial regime was already in place with Lord Birkett appointed as the new Chairman and former public servant Stanley Taylor taking the post of Executive Officer, following on from Henry Geddes, who had finally retired. Taylor had recently retired as Administrator of Hertfordshire Health Service. The view seems to have been that it was time for non-film industry personnel to take a more dispassionate view of the Foundation's management and finances. Pam Poll took the post of Secretary and long-time Foundation staffer John Gilbey became Stanley Taylor's personal assistant, reducing its central staffing from fourteen to three. Bob Kellett was also on hand to offer advice to the new Chair of the Production Committee, Ian Shand; Shand had directed two features for the Foundation a decade before for his own production company. The CFF would move from Great Portland Street to its new base at Elstree Studios in much smaller offices. Lord Birkett was to seek the permission of the acting union, Equity, to proceed with the television broadcasts. By 1983 the new arrangement was in place and the Foundation had changed its name to Children's Film and Television Foundation (CFTF). Lord Birkett announced that the new films would reflect the changing tastes of children, with a greater degree of sophistication and maturity in their content.[45] Ian Shand wrote to *Screen International* in October to remind the industry at large that the CFTF was still alive and kicking and would welcome project ideas from independent writers and producers. The initial roster of nine films was, he hoped, just a starting position.[46]

The first new release followed later in 1983 with Eyeline's gritty thriller *Break Out*, directed by Frank Godwin, and in 1984 a further batch of three films arrived. *Gabrielle and the Doodleman* was a familiar piece of whimsy with a striking supporting cast, including Matthew Kelly, Windsor Davies, Eric Sykes, Gareth Hunt, Lynsey De Paul and Bob Todd. *Haunters of the Deep* was an atmospheric ghost story set in Cornwall with a strong historical theme; it was selected for screening at that year's London Film Festival. The third release was *Pop Pirates*, which certainly had a contemporary feel and featured Roger Daltrey of The Who in a cameo. Three more films were released the following year. The first was *Exploits at West Poley*, its second version of the

John Krish's adult-themed *Friend or Foe* (1985)

Thomas Hardy novel, with Sean Bean and Brenda Fricker in its cast. This was followed by two of the most impressive films in the Foundation's entire output. John Krish's *Out of the Darkness* was a gripping ghost story based on historical events, which proved to be in equal parts disturbing and emotionally moving, while *Terry on the Fence*, adapted from a novel by Bernard Ashley and directed by Frank Godwin, was as morally challenging as it was toughly realistic. It even succeeded in sparking one of the Foundation's rare disputes with the BBFC.

By 1984 the BBC had begun to screen the first of its selection of Foundation films. This started rather half-heartedly with just one isolated screening of *The Boy Who Turned Yellow* for Christmas. It eventually established a regular late afternoon slot called *Friday Film Special*, which ran until 1987; it had to pay an additional fee for the extra year of screenings. Among the presentations were *Cry Wolf* (1968), *Sammy's Super T-Shirt* and *Haunters of the Deep*, with most of the choices coming from the 1970s. A 1986 letter to the *Radio Times* praising the films is indicative of the popularity of the broadcasts.[47] The ITV network broadcast its quota during 1986–7. A process of gradual commercialisation of the Foundation's rich back-catalogue had begun. One inadvertent consequence of the television screenings was that it diverted some of the catalogue away from the remaining Saturday clubs, whose attendances continued to fall.

Another important development came in 1985 with the appointment of Monica Sims as production head in place of Neil Shand. Appropriately enough her background was in television, having spent thirty-one years at the BBC, twelve of them as Head of Children's Programmes where she had overseen a near revolution in its output, discarding the cosiness of the 1950s for a much more contemporary and socially relevant approach. With the cost of production now running at £200,000 per film, the funding from Rank had stretched to just seven films rather than the projected nine. Early in 1986 Rank made clear its intention not to renew the funding; with financial challenges of its own, it could no longer act as a safety net for the CFTF. Any hope of extracting funds from the Eady Levy had died when the Conservative government closed it down altogether in 1985 and it rapidly became apparent that the domestic television broadcasters were not interested in extending their contractual arrangements with the Foundation. With the Rank deal over and the TV partnerships also at an end, Sims was left with the unenviable mission of trying to source other funding, a far from easy task considering the parlous state of the British film industry. By the close of 1986 the Foundation had effectively come to the end of its thirty-five-year existence as a producer of children's films.

From the CFTF to the Children's Media Foundation, 1987–

Ironically, considering the fragile state of the CFTF, the London Film Festival of 1988 celebrated the Foundation with a programme of screenings, an action that might have been interpreted by some in the industry as a requiem. In his programme notes for the screenings, Terry Staples reported that the CFTF was now using the remains of its capital funds to support projects through their early script stage in the anticipation that other companies would come in to bankroll the actual filming and release. He described how the Foundation would do this 'in the hope of breaking even, or perhaps making a profit, out of the film's general release and eventual sale to television'[48]. Any profits could go back into the kitty for the next project. These modest ambitions were achievable as there was still a little money left in the bank, plus some monies coming in from the handful of independents who still ran Saturday clubs (by the end of the decade this would come to an end), as well as income from overseas distribution.

The first fruit borne of this policy was *Just Ask for Diamond* (1988), a comedy crime story adapted by popular children's author Michael Horowitz from his own novel. It was directed by Stephen Bayly and supported with state subsidy through the organisation British Screen. The production partner who saw it through to release was Coverstop Films and the starry supporting cast included Patricia Hodge, Saeed Jaffrey, Jimmy Nail, Susannah York and Bill Paterson. This was followed by *Danny, Champion of the World* (1989), adapted by John Goldsmith from a Roald Dahl novel. There was another impressive cast featuring Jeremy Irons, Robbie Coltrane, Michael Hordern and Lionel Jeffries. Young Danny was played by Jeremy Irons's own son, Samuel. This time the co-producers were Portobello Pictures and Thames Television, with support from the Disney Channel in America. Although *Just Ask for Diamond* was poorly received and made little impact at the box office, *Danny* garnered strong reviews and solid box-office returns. Its welcome success enabled three more projects to reach completion by 1992. The first was a six-part serial, *The Torch*, adapted from a popular children's novel by Jill Paton Walsh. Featuring husband-and-wife team, Judi Dench and Michael Williams, it was co-produced on location in Greece by The Missing Piece and part-financed by the BBC, which subsequently broadcast it on television. The second project was *My Friend Walter*, this time from a Michael Morpurgo book and directed by Gavin Millar, who had also helmed *Danny*. Like *Danny*, it was a co-production with Portobello Pictures and Thames, which then had the UK television rights. Unfortunately, it did not replicate the success of *Danny* on large or small screens. The Foundation now found itself competing in a highly commercial environment where it was at the mercy of market-led trends. It would be another ten years before the CFTF was able to generate another film release. Its efforts were focused instead on facilitating the production of television serials and it was instrumental in developing a highly popular six-part adaptation of *The Borrowers* (1992) and subsequently the fantasy comedy *The Queen's Nose*, which ran for seven seasons from 1995 to 2003.

In 1989 in an attempt to generate much needed revenue, the Foundation gained the agreement of the unions to the commercialisation of its whole back-catalogue. This meant that more titles could potentially be released for television broadcasting or as videos. Unfortunately there were no takers on the television front and video deals were slow in coming to fruition. The number of releases was relatively small, as was the case when DVD technology arrived in 1998; perhaps tastes had simply moved on and it was too early for a nostalgia factor to have kicked in. Revenues were relatively modest. By the end of the 1980s even the most diehard of the Saturday clubs had closed. Although some cinemas retain special screenings for children on Saturday mornings to this day, these mostly constitute discounted reruns of films released six months previously and have little of the particular status enjoyed by the clubs in their heyday. As Terry Staples so beautifully put it: 'It is unlikely that children's cinema will ever again offer the anarchy, the social adventure, the solidarity and collective participation, and the occasional physical danger that came from being All Pals Together.'[49]

The major problem now facing the Foundation was its complete lack of financial backing. In July 1993 Lord Birkett spoke to the parliamentary magazine, *House*: 'Nowadays we are funded by no-one at all. We live, like Hardwick sheep in a snowdrift, on the fat in our wool. Are we, perhaps, the ideal recipient of capital monies from the National Lottery?'[50] However, such funds were not forthcoming at this point. In 1996 Monica Sims led a bid to the National Lottery for a niche children's film franchise but, despite being well received, it was not granted. The gloomy situation at the Foundation was also evident in an interview Stanley Taylor gave to *Empire* magazine in February 1995. He conceded that for the last few years the Foundation had been 'living off

Anna Home valiantly led the CFTF through its final years

our [sic] fat'. Rather than give up, he argued, it would continue to confine itself to assisting in script development: 'If we had the money we would make it ourselves ... we take the risk of paying a writer to develop the script. Then we sell it to someone else to make it.'[51] Unfortunately, it had little success in this regard until the very end of the decade.

In March 1998 Monica Sims retired from the CFTF and Anna Home took over. The move could hardly have been more sympathetic in that she had worked as a producer for Sims when she was head of BBC Children's. She had then followed in her boss's footsteps by taking overall charge of children's provision when Sims moved to the CFTF in 1985. They also shared a philosophy towards children's programmes that could be summed up in two words: *Grange Hill* (1978–2008). It was Anna Home who as a commissioning producer had brought the groundbreaking programme to the BBC with the support of Monica Sims. In an interview with the journal *Televisual* at the time of her appointment to the Foundation, she robustly defended her record of achievements at the BBC, citing the drama series *Byker Grove* (1989–2006) as an example of how children's broadcasting could be entertaining and yet still deal with serious issues in a way that didn't patronise a young audience.[52] With some prescience she went on to talk about the threat to children's media from globalisation and over-commercialisation. She also discussed the revised role of the Foundation, which was to continue to develop scripts with the hope of entering into co-productions so as to secure finance.

She certainly succeeded in bringing another belated surge of activity to the Foundation. In June 1998 it announced to the trade press the relaunch of its production arm, with two new titles in development: *Journey through Midnight* and *War Dogs*. Both were budgeted at £3 million and were to be co-produced in partnership with small independent companies, Catalyst and Green Umbrella respectively.[53] However, both met the fate of so many proposed film projects in this period: they never made it to the screen. The Foundation had more success in a supporting role, the development of television serials, including two seasons of *The Magician's House* (1999–2000) and a seven-part run of *Gypsy Girl* (2001). Eventually, after much campaigning on Anna Home's part, there was another film release: Harley Cokeliss's *An Angel in May* (2002), adapted from Melvin Burgess's novel and featuring actor Tom Wilkinson.[54] Working with four other production partners doesn't normally bode well but the film's limited theatrical release provoked a positive response and it was eventually broadcast as a four-part serial on ITV. It was also recognised with a number of international awards, as well as picking up an Emmy nomination. Sadly, it became the last release to bear the Foundation's name in any form. It was at least a pleasing film with which to finish.

As the new millennium progressed, Anna Home began to steer what remained of the CFTF into an advisory and campaigning role. Increasingly concerned by the cutbacks in ITV's provision of children's content and the commercial pressures facing the BBC, one of Home's new priorities was to influence the government's development of a Communications Bill. In 2002, while it was still in its draft stage, she wrote a piece for the journal *Television* entitled 'Don't Forget the Children', wherein she argued that the Bill should protect children's television in the UK in terms of the number of hours broadcast, the variety of programming, the spend and the content.[55] She also called for the creation of a new campaign group along the lines of the now defunct British Action for Children's TV.

The Foundation then received a belated boost to its hopes of continuing as a production body. In 2003 it was announced that for the next three years an annual sum of £500,000 Lottery funds was to be distributed via the UK Film Council to support the production of family films. Controlled by Grainne Marmion at the Film Council's Development Fund, the money was to be directed towards the BBC and the CFTF, who could use it as seed funding to help develop script ideas. The press statement issued said the initial success of the *Harry Potter* franchise (commencing in 2001) and of Aardman Animation's *Chicken Run* (2000) had shown that Britain could compete internationally in this market.[56] Sadly, although five 'family friendly' projects did receive support at script stage, none actually made it to completion and eventually the Foundation's Lottery support was withdrawn as part of a periodic government reorganisation, which also saw the demise of the Film Council.

The Foundation continued to look for ways in which to keep itself active. A new initiative was unveiled in May 2006 with the launch of the Film Street website. Backed by the Department of Culture, Media and Sport, the Film Council, the BFI and the BBC, it was designed to help children in the six-to-nine age group make their own films. Anna Home attended the press launch along with Greg Childs, who then headed up the BBC's digital content for children. This development was indicative of Anna Home's desire to widen the remit of the CFTF beyond just film and television. This type of activity was reinforced by its continuing role as an industry advisory body and commentator on issues relating to British children's media.

In 2012 the CFTF finally accepted the inevitable and abandoned any remaining dreams of acting as a producer. It also changed its name. Joining forces with the campaign group Save Kids' TV, it became the Children's Media Foundation (CMF) with

Anna Home as chair and the highly experienced Greg Childs, now working as a children's media consultant, as director.[57] Since then it has established an All Party Parliamentary Group to lobby MPs regarding media issues on behalf of children in the UK, as well as serving as a conduit for those interested in the area. Its espoused role is to represent the young audience itself, along with parents and other concerned groups, to both government and the industry, with the intention of promoting quality home-produced media for children. Both Anna Home and Greg Childs continue to share the conviction that children's media plays a vital cultural and social role, as well as generating income and providing jobs for the industry. The need for British children to see work on screen that reflects their own lives is central to the new organisation's aims. This links it back perfectly to the abiding concerns of the original Foundation. The CFF may be gone but its spirit lives on.

Notes

1. Terry Staples, *All Pals Together: The Story of Children's Cinema* (Edinburgh: Edinburgh University Press, 1997), pp. 1–2.
2. Ibid., p. 9.
3. Renamed as the British Board of Film Classification in 1985.
4. See Jeffrey Richards, *The Age of the Dream Palace: Cinema and Society in Britain 1930–1939* (London: Routledge and Kegan Paul, 1984), pp. 63–4.
5. Staples, *All Pals Together*, pp. 38–9.
6. See Richards, *The Age of the Dream Palace*, pp. 58–60 and pp. 67–85.
7. J. P. Mayer, 'Films for Children', *The Times*, 5 January 1946. See also Mayer's *The Sociology of Film* (London: Faber and Faber, 1946).
8. Geoffrey Macnab, *J. Arthur Rank and the British Film Industry* (London and New York: Routledge, 1993), p. 149.
9. Ibid., p. 148.
10. K. C. Wheare, *Report of the Departmental Committee on Cinema and Children* (London: HMSO, 1950).
11. Anon, 'Permanent Body on Child Film Making', *Today's Cinema* vol. 77 no. 6286 (4 July 1951), p. 3.
12. Mary Field, 'Children's Film Foundation', *Visual Education* (June 1952), p. 35.
13. Anon, 'Scheme for Distribution Now Ready', *Daily Film Renter* vol. 26 no. 6377 (25 August 1952), p. 3.
14. Mary Field interviewed in *Today's Cinema* vol. 79 no. 6570 (19 August 1952), p. 3.
15. As reported by Mary Field to *The Film Teacher* (Winter 1952), p. 3.
16. As reported in the *Daily Film Renter* vol. 26 no. 605 (29 October 1952), p. 8.
17. Anon, 'Rank Group Handles Child Films Abroad', *Today's Cinema* vol. 79 no. 6656 (17 December 1952), p. 7.
18. Sir Sidney Harris, 'The Child and the Cinema', *The Film Teacher* (Summer 1952), p. 3.

19. Anon, 'Saturday Morning Matinee', *Look and Listen: Modern Technologies in Education and Training* vol. 8 no. 1 (January 1954), p. 6.
20. Annual Report of the Cinema Exhibitors' Association (March 1953).
21. Anon, 'Can't Show Films We Subsidise', *Today's Cinema* vol. 80 no. 6725 (26 March 1953), p. 6.
22. Letter from W. G. R. Thom, Secretary of the Children's Film Foundation, to the editor of *Today's Cinema*, dated 7 July 1953, held in the British Film Institute archives.
23. CFF cinema survey (1953), held in the BFI archives.
24. Staples, *All Palls Together*, pp. 192–3.
25. *Report on the Work Done by the Children's Film Foundation, 1951–1960* (London: CFF, 1960).
26. Staples, *All Palls Together*, pp. 196–7.
27. Mary Field, 'The Beginnings', *Journal of the Society of Film and Television Arts* vol. 18 (Winter 1964–5), pp. 2–4.
28. Henry Geddes, 'The Present and the Future', *Journal of the Society of Film and Television Arts* vol. 18 (Winter 1964–5), pp. 23–5.
29. *Progress Report: The CFF in the Sixties* (London: CFF, 1964).
30. CFF archives held by the BFI.
31. John Davis, 'Films to Be Proud Of', *Saturday Morning Cinema: A Report of the CFF in the Sixties with a Full Catalogue of CFF Films* (London: CFF, 1967), p. 3.
32. See Chapter 2 for a full discussion of *Soapbox Derby* and *Go Kart Go.*
33. Interview with Henry Geddes, *Kine Weekly* no. 3138 (2 December 1967), p. 3.
34. Henry Geddes, 'The Economics of Children's Film Production' *Film Finance* vol. 3 (December 1970), pp. 21–3.
35. *Saturday Morning Cinema: 25 Years of Films for Children – The CFF Moves into the Seventies* (London: CFF, 1969).
36. Quentin Falk, 'Start 'Em Young Says CFF Chief Henry Geddes', *Cinema/TV Today* no. 10052 (6 October 1973), pp. 10–11.
37. See *Film and TV Technician* vol. 35 no. 295 (December 1969), *Sightlines* vol. 8 no. 1 (Autumn 1974) and *Films and Filming* vol. 28 no. 8 (May 1976), for example.
38. See *ABC Film Review* vol. 19 no. 3 (March 1969) and vol. 19 no. 4 (April 1969).
39. Anon, 'Saturday Morning Pictures', *Films Illustrated* vol. 6 no. 70 (June 1977), pp. 378–9.
40. Quentin Falk, 'The Case for a Top UK Export', *Screen International* vol. 132 (1 April 1978), p. 1.
41. Report in *Young Cinema International* (February 1977), pp. 19–20.
42. Anon, 'Children's Film Foundation Fights for Survival', *Film and Television Technician* (January 1980), pp. 1, 16.
43. *CEA Newsletter* vol. 173 (February 1980).
44. Quentin Falk, 'Whatever Happened to the CFF', *Screen International* vol. 371 (27 November 1982), pp. 1, 19.

45. Anon, 'CFTF Heads Back into Production', *Screen International* vol. 398 (11 June 1983), p. 13.
46. Letter from Ian Shand to the Editor, *Screen International* vol. 414 (1 October 1983), p. 4.
47. *Radio Times* vol. 251 no. 3280 (4 October 1986), p. 96.
48. Terry Staples, 'Alright for Kids', *Official Programme of the 32nd London Film Festival* (10–27 November 1988), pp. 23–4.
49. Staples, *All Palls Together*, p. 243.
50. Anon, 'Are You Sitting Comfortably?', *House* vol. 8 no. 603 (19 July 1993), p. 15.
51. Interview with Stanley Taylor, *Empire* vol. 68 (February 1995), p. 42.
52. Ed Waller, 'Once Upon a Time', *Televisual* (March 1998), pp. 25–6.
53. Reported in *Screen Finance* vol. 11 no. 12 (June 1998), p. 11.
54. See the interview with Harley Cokeliss in Chapter 3.
55. Anna Home, 'Don't Forget the Children', *Television* vol. 39 no. 8 (September 2002), p. 19.
56. Anon, 'Child Support', *Screen International* vol. 1425 (17 October 2003), p. 4.
57. See Chapter 5 for detailed coverage of the aims of the CMF.

2 The Films

This chapter examines some of the most significant, and typical, releases from the nearly thirty-five-year back-catalogue amassed by the CFF and the CFTF. The catalogue itself, a paper list that circulated to cinemas and other venues that had signed up to take the Foundation's productions, grew over the years until in its later versions it contained in the region of 180 separate titles. A late version of this catalogue can still currently be accessed at the Foundation's website.[1] This does not, of course, account for all the productions made or released under the Foundation's banner. Occasionally films were pulled from the catalogue, usually because the prints were too worn to use. The Foundation also distributed films that were made by similar institutions operating overseas, particularly in Eastern Europe or the Commonwealth. Although hard to verify exactly, these films probably add another twenty or so titles to the roster of the Foundation, taking the total to nearly 200.

However, this figure can be expanded again. Some of the catalogue titles were actually serials or series each containing a number of individual episodes. For example, a title like *Ali and the Camel* consists of eight separate episodes of about seventeen minutes each. Counting these as individual titles takes the complete total to over 400. Then there were the sixteen editions of *Our Club Magazine* (1952–6), reissues of films that predated the Foundation such as those from the CEF, travelogues, educational documentaries and the later projects that benefited from CFTF support at script stage. The grand total of items bearing the Foundation's name in some form is more like 450. In addition to this, the Foundation regularly produced promotional trailers and short compilations to advertise its own work, both forthcoming attractions and the back-catalogue itself. These formed part of the programmes shown at children's film clubs. For a not-for-profit producer the figures are remarkable. A full list, as near as possible, is included at Appendix 1.

The output of the Foundation can be grouped under a number of main headings. There are the feature films, which remain its signature pieces. These productions were the most widely seen and accounted for the bulk of its expenditure. There are close on 135 of these, disregarding the imported films distributed by the Foundation. These had a running time of between fifty and sixty minutes and usually formed the second half of children's matinee screenings. The Foundation also made a number of serials and series. A series can be defined as a sequence of stand-alone episodes with self-contained plots but a consistent group of characters, such as *The Chiffy Kids* or the much-loved *The Magnificent 6½*. Humour was foregrounded. The serials featured characters and plotlines that developed from episode to episode in a linear structure, often with a cliff-hanger ending in each instalment, such as *Five Have a Mystery to Solve* or *Valley of the Kings*. The episodes were typically fifteen to twenty minutes for both serials and series. There were occasional documentaries (frequently with fictionalised narrative elements) in both short and feature lengths, many with wildlife subjects like *Fern, the Red Deer* (1976) or *Flash the Sheepdog*. Other dramatised documentaries provided a snapshot of a job or a particular way of life, such as the series *A Letter from ...* . These productions usually appeared in the first half of a children's matinee before the interval.

Patterns of emphasis in the Foundation's work emerged over its thirty-three years in production. From early on the feature film became the Foundation's staple but the 1950s saw a leaning towards gentle detective stories, period settings and sports or music-based competition. These subjects also appear in the cliff-hanger serials common at this stage and into the first half of the 1960s. Although animal stories were always popular, they are more frequent in the 1950s and early 1960s, as are the films with foreign settings. These subjects never went away but as the 1960s progressed into the 1970s the Foundation started to edge away from adventure serials and documentary subjects, putting greater emphasis on the comedy series, as well as the ever present features. By the end of the 1970s the comedy series had also gone. The features now showed a shift towards humorous fantasy and science fiction stories on the one hand and darker, more realistic crime narratives on the other. This reached its apogee in the 1980s with the CFTF's final films, which are ambitious and sometimes deal with quite adult themes, such as in *Out of the Darkness* and *Friend or Foe*.

A comparison between the years 1958 and 1978 illustrates this broad pattern. The output for 1958 includes *Blow Your Own Trumpet*, a forty-one-minute feature film with a young Michael Crawford competing to play in his local brass band, an eight-part detective yarn called *The Carringford School Mystery*, *The Cat Gang* (children help customs officers catch smugglers) and John Krish's charming feature *The Salvage Gang*. The year 1978 offers the final six-part comedy series of *The Chiffy Kids*, more slapstick shorts in the final series of *Chimpmates*, two comparatively hard-edged crime stories in *Deep Waters* and *Black Island*, the Dr Who-inspired fantasy of *A Hitch in Time* with Patrick Troughton, more fantasy in the environmentally themed *Mr Selkie*, another crime drama, this time with animals, called *The Peregrine Hunters* and the fantasy sports spoof of *Sammy's Super T-Shirt*. Some things always abide, from animals and eccentric inventors, to smugglers and hidden treasure, but a change is perceptible. It's hard to imagine the realistic and morally ambiguous *Terry on the Fence* from 1985 being made in the 1950s, just as it's difficult to detect much sign of the nostalgic crime solving of 1956's *Treasure at the Mill* in the 1980s.

The films selected for inclusion in this chapter approximate roughly a quarter of the titles listed in the catalogue. Covering all of the Foundation's work would not only be a daunting task but a redundant one. Much of its output was necessarily formulaic and narratives were often repeated with small variations. The similarities and consistency are evident, for example, in the succession of animal subjects from *The Adventures of Rex* in 1959, through *Ali and the Camel*, *Beware of the Dog* (1963), *Calamity the Cow*, *Anoop and the Elephant* (1972) and *A Horse Called Jester*, right through to *High Rise Donkey* in 1980. In a remarkable number of the features and serials a small group of children on holiday come across a map or book revealing clues to the whereabouts of long-lost treasure, or they accidentally overhear the plans of a gang of smugglers or would-be thieves. With negligible help from the adults, they manage to thwart the villains' plans and retrieve the loot. Rather than fall into repetitive coverage, this chapter focuses on a representative number of productions that illustrate the typical output of the Foundation. By arranging the work chronologically the shifting patterns in its production ethos also emerges. The range of formats and narratives is covered but the selection also has an eye to the exceptions. The series *A Letter from ...* is not typical but is interesting for that reason. Similarly, *The Boy Who Turned Yellow* takes the Foundation's fantasy formula and, in the hands of Michael Powell and Emeric Pressburger, turns it into something unique. Many of the Foundation's finest, most celebrated and popular films have been included too. The choices are bound to leave some fans dissatisfied, and here nostalgia can be a powerful factor, but hopefully the selection succeeds in providing a good sense of what the Foundation was all about.

In making these selections thought has also been given to commercial availability and the opportunities that a reader might have to see the films for themselves. The vast majority of the back-catalogue is held in the archives of the British Film Institute, which has embarked on a programme of remastering. DVD releases are occurring at intervals of roughly six months and a number of titles are already on the market. The selection here has attempted to include all of those available at the time of going to press. Additionally, some titles have emerged via other legitimate sources. Under an earlier deal, a handful of the Foundation's films were licensed for DVD release via Carlton and other companies in the early 2000s. These are long out of print but do appear occasionally on eBay. All of the titles in those releases are discussed here. The selection has also sought to go beyond what is currently commercially available to cover a wider range of films.

Like any long-running franchise, there is a strong element of repetition in the Foundation's output. Familiarity was, after all, part of the appeal that brought young audiences back week after week hoping to see more of what they had enjoyed previously. This selection seeks to illuminate the stable elements that were part of that appeal. At the same time, it sets out to demonstrate that within the formula some startlingly individual achievements were possible. Who, after all, would want to miss the beautifully crafted period shocks of *The Man from Nowhere*, alongside the more comforting charms of *Five on a Treasure Island*.

John of the Fair (1952)

The CFF's first batch of releases for 1952 included four short subjects and just two of the hour-long features with which it would become most associated. *The Stolen Plans*, with its story of two children foiling a gang of spies who try to steal the plans for a new aircraft from its designer, supplied the prototype for many features to come. *John of the Fair* is a more unusual project with few subsequent imitators. Its most untypical aspect is its historical setting in eighteenth-century England, a narrative device which the Foundation, with its desire to encourage identification between its young audience and the subject on screen, only rarely returned to.

Young John (John Charlesworth) has been brought up by Doc Claydon (Arthur Young), a struggling fairground hawker who sells herbal remedies. As the narrative unfolds we discover that John is really the heir to a country estate and that his rightful inheritance has been stolen by his uncle, Sir Thomas Renton (David Garth). Doc was supposed to take the boy away from the area forever but their inadvertent return causes Sir Thomas to have John kidnapped and put aboard a ship. When this fails he attempts to have John killed, resulting in the death of Doc. His final scheme sees John framed for Doc's murder. Simultaneously, John and his friends try to find the only witness who can prove his true identity. The inevitable happy ending arrives with a last minute rescue at John's trial.

The film, produced by Merton Park, is a handsome affair that skilfully disguises its low budget. Despite some obvious sets, the costumes and décor are convincing and the orchestral score lends the film a cinematic feel. The story is constructed around a series of chases and escapes, an episodic structure that became characteristic of the CFF. Our hero is supported by a cast of experienced actors who bring polish to the film and the action is balanced with humour throughout, with the two combined in a number of the fight scenes. The various characters of the fairground world, who come together to help John, provide a deal of colour. The Foundation's decision to focus on more contemporary subjects appears to have resulted from a mixture of the costs associated with historical settings and the positive international response to *The Stolen Plans.*

The Dog and the Diamonds (1953)

In comparison with *John of the Fair*, *The Dog and the Diamonds* is highly characteristic of the Foundation's output for the next three decades, particularly in its combination of children combating a gang of villains with plenty of animal interest. The story centres on a group of youngsters who live in a London block of flats where pets are forbidden by the curmudgeonly caretaker, Forbes (played with relish by George Coulouris, who had made his name twelve years earlier in Orson Welles's *Citizen Kane*). Rather than face a constant duel with Forbes, the children transfer their animals to the outbuildings of a deserted mansion house nearby. At the same time, a gang of jewel thieves are using the main house as their base while they set about disposing of a haul of stolen diamonds. To add to this, two men from the council arrive to inspect the buildings as the possible site for a new youth centre. The plot strands draw together in a final chase with a stray dog coming to the rescue and the police arriving in the nick of time. Much to the chagrin of Forbes, the new youth club is established and provides a home for all the children's pets.

The film has many CFF traits but also feels like an early effort. The kids in the gang are barely differentiated so that no clear characters emerge and the pacing is slow, even in the truncated version screened in the 1970s. More typically we see our heroes, who are of various ages and both male and female, accidentally discovering the villains and then showing courage and invention in apprehending them. Also characteristic of the 1950s output are the cut-glass accents of many of the children. There are many incidental pleasures, not least the performances of George Coulouris and another veteran character actor, Kathleen Harrison, who plays Mrs Fossett, the eccentric owner of the local pet store. The film has the air of taking place in a gentler alternate reality, despite the gritty realism of the flats. With its reassuring outcome and sense of justice done, it's a fitting entry for Mary Field's era at the Foundation.

The film was scripted by Pat Latham from an original story by Mary Cathcart Borer, their first credits in what would be lengthy and influential careers with the CFF. It was produced by Peter Rogers, who was still a few years away from beginning the long-running *Carry On* film series, and directed by one of Rank's most reliable hands, Ralph Thomas (whose brother, Gerald, would direct all the *Carry Ons*, as well as *Circus Friends* for the Foundation).

A Letter from Wales (1953)

One thread running through the Foundation's output consisted of educational dramatised documentary shorts. These usually focused on natural history subjects, such as in *Swift Water* where Londoner Terry (Guthrie Mason) learns about sailing and birdwatching while on holiday in Devon. These were mainly products of the Foundation's early years and are redolent of Mary Field's approach. They rarely feature after the end of the 1950s.

One example is the series *A Letter from …*, which started with *A Letter from East Anglia* in 1953 and continued through *A Letter from Wales*, *A Letter from the Isle of Wight* and finally *A Letter from Ayrshire* (1954). Although released during 1953–4, some titles seem to have been shot as early as 1951. The main narrative device is a child writing a letter to a distant relative in which they describe their everyday lives. The intention was to choose locations that offered scenes of rural life and where the apparent lack of obvious excitements was revealed, through the detail of the letter, to be a false impression; everyday events would be shown to contain a wealth of small-scale adventures and pleasures. The films also afforded a glimpse at ways of life and regions rarely seen on British screens.

A Letter from Wales is a good example of the style and content. Made by the small London-based company Brunner Lloyd, which had connections to Wales, the film follows a boy called Rhys who introduces himself in voiceover as living on a farm with his family in North Wales. He sits at the kitchen table writing to his cousin in Australia, telling him about his week and we see various scenes as he describes them. There is breakfast with his brother and two sisters, followed by the walk to school during which he finds a bird's nest full of eggs and catches a trout in a stream. Rhys is late for school and sneaks into class but is caught in the act. His fish is confiscated and he is not allowed any lunch but in a neat reversal the fish is then brought in on a plate, having been cooked for him. After school, he rescues a stray lamb caught in a hedge and takes it safely home. In the film's final sequence, Rhys makes a trip to a nearby harbour with his friends. He spies seagulls circling and informs the sleeping fishermen who set off to make a catch. The kids are rewarded with a trip out on the lifeboat.

Like most of the Foundation's documentaries, actuality footage shot on location with local people is combined with a structured storyline to produce a form of dramatised documentary. The film is charming, with an unforced lyricism, and succeeds in capturing a lifestyle that was already under threat of extinction. Its limitations are attributable to CFF editorial decisions, encompassing the now dated received pronunciation of the child actor providing the voiceover and the unconvincing adult sentiments that he often expresses. After some petitioning, the Foundation released a version in Welsh, which is certainly appropriate considering this is the language spoken by the film's performers. These features are trademarks of the Foundation in the 1950s and can be traced to the position adopted by Mary Field. The condescending nature of this approach is particularly noticeable in the short documentaries and played its part in their being abandoned after Field's tenure ended.

Johnny on the Run (1953)

Johnny on the Run is one of the most striking of the CFF's early features, with a seriousness of intent that helped establish its international reputation. It shows a willingness to engage with topical subjects not always evident in later 1950s output but that made a return in the 1970s and 80s. Here the topic is the treatment of refugees displaced in the aftermath of World War II and in particular the plight of orphaned children.

Johnny, or rather Janek (Eugeniusz Chyiek), is from Poland and is being fostered by a less than welcoming family in Edinburgh. The mother, Mrs MacGregor (Mona Washbourne), is more interested in the money she gets for his upkeep than his actual welfare and her eldest son resents this cuckoo in the nest. After being neglected at home and bullied by children in the street, Johnny runs away to try to get back to Poland. On his travels he first falls into the clutches of two inept housebreakers played by Sydney Tafler and Michael Balfour but eventually finds his way to a special village in the countryside entirely made up of war orphans. Remarkably, this place actually existed in Renfrewshire, 640 orphaned children living together in their own community under adult supervision. Johnny is finally happy but his security in this new home is threatened when the two crooks turn up looking for their lost booty and then Mrs MacGregor arrives on a not dissimilar mission.

Johnny on the Run (1953) was an important early success for the Foundation

The film benefits from location shooting in a misty Edinburgh and the Scottish countryside. The children's performances are unforced and supported by effective turns by the adults. The director was Lewis Gilbert, who would go on to a distinguished career, including three James Bond films and the popular successes *Alfie* (1966) and *Educating Rita* (1983). The style and pace he brings to the film mark it out from the conservative approach to camera and editing evident in the Foundation's 1950s films.

The film's real achievement, however, is in combining an exciting narrative with a sober message about tolerance and understanding between nations in the postwar era. The action is often played for laughs but builds to a dramatic finale involving the village boys in a paperchase, while the girls try to capture the crooks and help Johnny. Underlying this is a sympathy for Johnny's plight that is genuinely touching. The depiction of the village, an idyllic setting where the children tend animals and operate a democratic system, electing their own president, offers a vision of postwar progress and consensus. Pat Latham's script even manages a gentle commentary on inequality when Johnny finds that the cost of a ticket to Poland is the impossible sum of £17 while at the same time the parents of a rich child are seen buying him a radio for the same amount.

Supersonic Saucer (1956)

Supersonic Saucer has two claims to importance in the CFF canon: first, in initiating a long line of science fantasy films; and, second, for the earliest appearance of a friendly alien. The saucer concerned is from Venus and has lost its way in space, arriving at an English boarding school during the summer holidays. It turns into a decidedly cute creature swathed in a cloth and with beguilingly large eyelashes, looking like a forerunner of Steven Spielberg's *E.T.* (1982). Like the alien of that later film, it only wants to help the three children it befriends, the science-obsessed and arrogant headmaster's son, Rodney (Fella Edmonds), and two girls, Greta (Gillian Harrison) and Sumac (Marcia Monolescue), who are from Norway and South America respectively and who have been forced to stay at the school in the summer holiday. A series of comic misadventures follow, including an accidental bank robbery performed by the well-meaning alien, whom the children have named Meba. The inevitable gang of criminals appear and, with the help of the crooked school caretaker, try to abscond with both the school's silverware and the stolen bank loot. After further mishaps, Meba helps capture the villains before returning safely to his home planet. The reward money enables the two homesick girls to go home for the summer.

Scarcity of funds always presented the CFF's film-makers with a challenge when it came to special effects. Here the saucer is rendered with simple animated drawings superimposed over still live-action images. The creature itself is a glove puppet limited to simple movements and his special powers are largely achieved by running the film backwards or through jump cuts that make objects appear or disappear. Despite their basic nature, the effects prove charming and enhance the air of fairytale unreality. Less agreeable, with hindsight, are the usual acting school accents of the children, even down to Greta and Sumac. The gender stereotypes of the period are initially upheld with Rodney portrayed as the science expert; his disparaging dismissal of the girls as 'foreigners' goes unchallenged. However, it is actually Sumac who comes up with a successful plan to rescue Meba from his captors and the alien only communicates telepathically with the two girls.

Made by regular CFF collaborators Gaumont-British, with Meba created by John Wright Puppeteers, the film was produced by Frank Wells from his original story. Wells had previously produced *The Stolen Plans* and *The Clue of the Missing Ape* and went on to be one of the CFF's most influential figures through the 1950s and early 1960s. In the end the children learn the valuable lesson to think carefully about what they wish for, as Meba's willingness to make their dreams into reality often ends in misfortune.

Treasure at the Mill (1956)

Treasure at the Mill is an archetypal example of the CFF's output in the 1950s and the basic elements of its plot were repeated many times. The film, from an original story by the popular and prolific children's writer Malcolm Saville, was simultaneously published as a novel. The screenplay was by Mary Cathcart Borer, who had been writing for films since the early 1940s. She was already a Foundation stalwart, providing the story for *The Dog and the Diamonds* and *Tim Driscoll's Donkey*. Mary Field collaborated with Saville on the short film *Trouble at Townsend* (1944) when at the Ministry of Information and clearly liked his work as she commissioned *Treasure at the Mill* from him personally. Saville's writing is known for its use of rural settings, particularly Shropshire, and often evokes a pastoral idyll. A good deal of that flavour translates into the film, which opens with a characteristically romantic view of our hero, John Adams (Richard Palmer), emerging from his den to feed swans on the river before setting off in his canoe. He longs to buy the deserted cottage he has found so that he and his mother can live there; as is the case with many CFF heroes, his father is absent.

Through reading a book on local history and receiving family heirlooms from his mother, John uncovers the fact that treasure belonging to an ancestor, thought lost during the Civil War, may be hidden in the village's old watermill. The new owners of the mill, a boy and his two sisters (plus parents), first hinder and then aid John. Narrative tension is provided by a rival treasure hunter, in the form of miserly Mr Wilson (John Ruddock), for whom John's mother works as housekeeper. Wilson is on to the clues as well and a cat-and-mouse story develops as they compete to get to the treasure. Excitement is created by cross-cutting between Wilson's climactic hunt for the treasure and John's efforts to escape from the workshop where he has been locked by Wilson, a technique common to innumerable Foundation films. John joins forces with the girls and turns the tables on Wilson, trapping him in the mill's water wheel and forcing him to hand over the treasure. He uses the money to buy the dream cottage for his mother.

The film's leisurely narration generates a little suspense but its real pleasures lie in the picture of rural contentment it paints. Shot at a mill in Essex, the film uses the family who owned it, the Pettits, who were known to Mary Field; the father, Harry, went on to illustrate the book. Their existence and presence in the film suggests a retreat to a calmer time and place. The mill itself is bathed in perpetual sunshine. A number of generic elements are apparent. The villainous Mr Wilson is more comic than sinister and gets his comeuppance as the children laugh at his plight stuck in the water wheel; it's remarkable how many of the Foundation's films end with the villain dunked in water while children look on laughing. The leading child actors have the clipped accents and drama school delivery favoured by Mary Field complete with exclamations of 'Gosh' and 'Smashing'. This is exaggerated by the use of post-synchronisation. In an interview on the DVD release by the Malcolm Saville Society, the now adult daughter of the Pettit family, Merrilyn, reveals that her voice and those of her siblings were dubbed over at the Foundation's insistence.[2] She also recalls attending the film's premiere at the Odeon, Marble Arch in January 1957 where it was rapturously received by an audience of children.

For all its limitations in terms of plot and performance, the film's appeal is its ability to conjure up a world which was already vanishing at the time of its making. There is no sign here of a nation in the grip of the Suez Crisis or on the brink of the cultural revolution of the 1960s. This is a world where villains are ineffectual, happiness is certain and summer days never end.

Five on a Treasure Island (1957)

In style and content, *Five on a Treasure Island* is a close relative to *Treasure at the Mill.* This eight-part serial is based on the first of Enid Blyton's popular, and occasionally mocked, Famous Five books. Originally published in 1942, it was followed by a further twenty-plus volumes detailing the adventures of siblings, Julian, Ann and Dick, their cousin George (actually Georgina but known as George because she's a tomboy) and George's dog, Timmy. The serial was scripted by Michael Barnes in his first assignment for the CFF; he went on to become one of its most reliable and versatile screenwriters. Frank Wells was in charge of the production and provided the initial treatment. The project was considered important enough for Rank itself to produce, with the experienced editor, Gerald Landau, in his only credit as director. The links with *Treasure at the Mill* are confirmed by the casting of Richard Palmer again, as Julian. As Norman Wright has pointed out, Barnes and Wells adhered closely to Blyton's work but 'introduced more action, a larger role for the villains and brought greater tension into the adventure'[3].

The CFF's format for adventure serials had been first established in 1955 with *Raiders of the River* and then consolidated by *Five Clues to Fortune,* both produced by Merton Park, but it was the popularity of *Five on a Treasure Island* that cemented the formula, one which the Foundation was to exploit for the next fifteen years. It was quickly followed by *The Carringford School Mystery, Mystery in the Mine* and, eventually, a direct sequel in *Five Have a Mystery to Solve.* The narrative unfolds over eight episodes of roughly fifteen minutes, each with a cliff-hanger ending followed by a title card encouraging the audience to come back next week. The next episode then opens with a recap introduced either by Julian or the villainous Jim (Nicholas Bruce), with brief clips from previous episodes.

The story finds the Five on summer holidays with George's parents on the south coast of England. George's father owns an island complete with ruined castle. Nearby is a shipwreck which may contain clues to the whereabouts of some treasure. The children find a box while diving at the wreck that contains a map that in turn leads them to a network of underground tunnels on the island and eventually to a hoard of gold bars. Two crooked antique dealers are also on the trail and the plot develops into a series of reversals as first the children and then the villains find themselves locked up on the island. Help eventually arrives from the mainland and the crooks are caught. The gold helps hard-up Uncle Quentin (Peter Burton) to pay his debts and keep the island in the family. The story is necessarily episodic but each instalment provides its own self-contained chase sequences before climaxing in the expected cliff-hanger.

Like *Treasure at the Mill*, a good deal of the enjoyment stems from an idealised image of childhood summers, albeit privileged ones. The scenery (the film was shot at Corfe Castle and Lulworth Cove in Dorset) is striking and the story unfolds at an easy pace with little sense of real threat; the outcome is never in doubt. There is plenty of time for picnics. The children are loyal in their friendships, including that with Timmy the dog, enjoy untroubled relationships with the adults (other than the villains) and easily triumph through tenacity and courage. Blyton has been the subject of criticism from contemporary commentators for her alleged sexism, class consciousness and xenophobia. There is little evidence of the latter but there is material that falls into the first two categories. Despite his financial problems, Uncle Quentin lives in a mansion and he, along with all the other characters, have impeccable middle-class accents; there are plentiful exclamations of 'gosh', 'smashing' and 'old chap'. Both girls are involved in the action but George's tomboy status is confirmed by the now dated fact that her hair is short. She also suffers the indignity of being told at the film's conclusion, as an intended compliment, that she couldn't have done better if she had been a boy.

These elements, along with a degree of padding (there are innumerable shots of the children walking to and from the castle), do tend to confirm the stereotype lampooned by *The Comic Strip Presents* in its 1982 parody *Five Go Mad in Dorset*. It's perhaps best now to recognise how the CFF sought to adapt what was already a popular, established generic formula for children to the cinema. If the attitudes are chauvinist and snobby, then the CFF was reflecting values held by parts of British society at this time. In this respect *Five on a Treasure Island* is indicative of a backward-looking conservatism that dominated CFF work in the 1950s and lingered into the next decade.

Soapbox Derby (1957)

Soapbox Derby is largely remembered now as one of the two CFF films to feature a young Michael Crawford, the other being *Blow Your Own Trumpet*, released the following year. However, the film is just as noteworthy as an early and typical example of the Foundation's penchant for stories with a competitive element, in this case the race of the film's title. It also taps into another narrative vein favoured by the CFF, that of an intrepid group of friends trying to build something together. All that's missing here is the usual crackpot inventor.

Peter (Crawford) is leader of the Battersea Bats. With his pals, Legs (Keith Davis) and Foureyes (Roy Townsend), he sets about making a kart that will win them the race. They are up against a rival gang, the Victoria Victors, which includes Lew (Alan Coleshill, playing a role many years too young for him), who has been kicked out of the Bats as a 'dirty fighter'. Supported by his dad, who owns a scrapyard, Lew resorts to various underhand methods to sabotage the Bats and win the climactic race. Lew is not averse to intimidating Foureyes' sister, Betty (Carla Challoner), by threatening to smash her favourite doll. He even enlists his dad's help in stealing the Bats' kart, but with the help of Grandpa (Mark Daly) it is retrieved and they go on to win the prize.

The story is punctuated by a number of chases and draws a simple but clear moral; it's not just about winning but about playing fair. Of course, this being a CFF film, the kids who play fair must also be seen to win, which rather confuses the point but ensures a happy ending.

The film deploys its London background to good effect, especially around the dockyards, which already seem neglected. It glancingly catches London on the cusp of major change. Scenes of still derelict bombsites contrast with the new estates and flats, and more comically with Grandpa's bizarre bubble car. The interiors were shot at Bushey Studios in Hertfordshire, a facility used for many CFF films and one of the longest running studios in the UK. A pleasure of the Foundation's films is their ability to capture the moment, enhanced by extensive location shooting (it was cheaper). Crawford is engaging, and immediately recognisable, supported by several other able child actors. He recalled for the BFI his happiness, as a former attendee at Saturday morning cinema, at 'being paid to do things you would ordinarily be arrested for!'[4] The CFF had begun to feature popular comedians and character actors in cameo roles and *Soapbox Derby* has a fleeting appearance by Harry Fowler as a barrow boy who comes to grief in an encounter with Grandpa's car. Fowler was already a veteran of British comedies where he invariably played genial cockney spivs.

One surprising aspect is the film's relaxed attitude to violence. It is punctuated by a series of punch-ups, with the children landing blows on each other. The first fight ends with one child having to be rescued from the Thames and Lew being ejected from the gang for kicking another boy while he is lying on the floor. Later, Legs is hurled to the ground by Lew's father, who is then nearly run over by Grandpa's car. Despite a comic music score, these incidents are unsettling for a contemporary audience. An oddly dark tone is also evident when Lew threatens Betty, a sequence that ends with her running into the road and being knocked down by a truck. More characteristic of this period is the misunderstanding and rift that occurs between Foureyes and Peter, which is only resolved at the end when the true events are revealed to Peter. Poor Betty is saddled with the usual role afforded to girls in the 1950s films, which is to generally get in the way and be a nuisance.

With its endorsement of playing by the rules and its confidence in the triumph of virtue, *Soapbox Derby* is a typical product of the CFF in the 1950s.

The Adventures of HAL 5 (1957)

The Adventures of HAL 5 combines two favourite CFF elements: gentle fantasy and nostalgic affection for vintage vehicles of various kinds. The vehicle here is an Austin 7 motorcar equipped with a simple animated face, which appears when none of the human cast members is looking. The film nods backwards to earlier British celebrations of charming vintage motors such as *Genevieve* (1953), as well as forward to Disney's almost human VW Beetle, Herbie, who was to make his debut in *The Love Bug* (1968).

The convoluted plot follows HAL 5 (his number plate) as he is sold to the unscrupulous manager of a garage, who in turn sells him on to a country vicar

(William Russell) at an inflated price, having first ensured that the car will break down and need expensive repairs. The car ends up back at the garage where the manager plans to have it stolen so he can claim the insurance on it. Fortunately, and with a strong element of plot contrivance, the vicar happens to know the car's original owner, as well as the man who actually owns the garage, and is therefore able to uncover the double-dealings of the garage manager. He is helped by his niece and nephew, the central child characters. The manager's attempts to dispose of HAL 5 are thwarted by the car itself which takes on a life of its own, deliberately driving him to the farm where the others are gathered. All ends happily with the manager fired and the car returned in pristine condition to the vicar.

As with *Treasure at the Mill*, the appeal, apart from the charming anthropomorphic car, lies in the presentation of a rural idyll. The story takes place in an unspecified village where everyone knows each other, the sun always shines for a picnic and the vicar trains the local youngsters to compete in a cross-country race. It has a dated air, so that the period could just as easily have been the 1930s as the 1950s. This is a Britain of ex-RAF officers with handlebar moustaches who say things like 'jolly good show, chaps' and of children who refer to adult males as 'sir' in painfully stilted accents. There is no evidence of a country on the cusp of the swinging sixties. The film is curious for placing the children at the fringes of the action with emphasis on an array of adult characters. There is the usual broad slapstick, mainly at the expense of the villainous garage manager, who inevitably ends up in the farm pond.

The film is an early work of director Don Sharp, who went on to a career in mainstream cinema and television; among his best-remembered films are lively entries for Hammer including *Rasputin: The Mad Monk* (1966). Sadly, there is little of that panache here. The pace is particularly leisurely. *The Adventures of HAL 5* is a film that belongs to the cosy style preferred by the CFF in the 1950s.

The Salvage Gang (1958)

Written and directed by John Krish, from an original idea by Mary Cathcart Borer, *The Salvage Gang* is one of the liveliest and least dated of the CFF's early features. Much of this is down to Krish's handling. He started his career in the 1940s with Humphrey Jennings at the Crown Film Unit and by the late 1950s had established himself as a leading documentary film-maker with work like *The Elephant Will Never Forget* (1953) made for British Transport Films. Just prior to *The Salvage Gang* he had switched to fiction subjects with crime stories for cinema and television. *The Salvage Gang* was made for the production company World Wide, which was following a similar path to Krish, moving from actuality into children's films. Krish would make two more features for the Foundation in the 1980s.

After the usual brisk credits, the film introduces the typical group of CFF protagonists: the leader, Freddie (Christopher Warbey), sidekick, Kim (Frazer Hines), youngster, Ali (Ali Allen) and token girl, Pat (Amanda Coxell). Frazer Hines belongs to the illustrious line of CFF child actors who went on to successful adult careers, in his case

The Salvage Gang (1958) is the first of three distinguished films directed for the CFF by John Krish

as Jamie in *Doctor Who* (1963–) and then Joe Sugden in a twenty-year run in the television soap *Emmerdale* (1972–). The plot is simple, even by CFF standards. Having ruined a saw belonging to Pat's dad, the gang set off to raise funds to buy a new one. This involves them in various episodes played largely for laughs. Their attempts to help paint a barge end in slapstick chaos, as does their effort at washing Mr Caspanelli's (Richard Molinas) car. The second half of the film revolves around a plan to make money by collecting scrap house to house and selling it at a yard. The ensuing confusion climaxes with a bedstead from Freddie's house being accidentally sold. The kids then chase all over London trying to retrieve it. This takes them initially on a bus journey and then on a long walk home as they push the bed through London's backstreets from East to West.

The humour is broad but engaging. The car washing sequence is typical with the vehicle gradually coming apart under the kids' ministrations. This is underlined by Jack Beaver's musical score, which gives Mr Caspanelli an operatic flourish. Everybody mugs enthusiastically for the camera. The film's comic highlight is a brief cameo by Wilfrid Brambell as a tramp who takes a liking to the bed and refuses to leave it; he is eventually tempted off by a ham roll. Although four years before *Steptoe and Son*, the short skit looks like a rehearsal for his later role. Krish recalled working with Brambell as 'a delight. He was always wonderfully kind and funny and hard working.'[5]

The film is hampered by the twee portrayal of the children, who seem to have been dropped in from a Home Counties fantasy of British youth. This caused Krish some irritation, as revealed in the interview with him later in this book. The ending is also tame as dad ends up ruining the new saw the children have bought for him; everyone laughs! Its lasting value lies in two areas. First, the inventiveness of Krish's direction with its fluent camerawork and well-chosen angles; in an interview given during the making of the film, Krish talks candidly about the challenges of working on a budget of £17,000 but also about the seriousness of his approach, particularly with his young actors whom he treats as professionals.[6] Second, in the vivid portrait of London unveiled by James Allen's striking cinematography. The children's journey takes them on a tour of London sights like Tower Bridge and St Paul's, but just as fascinating are the quiet backstreets they wander through, mostly empty of cars. This is a London in transition where one moment they are crossing vacant bombsites and the next passing a new block of flats under construction.

The Monster of Highgate Ponds (1961)

Despite its slender plot, *The Monster of Highgate Ponds* deserves mention for several reasons. First, the film was the only occasion on which the CFF collaborated with the company Halas and Batchelor, a surprising fact considering the latter was the premier producer of animation in the UK. The company was founded in 1940 by Hungarian-born John Halas and his English wife, Joy Batchelor. By 1961 it had built an international reputation through producing dozens of informational shorts for government departments, as well as adverts for commercial clients. It was best known for its adaptation of George Orwell's *Animal Farm* (1954), the first feature-length animation produced in the UK. Halas produced *Monster* himself, while Mary Cathcart Borer's script was developed from a story idea by Batchelor. Their influence is apparent in the stop-motion sequences showing the cute baby 'monster' as it emerges from its egg. These have a charm typical of Halas and Batchelor whose sensibility combined Disney-style anthropomorphism with a more European art aesthetic.

The second element of note was the distinguished director, Alberto Cavalcanti; the CFF was remarkably successful in drawing in renowned directors. Born in Brazil, Cavalcanti had worked in France before coming to Britain to join the GPO Film Unit, which he eventually headed. He then spent several years at Ealing before further travels. His remarkable output combines the realism he took from documentary with a taste for the surreal. Disappointingly, little of this is evident in *Monster*, with the exception of the grotesque old lady in the park. Vivien Halas, daughter of John and Joy, recalled that Cavalcanti regarded the project as something of a come-down and wandered the Hampstead Heath location 'clutching his head in despair'[7]. The film owes more to Halas and Batchelor's taste for whimsy.

The story combines several favourite CFF motifs. We have a small group of youngsters consisting of brother and sister, David (Michael Wade) and Sophie (Rachel Clay), and their friend Chris (Terry Raven), who are given an egg to care for by the siblings'

Uncle Dick (Ronald Howard), an explorer who works for the Natural History Museum. When the egg hatches, the story is about caring for an animal, albeit a kind of dragon, which was the basis for many CFF films. Add to this the fantasy element of the creature, who is almost David's imaginary friend during the first part of the film. This is the most successful section, with David hiding his new companion in his school desk and bedroom wardrobe.

The second half of the story devolves into a contrived drama, with the creature threatened by two fairground showmen who want to use it to draw customers to their failing sideshow. A series of chases follows as the narrative intercuts between the kids trying to keep the ever-growing monster safe and the inept efforts of the villains to discover its whereabouts. The action is played for laughs and shifts into farce, especially in a sequence where the monster, now living in the ponds on the Heath, appears in the women's bathing area and then the men's, causing chaos in speeded-up motion. As before, the London backgrounds provide much interest. The capital again seems caught between the past and a future heralding change. Here the past is seen in the form of the jovial policemen, whose helmets are stolen by the monster but who finally provide an escort to the docks. The children seem prematurely middle-aged. The opening family scene wouldn't have looked out of place in the 1920s.

Testing the film on my twelve-year-old daughter proved instructive. The clear engaging narrative held her attention throughout. However, the stilted dialogue and

The Monster of Highgate Ponds (1961): rudimentary special effects and an environmental message

dated accents caused unintentional mirth, as did some of the special effects. Children's media has moved a long way in fifty years and a man in a rubber dinosaur suit prompted howls of laughter. Worst of all were the early scenes when the monster appears to be a plastic toy that David carries under his arm. To my sympathetic, and aged, eye this suggested that the creature might be in the boy's imagination. The film also posits a gentle environmental message, with the monster returned to its natural habitat in the end.

Go Kart Go (1963)

Looking like a reworking of *Soapbox Derby* but with engines, *Go Kart Go* bears the unmistakable stamp of the Foundation's plan to imbue its films of the early 1960s with a contemporary feel. The brisk, energetic style here, combined with elements of realism, feels less dated than its typical 1950s work.

The story is on familiar territory with our gang (four boys and two girls of varying ages) making a go-kart to take part in races at a local track. They are up against a dastardly rival group who want to win at any cost, even stooping to sabotage. The good gang undergo the usual CFF trials and tribulations – no money to buy parts – but come through with the help of their parents (who club together to purchase a chassis) and a kindly scrapyard owner, played appropriately by Wilfred Brambell just a year after his first appearances in *Steptoe and Son*. The bad guys try to win the final race by sawing through the axle of their opponent's kart but a last-minute repair job saves the day. Their bullying leader, played with relish by Frazer Hines in his third and final outing for the Foundation, ends up in a pond, having tried to push another kart off the track. The cup is lifted by our hero, Jimpy, played in his first full CFF role by a fresh-faced Dennis Waterman (he had previously supplied a voiceover for *Ali and the Camel*), still many years from his best-known television roles in *The Sweeney*, *Minder* (1979–89) and *New Tricks* (2003–).

The film was written by Michael Barnes from an original story by Frank Wells. It was the sixth writing credit for Barnes and he would go on to script more than fifteen other productions into the 1970s. He had already worked with Wells on *The Piper's Tune*. Barnes had tended to create positive female characters, as evidenced here; the youngest girl reacts to her parents' suggestion that she should play with dolls rather than go-karts by running over one of her dolls with a toy lorry. However, other scenes demonstrate the CFF's chauvinism; in one the boys tell the girls to shut up as they are talking about important things. The film marks the CFF debut of director Jan Darnley-Smith who would go on to helm a further seven projects. He contributes greatly to the film's energy and realism. The normally static camerawork preferred in the 1950s has been replaced by a highly mobile camera. This is evident from the opening scene when we follow the kids on their homemade kart in a point-of-view shot that takes us tumbling down the Harrow hills. The go-kart racing sequences are staged with panache and the close-ups don't resort to the usual back projection, generating authenticity. Even the slapstick is handled with invention, as in a sequence where an out-of-control lawnmower heads around the suburban streets, shaving a rug that has been left out to air and conveniently chipping a bucket of potatoes ready for tea.

The contemporary tone is reinforced by a music score that sounds like the instrumental pop group The Shadows. Composer Ron Goodwin gets in a crafty reference to *Steptoe and Son* in the scenes with Wilfrid Brambell. The film has an undercurrent of class tension as our gang struggle to extract the money for their new kart from their cash-strapped parents. The clearly upper-class race announcer is mocked and Squarehead's (Jimmy Capehorn) dad is seen seeking gardening work from a middle-class man who runs the cricket club. Nonetheless, the moral is pure CFF: cheats don't prosper and those who play fair win in the end. An array of familiar comic actors help the fun including Graham Stark and Cardew Robinson as a policeman and postman caught up in the slapstick action. The *Monthly Film Bulletin* accurately described the film as 'an altogether admirable CFF production'[8].

Seventy Deadly Pills (1963)

Seventy Deadly Pills, along with *Go Kart Go*, was at the forefront of the CFF's new production ethos of the early 1960s. This is typified by the naturalistic acting of its young cast, including their authentic sounding working-class London accents, by the up-to-date nature of the dialogue exchanges between the children and through the realistically observed backdrops. There is a freshness and pace to the action that feels closer to the Foundation's later, gritty 1970s work than the reassuring cosiness of its 1950s productions.

Following the theft of a doctor's car, a bottle of dangerous pills becomes accidentally mixed up with a tin of sweets, which then falls into the hands of The Rockets, a gang of streetwise kids whose HQ in an abandoned house is directly above the garage where the villains have stashed a stolen car. What follows is a tense game of sustained suspense as the children unknowingly have a series of near misses with the pills. The pills come perilously close to being consumed on a number of occasions, while the police comb the streets trying to find them. One of the boys eats a sweet but it turns out to be harmless. Finally, Gertie (Sally Thomsett) succumbs to temptation and falls ill after eating a poisonous pill. Both the police and the gang members realise what has happened and set off separately to track down the remaining three members of the gang who have gone to Battersea Funfair. An exciting chase across London follows and Gertie is later seen recovering in hospital.

The film is directed with assurance by Pat Jackson from his own script. He had previously made his name with such distinguished documentaries as *Western Approaches* (1944) and he succeeds in bringing both realism and tension to the film. There are a number of anxious moments such as when one mother returns home to find her son apparently poisoned before realising that he is only sleeping. The handling of London locations and street scenes shows the influence of New Wave films like *Saturday Night and Sunday Morning* (1960). The London we see still bears the scars of World War II in its empty wasteland and derelict housing. The realities of the postwar world are alluded to in the depiction of one child whose single mum heads out to work evening shifts when he comes home for tea. This is a different world to the one depicted by Mary Field's CFF.

The adult cast sports the usual strong character actors with a memorable turn from Warren Mitchell among the villains. The children's performances are equally striking, with the intricacies of the gang's arcane rules eliciting a great deal of humour. Without being heavy handed, the film conveys its message about the need to beware gifts of unknown origin. The combination of this traditional sentiment with the reinvigorated film-making style indicates the new direction that the CFF was headed in.

Five Have a Mystery to Solve (1964)

Surprisingly, it took the Foundation six years to begin work on a follow-up to *Five on a Treasure Island*, its previous adventure serial based on Enid Blyton's popular sequence of Famous Five novels. This time it selected the twentieth, and latest, of the twenty-two books eventually produced by her. Although scriptwriter Michael Barnes was again on board, the rest of the production team was different, with Rayant Pictures handling the project rather than Rank. The film starred a new cast, even down to Timmy the dog, perhaps by necessity considering the time elapsed since the first series. According to Norman Wright, Barnes only used the bare bones of Blyton's novel this time, introducing a substantial new character in the form of Sir Hugo Blaize (Keith Pyott) and giving more time to the villains.[9] At six episodes rather than eight, the series is brisker than its predecessor too.

The content and format are as before, with a cliff-hanger ending to each fifteen-minute instalment and a concluding title card urging you to return for the next episode; a short recap at the start of each new part brings late arrivals up to speed. The children are on summer holiday again (picturesque location shooting at St George's Island, near West Looe in Cornwall) and set out to investigate rumours of illegal animal trapping at a nature reserve on nearby Whispering Island, owned by Sir Hugo. An added incentive is the treasure that may be hidden on the island. They are aided by the curious character of Wilfred (Michael Wennick), a young orphan who has a special, almost mystical ability to communicate with animals. Together they uncover the nefarious activities of Sir Hugo's two hired hands, who are trapping rare wild rabbits for the fur trade without his knowledge. They discover the whereabouts of the treasure, join forces with the wheelchair-bound Sir Hugo, and take on the villains in a cat-and-mouse contest to save the animals. Tension is escalated by a concluding race against time to escape a flooding dungeon.

Comparison with the first series shows how much the Foundation had changed during the intervening six years. Apart from the sharper cutting, the characters of the children are more developed, with George (Mandy Harper) taking time to warm to Wilfred and much bickering between all of them. The two villains are well played by

The CFF's second Famous Five adaptation, *Five Have a Mystery to Solve* (1964), marked the beginning of the end for its cliff-hanger serials

Robin Hunter and Michael Balfour, and the action shows panache, particularly underwater scenes shot in a large tank at Bushey Studios. However, some things never change and Anne (Paula Boyd) is still the perennial housewife-to-be; she can't wait to start housekeeping when they take care of Hill Cottage and is easily frightened by Wilfred's collection of snails, although she does gain his respect by dumping a bucket of water over his head. Class distinctions are clear: Sir Hugo is a sympathetic lord of the manor, while the villains are his unreliable working-class underlings. There is always time for a smashing tea and the Five are sustained in their adventure by a convenient bag of sticky buns. In the end, the villains fall out among themselves and Sir Hugo resolves to use the treasure to support his animal sanctuary and to help adopt Wilfred.

The Foundation had the rights to another of Blyton's Famous Five stories, *Five Have Plenty of Fun*, but this was never filmed. It seems to have decided that the time was right to move on.

Cup Fever (1965)

Cup Fever is illustrative of another of the Foundation's favourite themes, the sporting contest. Here the young players of Barton United in Manchester are taking part in their local junior cup competition when their efforts are sabotaged by the machinations of a corrupt local councillor (David Lodge). He turns them out of their home pitch, which is to become a car park; it just happens that his own son is captain of Barton's chief rivals, Tooley Green. What follows is a typical CFF adventure with the humble Barton United using all their ingenuity to find training facilities before the final against Tooley. The sort of class undercurrents evident in *Go Kart Go* emerge again. Tooley, aided by Councillor Bates, have the best facilities and kit, while Barton have home-made shirts, a shed for a changing room and train in the street. Despite this, they never resort to the underhand tactics used by Tooley – cutting off the studs on their opponents' boots, wrecking their pre-match plans to prevent the team turning up for the final – and end up triumphing. As always with the CFF, it's not just winning that matters but how you achieve the victory.

The film is unusual in two respects. First, it was shot largely on location in Manchester, a rare trip outside of London and the Home Counties for the Foundation. We are treated to fascinating glimpses of the suburbs, the town centre and older parts of Manchester, as well as a trip to Altrincham for the final. The second area of interest is the participation of Manchester United. When they hear of Barton's plight they offer a

Cup Fever (1965): the boys meet Matt Busby, manager of Manchester United

day at Old Trafford to train with the first team. They meet manager Matt Busby and then head onto the hallowed turf. Various United stars including Denis Law, George Best and Bobby Charlton are seen training with the boys in an extended sequence that serves as a centrepiece for the film. To add some balance for aggrieved Manchester City fans, the winners' trophy is presented by their former goalkeeping legend Bert Trautman.

The film's dominant realism is bolstered by its location shooting, right from the opening shot of a muddy football field fronting a block of flats. If the realism is indicative of the Foundation's revised style of the early 1960s, the attitudes to gender haven't shifted. This is very much a boys' film, with the girls reduced to the secondary role of washing the club's shirts or heating water for their improvised showers. The nadir comes when the girls are excluded from the Old Trafford excursion and volunteer to spend the time sewing new shirts for the boys. Another indicator that the Foundation was attempting to change with the times is the fact that the film features a black character and some Mancunian accents actually feature among the familiar London and Home Counties ones.

Cup Fever benefits from supporting cameos including a brief turn by Norman Rossington as an irate van driver. Most memorable is Bernard Cribbins as a sympathetic policeman; the team's attempts to avoid what they misconstrue as hostile intentions on his part generate much of the film's comic action. The principal girls are played by future stars Susan George and Olivia Hussey. The story reaches a lively finale with the team squad being delivered to the ground in a convoy of milk floats. As described by the *Monthly Film Bulletin*, this is 'a genial, lively and quite inventively scripted comedy, put over with considerable verve'[10].

Runaway Railway (1965)

Like *The Adventures of HAL 5*, *Runaway Railway*'s appeal relies on the presumed fascination that small boys have for vehicles of all descriptions. Here it's a steam train called Matilda that the heartless, bowler-hatted men from the ministry have decided is past its usefulness, along with the local station and the branch line on which it runs; shades of Dr Beeching's cuts to the railway network. In a manner reminiscent of Ealing's *The Titfield Thunderbolt* (1953), our gang of intrepid kids set out to save the train and the railway line. Hope is offered by the local gentry in the form of Lord Chalk (Gerald Case), who might be persuaded to buy the railway and Matilda with it, thereby keeping it in operation. The first half of the film treads familiar territory with its idyllic rural setting (Hampshire), comic adults, bursts of slapstick and gang of industrious children with a plan.

However, the second half of the film shifts gear substantially. Referencing the events of the Great Train Robbery of 1963, the children find themselves inadvertently caught up in an attempted raid on a mail train. After hair-raising near misses involving an express train, they foil the robbers and prove to Lord Chalk that Matilda can still cut the mustard, persuading him to continue funding the line. These latter scenes combine exciting footage of the trains, an elaborate chase and neatly worked slapstick, balancing thrills with humour.

The film brings together two CFF stalwarts in writer Michael Barnes (from a story by CEO Henry Geddes) and director Jan Darnley-Smith, although the material is not consistently handled with the assurance of their other work. The first half is sluggish, with weak performances and poor matching between location footage and studio close-ups. Much of the slapstick has a tired air, including the inevitable sight of a villain falling into a pond. There is an unconvincing rock 'n' roll party organised by the kids to raise money where our gang play the music. Gender bias is also in evidence with one of the girls given a cleaning kit to use on the train, indicating the role deemed appropriate for her. A bright supporting cast carries the interest, with Sydney Tafler and Ronnie Barker as the robbers, Hugh Lloyd as the pompous ministry man and future Doctor Who, Jon Pertwee as the station master. Most enjoyable is a comic turn by Graham Stark as a signalman whose attempts to cook sausages for his breakfast are ruined by the mayhem on the tracks.

Runaway Railway is a film caught between two eras of the Foundation, harking back to the nostalgia of the 1950s, while looking forward to the broad humour and irreverence of the late 1960s and early 1970s.

Operation Third Form (1966)

One thing quickly evident in *Operation Third Form* is that Britain has changed, and so have its children. Our hero, Dick (John Moulder-Brown), may look at first a typical well-scrubbed CFF posh kid but he, and his schoolfriends, talk in authentic working-class London accents. His home and school (St David's School, Hornsea) are ordinary and therefore easier for the young audience to identify with, and the dialogue between the children feels natural. There is more traffic on the streets now, as well as parked cars. The London backgrounds are less prominent than in *The Salvage Gang* but we do get a finale in Regents Park. The boys have longer hair and the attitude to girls is altering. Although initially dismissed by the boys as too young to help out, two of the girls end up performing a crucial role in the action, their bravery instrumental in catching the bad guys. Dick is played engagingly by Moulder-Brown, who was already a veteran of more than a dozen films including the Foundation's *Go Kart Go* and *Runaway Railway*; he would go on to appear in *Calamity the Cow* and later had his greatest critical success with the cult film *Deep End* (1970).

Some things have definitely not changed. The plotline conforms to the formulaic approach favoured by the Foundation even after fifteen years in operation. Dick's school has a naval tradition, evidenced by a ship's bell donated to them by a retired admiral. When it goes missing, Dick and his friends set about finding it and in the process discover that the owner of the local scrapyard (who has the bell) is a criminal planning to steal a valuable painting from the admiral's house. The kids keep watch on the villain, Skinner, played with camp relish by Derren Nesbitt, who would later appear as a wicked Nazi major in *Where Eagles Dare* (1968). When he takes the stolen painting to Regents Park to sell it on to a dealer, the kids lie in wait with most of the school's third year. Skinner ends up in the pond as the police descend and the kids are in fits of laughter. The bell is returned to the school and the kids are given a day off. Crime does not pay and justice is done. The handling by director David Eady, who became another CFF regular, is straightforward but lacks the invention that Krish brought to *The Salvage Gang*.

Nonetheless, as so often with the CFF, there are many incidental pleasures. An early scare sequence when Dick, looking for his French book in the school after dark, runs into the caretaker and some skeletons in the science labs, is funny with a frisson of fright. The kids plan their campaign to trap Skinner in a manner redolent of any number of caper movies, even down to creating an ops room with a blackboard covered in diagrams and plans. They utilise a range of methods more readily available to children, from following Skinner on roller-skates and bikes, and spying on him from behind a copy of *The Avengers* comic book, to using a doll's pram to tip him into the drink. These elements illustrate a crucial aspect in the CFF's success with its audience; it presented stories with which they could identify, however outlandish. This works well in *Operation Third Form*, even if the mugging of the adult performers takes away from the effect.

The Sky Bike (1967)

After the startling sight of the CFF logo in full colour, we move into an equally striking opening sequence. A boy is sleeping in his bedroom. The camera switches to a high angle and the image is tinted blue. Double exposure presents us with a ghostly version of him floating out of his body and flying around the room to inspect his many pictures of airplanes. With an accompaniment of psychedelic music, he is about to zoom out the window when his dad wakes him. His return to earth is confirmed when an attempt to fly downstairs by umbrella ends in a crash landing.

The Sky Bike is directed by Charles Frend. He started his career as an editor in the 1930s and worked with Alfred Hitchcock. He had a long stint at Ealing in the 1940s and 1950s where he made several memorable films including *The Cruel Sea* (1953) and *Scott of the Antarctic* (1948), before moving into television in the 1960s. The sober realism of his usual style is absent in this fantasy, which has affinities with Ealing's taste for quirky humour, but the deftness and sympathy he brings to the film distinguish it. He copes manfully with the low budget but struggles to suggest that the sky bike is actually flying with only the aid of a crane and some carefully angled shots.

The Sky Bike is a gentle, sweet film that harks back back to the nostalgic, comfortable world of the 1950s films, while mixing in swinging sixties psychedelia. A bike ride takes Tom (Spencer Shires) to a disused aerodrome where he encounters Mr Lovejoy (Liam Redmond), another in the Foundation's long line of nutty professors. He is building a flying machine in the hope of winning a competition for man-powered flight. Tom will help him and be co-pilot. The narrative continues along familiar lines. A rival group have their own machine in another shed nearby. They are led by Wingco (Bill Shine) and include David Lodge, both well-known faces from cinema and television of the period. The rivals are ruthless, in a relatively harmless way, and try all kinds of underhand tactics to win, including locking Mr Lovejoy up and vandalising the sky bike. Tom is aided by Porker (Ian Ellis) and his sister, Daphne (Della Rands), and eventually succeeds in getting their machine to fly, enabling them to win the climactic race. Wingco inevitably falls into a ditch full of water and David Lodge's villain is chased off by his own guard dogs. Daphne is regulated to the usual female role, helping to repair the sky bike's sails with her sewing machine. A (much used) subplot entails a misunderstanding between Tom and Porker that drives the latter temporarily into the arms of the rival team, but the two are reconciled and Porker takes over as co-pilot from the exhausted Mr Lovejoy at the finale.

The film's moral is conveyed by Tom's father, who tells him that 'It doesn't matter if you lose as long as you have a go.' Yet the film's pleasures lie elsewhere. Tom is a lonely figure, playing on his own and living in a dream world where he imagines himself as an airline pilot. Tom's parents, although kindly, are distant figures who take him on a stuffy summer holiday to a lakeshore where he distracts himself with thoughts of the flying machine. His conventional, middle-class home is in a leafy suburb where everyone knows each other but little happens. There is the sense here that, as with other fantasy films by the CFF, the whole story might be something he has imagined. This is how the film exerts its emotional pull, inviting us to join in Tom's dream, one where a boy really can fly with a little help from his friends.

Cry Wolf (1968)

Cry Wolf is classic CFF material, an exciting story that builds to a dramatic finish, with a simple message for its young audience. Tony (Anthony Kemp) is a victim of his own vivid imagination, with a reputation as a teller of tall tales. His most recent offence has been to mistakenly accuse a team of surveyors from the council (including Ian Hendry in a cameo) of being bank robbers. His stories are a source of embarrassment to his father who, as the town's mayor, is preparing for the visit of a foreign prime minister. However, Tony has the loyal support of Mary (Mary Burleigh) and eventually of the sceptical Martin (Martin Beaumont). Tony accidentally uncovers a plot to kidnap the PM but can't convince any adults he is telling the truth. He is further confounded by a journalist named Stella (Judy Cornwell) who pretends to believe him but who is actually the leader of the gang planning the kidnapping. After various plot twists including Tony being held prisoner by Stella, he succeeds in foiling the kidnappers and exposing their plot. He is finally vindicated in the eyes of his father.

The action is handled with verve by director John Davis, who went on to make *Danger Point* for the CFF in 1971. The finale is impressive with stylish use of close-ups, crash zooms and rapid cutting as Tony and his friends tackle the kidnappers and prevent their marksman from shooting the PM. The film also benefits from the attractive location work in Margate and features the customary guest appearances, notably from CFF regular Wilfrid Brambell as an accident-prone bicycle delivery man who furnishes the comedy relief.

The moral might seem obvious enough: if you regularly tell fibs, no one will believe you when you're telling the truth. In reality the film's message is more subtle and typical of the child-friendly attitude of the Foundation. It's not Tony's vivid imagination that is at fault so much as the failure of adults to appreciate the worth of a boy with an inventive mind and a good eye for adventure.

The Magnificent 6½ (1968–71)

The inspiration for *The Magnificent 6½* was an earlier serial by the Foundation called *River Rivals.* Produced by Roy Simpson through his company, Century Films, and directed by Harry Booth, this seven-part adventure followed the Holmes children as they build their own boat and beat their rivals, the Craigs, in a local regatta. From this, the CFF has adapted the framework of a gang of kids who could be involved in various ongoing adventures – hardly groundbreaking for the CFF; the twist was that each standalone episode would feature the same characters in a new, self-contained story allowing for an unlimited number of instalments. Comedy also took priority over plot or action. The result was *The Magnificent 6½*. The format proved immensely popular and other variations followed such as *The Chiffy Kids.* By the 1970s these comedy series largely took the place of the cliff-hanger serials previously favoured by the Foundation.

For the first series of *The Magnificent 6½*, released in 1968, the scripts were the work of director Harry Booth and Glyn Jones, who had appeared in *River Rivals.* The first instalment, *Ghosts and Ghoulies,* introduces the characters who make up the gang: the leader is Steve (Len Jones); Dumbo (Ian Ellis) is oversized and dopey; Stodger (Lionel Hawkes) can't stop scoffing sweets; and Toby (Brinsley Forde – later of reggae group Aswad) is the group's joker. The brains of the outfit is bespectacled Whizz (Michael Audreson) and the two girls are tomboy Liz (Suzanne Togni) and pint-sized Peewee (Kim Tallmadge), who counts as the half in the title. Their HQ is an old van in the local scrapyard that they convert into a den. The first series ran to six fifteen-minute episodes, each one introduced by music parodying the theme from *The Magnificent Seven* (1960), complete with gunfire.

The fifth episode, *Bob a Job,* gives a good sense of the overall style. The kids are making their way around a suburban housing estate offering to carry out small tasks to raise money for the church youth club. They are hampered by a mean-spirited householder, who engages them to carry out several jobs and then rewards them with just one shilling between the gang. However, they inadvertently get their revenge when their efforts at his neighbours' homes lead to various slapstick accidents which rebound on him. His garden ornaments are smashed and plants cut down before a friendly policeman arrives and extracts proper payment. The kids are treated to tea and cake with the neighbours and the whole thing ends in a speeded-up chase involving all the cast. Plot is minimal and the film's tone is that of a Keystone Kops silent comedy with lots of visual gags.

A second series of six was commissioned from Century in 1969, again with Booth directing; the new title cards inform us that they are back 'by popular demand'. This time a number of scriptwriters were involved, including Yvonne Richards, Don Nichol, Wally Basco and inevitably Michael Barnes, as well as Glyn Jones. The only cast change was the replacement of Len Jones as Steve by Robin Davies, and the absence of Brinsley Forde from several episodes despite being listed in the cast. The format remains the same involving plenty of slapstick, although some episodes' plotlines are more developed, with the feel of a sitcom. An example is *The Astronaughts* where the gang build a space rocket and mistakenly think they have taken off when it is lifted by a crane. There is more dialogue here, with rounded characterisations amplifying the humour. Both series feature comic cameos from adult actors in the usual style. These include Cardew Robinson, Deryck Guylor, Julian Orchard, Sheila Hancock and George Roderick, who crops up regularly as the local bobby.

Following the popularity of the first two series, Simpson and Booth wanted to offer a third series for television, a move contrary to the CFF's policy. This led to a parting of the ways. Century took the new version to the BBC, which turned it down, but backing was then procured from American producer Twentieth Century-Fox. The result was the highly successful *Here Come the Double Deckers!*. Seventeen episodes were made and broadcast initially in the US; ironically it was the BBC who then picked up the series for broadcast in Britain. Oddly, the BBC had previously had its own go at covering the same territory with *Adventure Weekly* (1968), another 'our gang'-style series that included cast members Len Jones and Ian Ellis from *The Magnificent 6½*. The cast for *The Double Deckers* was mainly new with the exception of Michael Audreson, who was renamed as Brains, and Brinsley Forde, who became Spring. Melvyn Hayes, who played occasional supporting roles in *The Magnificent 6½*, appeared as street cleaner, Albert, the only consistent adult character. The setting of the scrapyard was retained but their den was now a disused double-decker London bus. The slapstick was supplemented by stronger characterisations and even some musical numbers.

Despite this blow, the CFF continued with a third series of *The Magnificent 6½* in 1972 but with an entirely different cast and a new production company, Lion Pacesetter. The character of Liz returned, while others simply changed names: Whizz became Genie, while Stodger and Dumbo were combined to become Podge. However, the series was a failure and didn't achieve the audience response of the first two. Although overshadowed by the success of *The Double Deckers, The Magnificent 6½* was significant in its own right, both in terms of its considerable popularity and in its use of broad slapstick, which was to be a dominant feature of much of the CFF's 1970s output.

On the Run (1969)

If the early CFF could be accused of holding reactionary attitudes towards gender, class and race, then there is certainly evidence of the latter in this thriller. Ben (Dennis Conoley) is reunited with his father (Gordon Jackson), who is often abroad with his work. While playing tennis he meets Tom (Robert Kennedy), an African boy who is in exile from his homeland and in the care of his Uncle Joseph (Bari Jonson). He also encounters Lil (Tracey Collins), who has run away from home to avoid being taken in by social services while her mum is in hospital. The children brandish a variety of accents from acting school cut-glass to Tracey's broad cockney. Uncle Joseph is revealed as a traitor who plans to kidnap Tom as part of an elaborate plan to depose the latter's father back home. Ben and his two new friends flee to his aunt's house on the coast pursued by Joseph and his henchman, Baldy (John Hollis). The finale takes place on the beach as the children find themselves trapped in a cave by the villains. Ben manages to climb the cliff, find his father, and bring the police to the rescue just in time.

The film is hampered by poor acting and unconvincing physical action, despite the employment of Ealing veteran and distinguished documentary film-maker Pat Jackson as director, here making his second feature for the CFF after *Seventy Deadly Pills.* There is evidence of changing attitudes to gender – the two boys leave Lil behind at one point with the usual excuse that girls get in the way but change their minds and include her in the adventure – but it's the film's racial attitudes that are problematic. Uncle Joseph is a caricature African villain, completely untrustworthy and corrupt. He hails from an unspecified nation where political assassination seems to be the order of the day. Cruder still is the casual racism of references to the jungle and to tribal war cries when he is climbing the sea cliffs to get into the cave. Although clearly intended to add exoticism to the film, these elements consign it to the past. At a time when Britain was undergoing radical changes in its racial mix, the film is backward-looking. Fortunately, the Foundation's output in the 1970s was soon to show signs of real alteration.

Egghead's Robot (1970)

A decided air of whimsy, combined with broad humour and fantasy, had become evident in the Foundation's output of the late 1960s and early 1970s. This is typified by the ramshackle *Egghead's Robot.* The film marked the CFF debut of Keith Chegwin, who plays eccentric boffin, Egghead Wentworth. He went on to appear in a direct sequel, *The Troublesome Double,* and *Robin Hood Junior,* as well as playing himself in *High Rise Donkey.* He is joined here by his brother, Jeffrey, who plays the robot.

The plot follows the misadventures of Egghead as he makes use of an abandoned robot created by his inventor father (Richard Wattis), which happens to be his double, to avoid chores like weeding the garden or mowing the lawn, as well as letting it take his place in the cricket team. The film is pure farce as Egghead and the robot are mistaken for each other and various changes of clothing, including a bit of cross-dressing, are required to keep the ruse going. The robot is a success at cricket, courtesy of rudimentary special effects involving speeded-up motion. However, accidents occur as the controls fall into the wrong hands and the robot causes chaos with a cricket ball at a hospital. Much of the comedy is provided by Roy Kinnear as a grumpy park keeper whose attempts to get to the bottom of things inevitably end with him falling into a lake of liquid compost.

Unfortunately, the film is mainly of interest as an example of how the formulaic nature of the CFF's output could produce a tired, threadbare result. The acting is poor, particularly from Jeffrey Chegwin as the unconvincing robot, endlessly repeating the same line: 'Two choc bars in a bag please.' The humour is laboured and the plot makes little sense. The film has an amateurish quality, which even seasoned performers like Kinnear, Wattis, and Patricia Routledge as mum, can do little to combat. The setting is a fantasy of suburbia shot in Wimbledon with accents to match; even Keith Chegwin tries to mask his trademark scouse. On a more positive note, the film is attractively photographed by another CFF regular, John Coquillon, who went on to shoot such feature films as *Straw Dogs* (1971).

One inadvertently funny line provides period interest: when confronted by the sight of Keith Chegwin in his swimming trunks, Patricia Routledge comments, 'Do you think this is the Kings Road, Chelsea – get some clothes on.' The door is left open for the sequel when, after the demise of the robot, Egghead reveals a new robot copy of his sister, complete with trendy sixties gear.

Junket 89 (1970)

Junket 89 is another comic science fantasy redolent of this period, albeit one that is shot against a realistic backdrop. Junket (Stephen Brassett) is the surname of our unfortunate hero who is always in trouble at school, despite being the innocent party. His farcical adventures centre on a transportation device created by his absentminded science teacher, Mr Potter (Richard Wilson), in the school labs. The film shares similarities with later films such as *The Boy Who Turned Yellow* and *A Hitch in Time* in that the humour and plotting depend on characters appearing and disappearing as they move between Junket's school and various other locations, including a tropical island where he is waited on by a uniformed butler and a French maid.

The playful tone is established from the opening credits where the cast clap and jump, chanting the film's title, openly acknowledging the camera. The two school bullies are absurd in matching braces, the head is an accident-prone buffoon (Christopher Benjamin) preoccupied with trying to impress a wealthy parent, Mrs Trowser-Legge (Fanny Carby) whose son, Boofles (Mario Renzullo), is joining the school. There is much chasing about the school and jumping from location to location as Junket, his friends, Boofles and even the Head and Mrs Trowser-Legge find themselves transported by the machine, usually from Junket's locker, number 89, hence the film's odd title.

Some of the comedy is decidedly surreal, as in a sequence where Junket and his friends help a nature photographer capture the eggs of a rare bird. The finale sees most of the cast chasing a malfunctioning control box in the shape of a cricket ball, which ends up at Lord's Cricket Ground in the hands of Gary Sobers, the West Indian all rounder. Things aren't helped by unexplained leaps in the plot or by special effects consisting of jump cuts and tame pyrotechnics. The film's interest lies in the realism of its setting and performances. The school used for filming is clearly genuine, with the rundown appearance of many state schools in the 1970s. A rough edge is provided by the young actors from the Anna Scher Children's Theatre, who were often from under-privileged homes. They bring an energy and naturalism, not least in their accents, to the film. Among them are Linda Robson and Pauline Quirke, who later starred together as adults in the BBC sitcom *Birds of a Feather* (1989–98 and 2014–). The greater realism prefigures the direction the Foundation would take in the decade. The CFF must have considered it a success as it commissioned a follow-up featuring most of the same characters in the form of a comedy serial called *The Trouble with 2B.*

The Johnstown Monster (1971)

The Johnstown Monster is one of the CFF's periodic excursions outside the UK. It was shot on location around Lough Derg, County Tipperary in the Republic of Ireland with postproduction work in London. The landscape makes an attractive background, although sometimes with a slightly bleak aspect due to being shot in winter. The whimsical story plays on stereotypical views of Ireland complete with folk music and a half-mad gypsy figure who roams the countryside and eventually helps the children.

The story begins in classic style with Jock (Simon Tully) on a camping holiday with his sister and father. He makes friends with a local boy, Dominic (Connor Brennan) and his family. Jock and Dom hatch a plan to help the nearby town by bringing in tourists. They fake a photograph that purports to show the Irish equivalent of the Loch Ness Monster. They fend off the attentions of a couple of neighbourhood bullies and soon the tourists are rolling in, including a sceptical American and his wife. The boys decide a fullsize monster is required and use the 'haunted' castle as a base to make their inflatable creature. Soon television news teams arrive and business in the pub is booming. However, the nosy American, aided by the bullies, discovers the truth and sees the monster off with the aid of an airgun. Or does he ...

The film has a jolly swagger to it and is directed by the actor and artist Olaf Pooley from his own script in his only directorial credit. The eccentricities are reminiscent of the Ealing comedies and typical of the Foundation's films of the early 1970s. The ambiguous ending is also effective. However, the attitudes to gender on display are archaic even by CFF standards, with the girls relegated to acting as lookouts or nursemaids to the boys and Jock's sister referred to as good wife potential because she can cook. The 'real' monster seems to be a small reptile photographed in murky close-up in a tank of water and the Irish clichés, topped by the characters performing a song they have collectively written, nearly sink proceedings to the bottom of the Lough. When on its travels the CFF was prone to casually replicating national stereotypes.

The Boy Who Turned Yellow (1972)

The Foundation's proficiency in securing the services of distinguished professionals behind the camera was never more impressive than here. Few would dispute the reputation of Michael Powell and Emeric Pressburger as the finest film-making partnership in British cinema. They made nineteen films together over a period of nearly twenty years, including such classics as *A Matter of Life and Death* (1946), *Black Narcissus* (1947) and *The Red Shoes* (1948). Their partnership ended in the late 1950s when Pressburger went into semi-retirement, while Powell's career suffered after the critical

The CFF turns psychedelic: Powell and Pressburger's *The Boy Who Turned Yellow* (1972)

mauling afforded the now highly regarded *Peeping Tom* (1960). *The Boy Who Turned Yellow* reunited them for what was the last feature made by either. Powell directed, while Pressburger scripted and produced the film. They also drafted in one of their earlier collaborators, the gifted cinematographer Christopher Challis.

The film opens quietly enough with a pre-credit sequence showing John (Mark Dightam) on a school trip to the Tower of London where he loses his pet mouse, Alice. However, from the beginning there are interesting diversions. Pre-credits sequences are rare for CFF films but this one combines beautifully photographed travelogue shots with fluent editing and voiceover to convey a tremendous amount of narrative at pace. We go into the credits with 'Three Blind Mice' being whistled on the soundtrack. The choice of the name Alice isn't accidental, as what follows is an hour spent inside the imagination of a young boy who might just have been reading Lewis Carroll. The film does entail an educational dimension, imparting much information about the nature of electricity and its uses, but this is frequently mocked (rather as Carroll's Alice books mock the didactic nature of Victorian literature for children).

The story concerns John's attempts to recover Alice with the help of an extraterrestrial. Having been sent home from school for falling asleep in class, John is on a tube train (with a woman reading Steinbeck's *Of Mice and Men*) when suddenly the compartment turns yellow, along with John and the woman. In a wonderful sequence, especially considering the budget, the now yellow train arrives at the platform, causing pandemonium. It seems that a virus has hit London, turning a number of people yellow. That night, the alien, whose name is Nick (Robert Eddison), as in electro-nic(k), appears via the family's television set and whisks John off to the Tower to look for Alice. Nick has a fascination for electricity and eats the stuff. He explains that those who have turned yellow have been identified by the aliens as helpers. The limited funds don't hamper the neatly executed special effects, which include jump cuts to allow people to appear and disappear and coloured strobe lights to suggest how the two travel via the television. Nick's appearance is odd, with yellow overalls and a crash helmet topped with a flashing light; his travelling is assisted by a pair of yellow skis. The pair enlist the help of John's brainy classmate, Munro (played by Lem Kitaj, son of the noted artist R. B. Kitaj, who went on to be a screenwriter himself under the name Lem Dobbs).

Commonplace in CFF productions is a suggestion that the central character might be imagining events, especially when it comes to fantasy creatures or alternative worlds, but here this idea is made explicit. At the end of the film Nick disappears and John finds himself back in school just at the moment he was about to fall asleep and be sent home. Now he is able to answer questions on electricity and stays in class. His journey home is without incident and he doesn't turn yellow. The cause of his daydreaming is revealed to be anxiety about his pregnant pet mouse; John's mother had told him she would drown the babies. However, when he gets home and finds that the babies have been born, his mother relents and decides he can keep them. He hugs her. Rather touchingly, the dream world John has retreated into is revealed to be compensation for the stresses caused by the adults in his life. As with the strongest CFF films, thoughtful undercurrents have been incorporated into a light-hearted narrative.

Another pleasure is the abundance of well-executed jokes and topical references. When Nick suggests the supply from a power station isn't to his liking, John replies that this might account for the number of power cuts they have had. John earns Nick's trust due to his liking for yellow, which stems from his support for Norwich City football team. One smart sequence sees John accidentally deposited into a football match being watched on TV by the Tower's Beefeaters, with much comic confusion. A number of the Beefeaters turn out to be frightened by mice. In another sequence John uses his last request (before being beheaded) to watch television, despite the fact there is nothing on in the morning. A final caption at the end of the film matches this tone by thanking various institutions, including the Tower of London staff, for not minding being turned yellow.

The film is a fascinating barometer of changing times. The Britain of *The Boy Who Turned Yellow* has been through the swinging sixties and come out the other side. The schoolboys sport tie-dye shirts and flares and have long hair. The woman John encounters on the tube looks as if she's stepped out of Biba and the soundtrack moves to a jazz guitar score. Even John's mum looks like a figure from a Laura Ashley advert. The styling of the film, with its exuberant colour, shows the influence of psychedelia.

With so much of interest in the film it's unsurprising that it went on to win several Chiffy awards from the CFF audience and became the first of the Foundation's films to appear on television when the BBC screened it for Christmas 1984. Although, as Michael Powell later revealed in his memoirs, the project was only approved by the CFF because Powell himself was on the board, and the Foundation subsequently tried to shelve the finished film.[11] The tension between caution and innovation was a frequent undercurrent in the CFF's work. It is fortunate that Powell won out as this remains one of the most unique films in its entire output.

Hide and Seek (1972)

As the 1970s progressed realism played an increasing role in the CFF's projects. Alongside this was a gradual turn towards adult subjects, with the moral certainties of its earlier work softened by ambiguity. Nowhere is that trend clearer than in *Hide and Seek*, which has retained a cult following of CFF fans. The story follows Keith (Peter Newby) who runs away from the Approved School where he lives and heads for London in search of his father; his mother died years before. He has had a letter from his dad, who has remarried and is about to set off for a new life in Canada. Living rough in an abandoned basement in Deptford, Keith survives by stealing food from local shops while trying to locate his childhood home in the hope of rejoining his father. He is helped by two other kids, Chris (played by future Spandau Ballet star Gary Kemp) and Beverley (Eileen Fletcher), who conceal his whereabouts from her policeman father.

Unfortunately Keith's dad, Ted Lawson (Terence Morgan), turns out to be a criminal who is masterminding a bank robbery, while his new wife (Liz Fraser) has no intention of letting Keith join them. The narrative develops in conventional CFF style as the kids work together to uncover the plans for the heist and then help foil it. However, there are substantial differences between this and earlier Foundation caper films. Ted is an ambivalent figure who is both villainous and sympathetic. We only make our minds up about him when he finally rejects Keith in a scene of real emotional impact. When he is arrested there is a moment of redemption as he asks the police to look after his son. Similarly, Keith himself is a morally unstable character for much of the film. Initially he lives by stealing and brusquely refuses help, earning himself the nickname of 'The Deptford Dodger'. When he discovers what his father is doing he wants to join him and when rejected his first reaction is to go on the run. In his world, crime is often a necessity. It is only when Beverley and Chris are in danger that he changes his mind and returns to rescue them. He is rewarded in the film's final scene where we see him being removed from the Approved School to become part of Beverley's family.

The script is again by Michael Barnes, working here with the director David Eady. They first teamed up on *Operation Third Form* and went on to form their own production company, Eady-Barnes, for *Scramble!*, making a further four titles for the Foundation during the 1970s. Although their work together and separately is varied, they bring a rawness and grit to *Hide and Seek* that is striking for this time in the CFF's history. Gary Kemp attested to this in his own autobiography when he remembered having to dodge milk bottles thrown at him by the local Deptford gangs during filming.[12]

The cast is liberally sprinkled with star cameos, some rather surprising. A throwaway slapstick sequence at the start features the briefest glimpses of Graham Stark, David Lodge and Alfred Marks as victims of Keith's pilfering. Roy Dotrice plays a crotchety pensioner who helps him, but most startling is the appearance of Robin Askwith, soon to become a top box-office draw in the UK with the *Confessions* films (1974–7), and Alan Lake as two inept crooks unconvincingly disguised as policemen. Lake turns in a highly effective performance. The location shooting around Deptford shows a capital city in obvious economic decline; graffiti for the BNP is clearly visible at one point. The film's rough-edged quality extends to the use of a form of juvenile swearing with the 'f' word translated into 'flamin''. *Hide and Seek* was, in its own way, a groundbreaking film for the CFF.

Kadoyng (1972)

Kadoyng belongs in the CFF tradition of gentle science fantasy films that reaches back to *Supersonic Saucer* and that had its heyday in the early 1970s. It also sits in a second strand of films featuring friendly aliens who take the role of the perfect imaginary friend. This links the film both backwards to *Supersonic Saucer* and forwards to *The Glitterball.* In addition, the film has a strangeness all of its own. It was the brainchild of television actor Leo Maguire, who both wrote the script and plays the naïve alien who gives the film its title; his performance is oddly understated, presumably intending to convey a childlike innocence. He went on to script two further CFF features and supplied the story for an episode of *The Chiffy Kids.* The film was directed by Ian Shand for his own production company and produced by Roy Simpson. For Shand it was the second of his three outings for the Foundation as either director or producer and for Simpson it marked a return after his falling out with the CFF over *The Magnificent 6 ½*; he went on to work with Leo Maguire again on *Professor Popper's Problems* (1974), demonstrating the Foundation's preference for familiar faces.

We are in well-worn territory here when Kadoyng arrives in the picturesque village of Byway whose pastoral calm is threatened by the building of a new motorway. Kadoyng decides to help three local children in their attempts to foil the bullying developer, Mr Fritton (Bill Owen) and the government minister he has in tow (Dennis Ramsden). Eventually he sabotages the motorway by turning the land into a watery bog, a skilfully achieved visual effect. The film's environmental message and celebration of small is beautiful place it in the Ealing vein within the Foundation's work. In typical CFF style the simple special effects involve jump cuts, which act to transport people through space, and speeded-up motion. Among the oddest elements are Kadoyng's antennae with which he can control puny earthlings; they sprout from the top of his head and have to be hidden under a top hat at one point. There are surprisingly satirical scenes as when Kadoyng makes the minister talk literal gibberish to a public meeting, alongside the usual broad slapstick.

Many of the film's incidental pleasures come from its period references. Along with an array of painful 1970s fashions, including one especially lovely tank top, there are several contemporary jokes as when someone asks Kadoyng if he can pick up Radio Luxembourg via the antennae. Slow and rambling as it is, *Kadoyng* is a curiosity with more than a whiff of 1960s bedsit radicalism about it.

The Boy with Two Heads (1974)

Also known as *Chico the Rainmaker*, the title used for its US television broadcast by CBS, *The Boy with Two Heads* is a late example of a CFF cliff-hanger adventure serial, albeit one with strong elements of slapstick and fantasy that place it in its 1970s output. Each of its seven episodes opens with a catchy theme tune, followed by a quick voiceover recap of the story so far. This concerns brother and sister, Chris (Spencer Plumridge) and Jill (Leslie Ash), who discover a shrunken head inside a box given to them by Ben, the owner of an antiques shop. Chico comes to life when Chris hits a drum and Jill plays a tune on the panpipes that also came from the shop. The kids try to help Chico return to the South American tribe from which he has been stolen, while two heavies (Stanley Meadows and Louis Mansi) aim to recover him for a crooked antiques dealer, Mr Thornton (Lance Percival). The theme song is repeated at the end of each episode with on-screen lyrics so the audience can join in.

Each instalment adheres to a set format. The criminals try to steal Chico from the kids – he's worth a small fortune – but are foiled, thanks partly to Chico's talent for magic. The action is played mainly for laughs and Chico's supernatural abilities rely on simple in-camera effects. Typical of this is a long sequence across two episodes where Chico is hidden in a football that then flies about the streets causing chaos before falling into a river where the villains pursue it by dinghy. They, of course, end up in the water. The episodes are repetitious but build to an entertaining finale in which the children help Chico to transform into a bird so that he can fly back to his village where the inhabitants need his skills to make rain for their crops.

The film's most bizarre aspect, and the reason for its small cult following, is Chico himself. The puppet head with its moving eyes and mouth is decidedly creepy, as evidenced by the reaction of my own twelve-year-old daughter. The discussion boards on the Internet Movie Database bear further testament to this with one person remembering being traumatised by Chico when first seeing him in the cinema. The series was the work of writer C. M. Pennington-Richards and Foundation regular Frank Godwin. Godwin also produced for Eyeline, which had begun its work for the Foundation with the equally unusual *The Sky Bike*.

Robin Hood Junior (1975)

As well as marking Keith Chegwin's return to the CFF, *Robin Hood Junior* belongs to a select group of films with historical settings. These include *John of the Fair*, *The Piper's Tune*, and the serials *Night Cargoes* and *The Young Jacobites*. By the 1970s they had all but vanished from their output. However, its popularity led to a sequel in the form of the serial *The Unbroken Arrow* made by the same company, Brocket Production, although without Keith Chegwin.

Despite the typically restricted budget, *Robin Hood Junior* looks impressive, thanks to beautiful costumes and location filming at Allington Castle in Kent. The same cannot always be said about the fight sequences and stunts, which are not up to the standard expected in modern television successes like *Merlin* (2008–12). The story effectively repeats the legend of Robin Hood but in juvenile form with our young hero, played with an unlikely Merseyside accent by Cheggers, taking on the wicked Black Baron (Maurice Kaufmann at full throttle). The Baron has arranged for the murder of his own brother, who is away at the crusades, and then tries to steal his lands and castle from his daughter, Marion (Mandy Tulloch). Robin comes to the rescue, leading the Saxon villagers in a struggle against the cruel Normans. Comic relief is provided by Andrew Sachs as the Friar and there is plenty of knockabout between the chases and fights.

The film suffers from the anachronisms that frequently beset this kind of period adventure, so that the dialogue veers between contemporary speech and a form of pseudo Middle English. The adults tend to overact, lending the piece the tone of a goodnatured pantomime romp. A similar strain is evident in the switch between humour and action. Nonetheless, *Robin Hood Junior* is an ambitious piece and a rarity for the CFF at this point. With its focus on direct audience identification, the Foundation only occasionally stepped away from contemporary settings.

Hijack! (1975)

Nautical settings were popular for CFF adventures. *Hijack!* belongs in a long sequence with *The Sea Children* (1973), *Wreck Raisers, Danger Point, All at Sea* (1969), *Escape from the Sea* (1968), *River Rivals* and *Davey Jones' Locker*. The film is packed with enough detail to pass for a visual manual on how to sail a small craft at sea. Siblings, Jack (James Forlong), Jenny (Tracy Peel) and Lucy (Sally Forlong), are kidnapped at knifepoint by escaped convict Colin (Richard Morant). He forces the children to sail him to France in their parents' boat. The tightly scripted narrative sees a number of twists as Colin and the children decamp to a speedboat taking part in a race, only to end up back on the family's yacht. In characteristic fashion, the children prove resourceful and succeed in turning the boat around unbeknownst to Colin and heading it back towards England. They survive a storm at sea and are eventually rescued by the coastguard and the police in an exciting conclusion.

The film makes excellent use of its confined setting aboard the boat and features a strong central performance from Richard Morant, a regular face on British television in villainous roles. He manages to make Colin a believable figure, sometimes dangerous and bullying but at other times helplessly reliant on the kids, and frequently in awe of their skills. Colin belongs with the increasingly ambiguous villains of the later CFF output. The Foundation struggled with how to convey a convincing sense of threat in a children's film without employing actual violence; comedy often provided a way out of this bind. Here Colin wields a knife and carries a hand grenade that he repeatedly threatens to explode. At the same time, the audience is made conscious of the fact that Colin is not as ruthless as he tries to appear. His motivations are desperation and fear. By making him a rounded figure the challenge of balancing threat with restraint is resolved.

Shot on the coastline around Swanage in Dorset, the film was written, produced and directed by the New Zealand-born James Forlong and features his own children in two of the leading roles. The film was the fourth of his five assignments for the Foundation and ranks as one of its best seafaring adventures.

The Battle of Billy's Pond (1976)

The Foundation's willingness to tackle topical issues, evidenced early on with *Johnny on the Run*, became increasingly evident during the late period of its operation in the 1970s and 1980s. *The Battle of Billy's Pond*, directed and co-written by the American-born Harley Cokeliss whose background was in documentaries, is one of the best examples. The story follows Billy (Ben Buckton) and his best mate, Gobby (Andrew Ashby), as they investigate the poisoning of the pond where Billy likes to fish. With the help of Gobby's scientist dad they discover the reason for the fish's demise: a local chemical company is illegally dumping waste in a disused quarry, which is then escaping into the pond via an underground river. An added level of irony is introduced by the company's television adverts, seen several times in the film, which promote a detergent called Breezee that promises to wash clothes 'nature's own way with a new organic detergent that whitens the same way as sunshine'. This is accompanied by idyllic shots of children running through cornfields in the sunshine.

In addition to the film's prescient environmental theme, it is effective as a thriller. The boys turn detectives to unmask the villains, using maps from the local library, and come into contact with the unhelpful local police (Geoffrey Palmer) and a supportive eccentric (Talfryn Thomas). Suspense is skilfully built as they are menaced by an ominous truck and we see glimpses of the sinister criminals in orange overalls, their faces masked by breathing equipment. One thrilling sequence finds them caught in the tunnels of the quarry as toxic waste is being dumped down onto them. The action is undercut by clever gags and comic cameos by the likes of Miriam Margolyes as a visitors' guide at the chemical plant without detracting from the drive of the central narrative. The direction has flair with fluent camerawork and cross-cutting. In more familiar CFF style, Gobby is an amateur inventor and his gadgets, including homemade cameras and sound gear, are used in the film's finale as the villains are caught red-handed dumping the poisonous waste.

The fact that the film delivered a message indicates that the Foundation was a place where young directors with something to say could make their mark and demonstrate their technical skills.[13] In this way, it prefiguress later CFF work from John Krish with *Out of the Darkness* and *Friend or Foe*.

Night Ferry (1976)

Night Ferry is noteworthy as an illustration of the inherent conservatism of the CFF and the formulaic elements embedded in its methods. It also highlights the challenge of trying to depict realistic villainous characters or action scenes without scaring a young audience. Young Jeff (Graham Fletcher) and his friend Nick (Engin Eshref) uncover the shady activities of a gang operating out of a lock-up in the railway arches at Clapham.

Joined by Carol (Jayne Tottman), they discover that the criminals have stolen an Egyptian mummy that they intend to smuggle to the continent in a shipment of showroom dummies on the night train through Dover. They spy on the gang, follow them onto the train, and eventually apprehend them with the help of the transport police.

Familiar elements abound. Jeff needs to redeem himself because his recklessness, running onto a train line while chasing his model airplane, precipitated an accident. The villains are hopelessly inept, led by Pyramid, a master of disguise played by Bernard Cribbins, the popular star of children's television and comedy films, here trying out various outfits and voices. Although Carol takes some part in the action, she is still viewed as having secondary status by the boys, who carry the narrative. The story unfolds in a series of chases, with the obligatory sequence involving our hero being locked up. A number of character actors appear, including Aubrey Morris as Soapy, a cowardly gang member easily frightened by the boys. The action turns into farce and is played for laughs, with a good deal of running in and out of compartments on the train, with mummies (real and false) causing mayhem. Pyramid doesn't end up in the pond but he does get stranded on a gangplank suspended in mid-air. Niche interest is added by sufficient shots of trains to keep any enthusiast happy.

Considerable effort has gone into grounding the story in realistic settings to encourage audience identification. Apart from the genuine British Rail rolling stock, the film uses London locations and features youngsters who look and sound true to life. The dialogue feels genuine and the acting unforced. We gain another glimpse of a changing Britain and one that seems a world away from the colourful post-1960s fizz of *The Boy Who Turned Yellow*. The London here has an air of decline; it is shabby and tired, its streets full of litter.

These backgrounds lend the film immediacy but also emphasise the fantastical elements of the plot and their absurdity. The actors portraying the villains face a dilemma. If their performances matched the children's commitment, the film would have gained a real edginess but would also have strayed beyond the parameters set by CEO Henry Geddes. Instead they opt for a pantomime approach, complete with overreaction and silly voices. The results jar against the film's locations and the naturalism of the children. It also means there is never any sense of threat and therefore little narrative tension. Children's films have always had to tread carefully but *Night Ferry* was released a year after *Jaws* had played to packed houses including pre-teens. *Night Ferry*'s caution leaves it stuck in the past.

The Man from Nowhere (1976)

The Man from Nowhere is one of the most unusual and memorable of the CFF's films. Its period setting, although not so unusual in the 1950s, had become rare for CFF films by the 1970s. It's also a ghost story but one that plays its supernatural elements straight rather than for humour. It creates a proper sense of unease and manages shock moments that might make contemporary audiences jump. Much of the credit for this must go to the director, James Hill, a veteran of film and television, best known for *Born*

Victorian chills in *The Man from Nowhere* (1976)

Free (1966). He had previously made four films for the Foundation including its first feature, *The Stolen Plans*, but had not worked for it since 1959's *Mystery in the Mine*.

The opening might qualify for a children's version of a Hammer film. Orphaned Alice (Sarah Hollis Andrews) arrives at a country railway station and is making her way towards her new home when a dark stranger suddenly emerges from the bushes with a warning. Hill employs a startling cut to introduce the spectral figure, after creating a falsely idyllic mood to distract us. Victorian Britain is skilfully suggested with a few well-chosen locations and costumes, despite the customary low budget. There is fluency to the camerawork, with a reverse tracking shot following Alice along the path.

The plot is fairly well worn. Alice is the only surviving relative of wealthy Uncle George (Ronald Adam), who lives alone but for his footman and faithful housekeeper, Mrs Smee (Gabrielle Hamilton). Uncle George is unwell and may die at any moment, leaving Alice as his heir. The dark figure keeps appearing when Alice is alone, warning her to leave her Uncle's house, but if she does she will be disinherited. No one else sees the figure or believes Alice, except for a group of street urchins led by Spikey (Anthony McCafferty) who live semi-wild in the local woods. With the help of Spikey and his friends the true identity of the ghostly figure is revealed as Mrs Smee's brother, who is employed at the railway station and is in cahoots with the housekeeper to frighten Alice away; Mrs Smee was previously to have been the beneficiary of Uncle George's will. The finale features many classic CFF elements, including a chase through the wood with the boys working together to outsmart the villains, but even this has a fresh feel as they improvise traps to thwart Smee's brother. They even manage to trap Smee into an inadvertent confession with the help of a disguise.

The story might sound like an episode of *Scooby-Doo, Where Are You!* (1969–71) but the handling has panache and generates a number of alarming moments. The man in black materialises suddenly from behind gravestones (an effect admired by the film's writer, John Tully)[14] or outside the lawyer's office to the accompaniment of unnerving electronic music. Hill's camera glides and tracks, giving the impression that something is lurking just outside the shot. The most startling moment occurs when the figure is reflected in a kitchen mirror at a point when it has been clearly established that he cannot get into the house. When the villains are caught it's a satisfying conclusion. The urchins are rewarded with jobs at the grand house and Alice is seen driving out with her uncle. In a charmingly quirky touch, the cast walk out to the camera to bow, before the curtain falls, as if in a ghostly play that might have been enacted for a Victorian Christmas.

With its neat execution and chilling atmosphere, *The Man from Nowhere* remains a fine example of how the Foundation could step outside of its formulaic remit and produce something to challenge the audience's expectations.

Sky Pirates (1976)

The Foundation was always on the lookout for a new spin to put on the familiar theme of children taking part in a competition or pursuing a hobby. After go-karts and flying machines, motorbikes and even hovercraft, here we have remote control airplanes. In addition, the film-makers throw in another standby, kids uncovering and apprehending a gang of criminals. Even after twenty-five years the old formulas were still in operation.

Brothers Mike (Adam Richens) and Harry (Michael McVey), make friends with Maggie (Sylvia O'Donnell) and her dad, Charlie (Bill Maynard) at an event for radio control enthusiasts. Also there are Eddie (Reginald Marsh) and his son, Sidney (Jamie Foreman), who are seeking a robust aircraft to send across the Channel to pick up a stolen diamond from their fellow criminals in France. Eddie owns just such a machine, so the villains use a powerful transmitter to take control and divert it off to their hideout at a country mansion. The children are soon wise to the criminals' plan and, with the help of a tracking device, are waiting when the plane returns from the Continent with its illicit cargo.

The film has a well-staged climax. With shades of the Battle of Britain, the children and Charlie arm their model aircraft with weapons to shoot down the criminals' plane. A dogfight ensues with our heroes communicating by walkie-talkie. The scenario may be implausible but it's effective with the World War II references reinforced by the fact that Charlie had been a fighter pilot. The enemy aircraft is shot down; the villains are rounded up by the police; and the boys are rewarded with two new planes courtesy of the company that insured the diamond. The action is complemented by slapstick from the semi-comic villains and plenty of incidental information can be gleaned about the world of radio-controlled models. There are some unintentionally amusing scenes allegedly set in France, indicated by a roadsign for Calais, with villains speaking in accents that would have embarrassed Inspector Clouseau.

Written and directed by former cinematographer C. M. Pennington-Richards, whose earlier work for the Foundation included *Danny the Dragon* and the script for *The Boy with Two Heads*, *Sky Pirates* is indicative, for all its entertaining elements, of the CFF's propensity to rely on tried and tested formulas.

The Glitterball (1977)

The second CFF feature directed and co-written by Harley Cokeliss, *The Glitterball*, became one of its most popular films during the last ten years of its operation. The story is a science fantasy adventure with the emphasis on humour, and a gentle message about the value of friendship. Max (Ben Buckton) discovers a visitor in the new family home in the form of an alien creature. Considering that the creature is basically a silver ping-pong ball, the film manages to convey the impression that this is a real character remarkably well. Max and his new friend, Pete (Keith Jayne), try to help the alien return to its own planet – it's only on Earth due to a malfunction in its tiny space ship – and to shield it from the attentions of a local petty crook, Filthy Potter (Ronald Pember). Meanwhile the RAF is also trying to track down the cause of the strange readings on its equipment, with Max's dad (Barry Jackson), who works for the RAF, leading the efforts.

The film boasts plenty of trademark slapstick, mainly at the expense of Potter, but what makes it work are the inventive visual gags involving the creature, supported by surprisingly polished special effects. Although most of these utilise very old in-camera tricks like reversing the film or stop-motion animation, they imbue the film with real charm. Cokeliss was adept in overcoming his small budget enlisting some creative friends.[15] The alien glitterball scoots around the house, jumping through letterboxes and heading up the stairs. It devours fruit left on a table, proves to have a liking for custard – a particularly nice effect sees the creature swallowing a bowl of the stuff – and spells out messages by rolling in paint. The film's ending sees a whole army of its fellow creatures arrive and attack Potter, sliding him away to the sound of Wagner's 'Ride of the Valkyries'. The shots of the alien's mothership are all the more remarkable for having been achieved on such a tight budget.

The film's appeal also derives in part from setting these effects against a realistically observed backdrop of ordinary shopping centres and suburbs, so that this becomes a fable about friendship rather in the mode of the celebrated *E.T.* (1982). It also continues a well-established CFF tradition whereby children prove their moral character by helping protect a magical being, as in *The Monster of Highgate Ponds.* In the end, the police nab Potter and the RAF arrive too late to see the alien departing after saying farewell to the boys. *The Glitterball* set a high standard for fantasy humour at the CFF, which was to be matched the following year by *Sammy's Super T-Shirt.* Harley Cokeliss went on to work for George Lucas on the second *Star Wars* (1980) film.

A Hitch in Time (1978)

A Hitch in Time demonstrates that late into the 1970s the CFF was still relentlessly mining familiar territory, but also willing to tap into popular trends; this time-travelling fantasy owes a clear debt to the BBC's long-running science fiction series *Doctor Who.* It even stars the second Doctor, Patrick Troughton, offering a reprise of his take on the character but as an eccentric inventor who has created a time machine, albeit one with a habit of malfunctioning.

In time-honoured CFF tradition, our two heroes, Paul (Michael McVey) and Fiona (Pheona McLellan), stumble across the secret laboratory of Professor Wagstaff (Troughton) inside a neglected castle. They help the Professor in his experiments and he sends them back in time, although machine errors result in them hopping erratically from one period to another. They encounter the ancestors of their current drama teacher, Miss Campbell (Sorcha Cusack), and of their unpleasant history teacher, Sniffy Kemp (Jeff Rawle), who turns out to have always been a villain. The historic scenes include Elizabeth II's coronation, an encounter with a highwayman and even prehistoric times. The educational content is self-evident, if laboured (with the exception of the darkly realistic World War II section). Twin climaxes are reached as the kids work together to escape the historical version of Sniffy, while in the contemporary world he wrongly identifies the lab as a bomb factory (a jarringly grim detail referencing the Troubles in Northern Ireland), bringing in the police and his headmaster, who unmask his embarrassing mistake. A final twist takes us back to the start of the film, in a manner reminiscent of *The Boy Who Turned Yellow,* as the kids are about to meet the Professor for the first time all over again.

The film reveals just how repetitive the Foundation's work had become by this stage. The special effects, hampered by budget constraints, consist of a few jump cuts, some basic superimposition and a few coloured lights. The set for the Professor's laboratory, along with his computer called OSKA, have the solidity of hastily assembled cardboard and the explosions are small puffs of smoke. The prehistoric sequence takes place in a papier mâché cave as the children are pursued by a bear that is all too obviously a man in a costume. Troughton puts in an entertaining turn but many sequences possess a pantomime quality, as the actors run around the ruined castle and its surrounding field in various period costumes.

There are a few nods to changing times, such as the inclusion of a then fashionable kung fu fight scene. More significantly, Fiona is accorded a greater role, taking the lead when rescuing the stranded Paul. Despite a script by T. E. B. Clarke, beloved writer of such Ealing classics as *The Lavender Hill Mob* (1951), the mechanics of the plot feel worn out and dated.

Sammy's Super T-Shirt (1978)

The 1970s is often considered a golden age for British television, a fact that inadvertently played its part in the demise of the CFF, but also proved an inspiration for its work. *Sammy's Super T-Shirt* shows the influence of the popular American-made series *The Six Million Dollar Man* (1974–8), which had its initial British run in the late 1970s. Fortunately for Sammy, he doesn't have to be rebuilt with cyber technology, he just gets his t-shirt zapped with special rays created by another of the CFF's mad scientists.

Sammy, played with great sympathy by Reggie Winch, is the typical skinny geek of any number of superhero comics. He is determined to get fit, with the help of a training cassette tape, so that he can win the big race. Another popular TV series is referenced by the word 'superstars' on a poster for the race, *Superstars* (1973–85) being a long-running BBC sports show. Sammy is bullied by other kids, who steal his lucky tiger t-shirt and throw it through the open window of a science lab. By the time Sammy and his pal, Marvin (Lawrie Mark) retrieve it, the shirt has been transformed. Wearing the shirt gives Sammy extraordinary sporting powers and leads to a series of genuinely funny gags. The shirt can cause bullets to shatter and makes a cosh bounce off. Escaping from the labs, Sammy finds he can jump over walls and move faster on foot than Marvin can on his bike. All of this is depicted with a mixture of slow motion and speeded-up shots accompanied by sound effects that directly parody *The Six Million Dollar Man.* One of the funniest sequences sees Sammy encounter the boys who bullied him. He kicks a football into orbit and fells both of them in a scene that has the anarchic quality of a Dennis the Menace comic strip.

The plot follows the usual formula. The scientist and his boss want the shirt so they can exploit its commercial possibilities. They kidnap Sammy and Marvin, who then escape. The film resolves into a series of chases, which end with the villains coming off the worse for wear. The finale is at the race where Sammy arrives with the bad guys in pursuit. The shirt's magic powers fail but Sammy is inspired to win under his own steam; the boffins are blown into a tree by the exploding shirt. The moral, that hard work pays off and that the small guy can triumph, is handled with a commendably light touch. It may be familiar stuff but it works wonderfully thanks to the parody, which is sustained right to the final shot of a remaining scrap of t-shirt, its tiger eyes glowing while eerie laughter echoes on the soundtrack.

There is considerable nostalgic value in the 1970s fashions: Sammy sports flares and long hair, while Marvin has a fantastic afro. The streets, parks and homes are thoroughly ordinary and would have been immediately identifiable to children of the period. Small details, like the picture of Formula One hero James Hunt on Sammy's bedroom wall, catch the eye. Even the familiar elements are given a twist, so that when the bullies inevitably fall into the mud, this is accompanied by an animal roar from Sammy's tiger shirt. Some gags, like Marvin's attempt to make a fake t-shirt to fool the villains, fall flat but overall this has an invention that stands out, a fact that my young daughter confirmed with regular fits of laughter throughout. The film was one of the most popular with Saturday club audiences.

Sammy was written and produced by Frank Godwin, who started his career at Gainsborough in the early 1940s. Despite the dubious distinction of having been chief cost accountant at Rank, he was also producer of several innovative British films such as *Woman in a Dressing Gown* (1957). He began working for the CFF late in his career, sometimes with his own production company, Monument. His decision to cast the West Indian actor, Lawrie Mark, as Marvin was a deliberate one, intended to reflect the increasing multiculturalism of the CFF's urban audiences. It won Godwin praise, as well as an award for promoting 'understanding between ethnic groups' from the Strasbourg Film Festival.

Black Island (1978)

Black Island is a tough and taut suspense thriller with the slightly rougher edge that had crept into the Foundation's work during the 1970s. In an extended pre-credits sequence we see a school class out on a nature trip. Two of the boys, Mike (Martin Murphy) and Joe (Mike Salmon), set out across a river in a leaky boat and end up stranded on an island. The boys soon discover that they are not alone, as the island is being used as a refuge by two escaped convicts: an older man, George (Allan Surtees) and the thuggish Jack (Michael Elphick). An exciting pursuit follows culminating in the villains catching the boys as they try to escape on a homemade raft.

Tension is maintained as Jack forces the boys to carry out chores, while the kindly George sneaks food to them. A second escape attempt, this time in the convicts' dinghy, is thwarted and then Mike is forced to go foraging for food on the mainland with George (which proves a futile exercise) while Jack holds his friend captive. The two convicts are increasingly at odds with each other as supplies run low, until an accidental fire finally attracts the attention of the river police. A vicious fight breaks out between the boys and Jack before they are rescued. Directed with economy by Ben Bolt, the film maintains its grip throughout.

The film's chief virtue is its uncompromising rawness. Michael Elphick is seriously alarming as the brutish Jack, who treats the boys with contempt and is not averse to threatening to kill them. Stalking around the island with his double-barrel shotgun over his shoulder, he makes a menacing figure. The settings on the Blackwater Estuary are shot in an almost documentary style and the performances, particularly by the two boys, are naturalistic and convincing. The result is an exciting thriller with a realistic edge, which helps to cement the path from the earlier *Hide and Seek* towards *Terry on the Fence.* The film was one of those released for television broadcast in the 1980s.

Electric Eskimo (1979)

Electric Eskimo is a late entry in the series of quirky science fantasy stories that the Foundation made in substantial numbers during the 1970s, being particularly reminiscent of *The Boy with Two Heads.* It was released in the US as *Superkids.* With better special effects than was sometimes the case with the CFF, the film begins at a research station in the North Pole where an experiment with magnetic fields and electricity accidentally affects an Eskimo boy called Poochook (Kris Emmerson). He is suddenly endowed with remarkable powers and taken back to the UK (with his parents' permission) to be studied.

In Britain he is under the care of Dr Fielding (Ivor Danvers) and makes friends with the latter's two children, Kate (Debby Padbury) and Peter (Ian Sears). Enter the villains, intent on kidnapping Poochook to use his powers to generate electricity, but the children come to the rescue and fetch him away to the house of their aunt (Diana King). The story culminates in a lengthy chase around a car scrapyard. Poochook needs food, especially sugar, to generate his power but with the help of the children he is able to capture the two heavies in time for the arrival of the police.

The main attraction, as in *The Glitterball,* is the deployment of a number of cheaply produced but charming trick shots. When Poochook sneezes he causes the traffic lights to change and he sets off all the kitchen appliances at the children's house. In the science institute he makes equipment explode and electrocutes a boffin. In the final scenes he starts an airplane rotor and controls a crane as he tackles the villains. The mildly amusing stunts are achieved by an imaginative blend of sound effects and stop-frame animation. A simple message against exploitation of the natural world is conveyed without too heavy a hand. Frank Godwin handles things with typical aplomb, with the exception of an abrupt ending that leaves Poochook's wider fate unknown.

Electric Eskimo was awarded Best Film by the International Centre for Children's Films in Los Angeles and the Moscow Film Festival gave Godwin the Pravda Award for directing the most popular children's film.

4D Special Agents (1981)

4D Special Agents belongs to a small group of CFF films made in response to specific contemporary events or campaigns, such as *The Flood,* which reflected the flooding in East Anglia in 1963. Here, less dramatically, it was a scheme set up by South Yorkshire Police to engage children in crime prevention and safety. Kids could become 4D Special Agents and promise to help the police. The four Ds stood for a set of basic rules to be observed by the children, such as not talking to strangers.

Our heroes are the usual gang of assorted kids, designed to show that anyone can help the police, be they a clean-cut girl with a policeman father or someone living with a grandfather who has previously been in trouble with the law. The action takes place around a depressed-looking Isle of Dogs as the kids uncover the activities of a gang of jewel thieves who are planning to smuggle their ill-gotten loot out of the country in a boat. Complications occur when Steve (Dexter Fletcher, at the start of a still continuing career in films and television) decides to take one of the jewels for himself. This leads to Jane (Lisa East) being kidnapped by the crooks as they try to find the missing brooch. As the plot twists back and forth, there are a series of reversals culminate in a climax on the Thames as the crooks in their boat are pursued by granddad in his.

The film benefits from the rough edge of later CFF productions with naturalistic acting from the children, working-class accents in abundance and a slangy humour to the dialogue between the children. The villains generate a sense of menace far removed from the comic capers of earlier Foundation films, with Jane threatened with a beating and Steve thrown in the river to drown. The action is tough, with a convincing car crash that might have been taken from an episode of *The Sweeney*. The film shows development in the depiction of gender roles with Jane matching Steve for bravery and resourcefulness; it is Jane who saves Steve from drowning at the end of the film. The temptation to commit crime is depicted in a non-judgmental way through the role of Steve as he gradually comes to regret having taken the jewel.

The film was directed by Harold Orton, whose involvement with the Foundation dated back to the early 1960s, although his more common role was as a producer. Although conventional in many respects – the film is almost an updated Famous Five adventure – its streetwise energy is indicative of the changed approach that had taken root at the CFF.

Friend or Foe (1982)

After an absence of more than twenty years, John Krish returned to the Foundation to direct and adapt a story by successful children's author Michael Morpurgo. Morpurgo is renowned for his ability to tackle challenging moral issues within a narrative aimed at younger readers and that is certainly true of Krish's film. *Friend or Foe* also ushers in the final period of the Foundation's work when its projects were frequently ambitious in scope and production values, as well as in broaching new and adventurous subjects.

Friend or Foe tells the story of Tucky (Mark Luxford) and David (John Holmes) who have been evacuated to the West Country during the German air raids on London in World War II. Although some of the villagers are less than friendly and the local children tease them, they are made welcome by farmer Jerry (John Barden), and his French wife, Anne (Stacey Tendeter), where they are billetted. The boys witness a German plane coming down and go looking for the crew. While out searching, David falls in a river and is saved from drowning by one of the German airmen who has been hiding out with an injured compatriot. The boys are faced with an ethical dilemma: do they report the two fugitives as they should or do they repay their debt by protecting them? They decide on the latter, partly from a sense of honour but also because the locals have been so unfriendly.

The film poses a moral dilemma for its young audience, which needs careful weighing up. The ambiguities of the situation are intensified by the fact that David's father had been killed by Germans earlier in the war. In addition, the patriotism of the villagers seems little more than bigotry, while the German airmen veer between appearing brutal in their dedication to their own cause and sympathetic in the loyalty they show to the two boys who have protected them. Krish was convinced that children were capable of appreciating these complexities and does not shirk from depicting the difficulties of the situation.[16] At the film's conclusion the boys, like the audience, remain unsure whether they have done the right thing or not. It is left for Tucky to deliver the film's true message: 'I think that war is stupid.'

The serious themes of the film are conveyed by convincing performances, dialogue and settings. We are a long way from the familiar knockabout humour and formulaic plots that had become the Foundation's standby. This is a complex, thought-provoking film that ranks among its finest achievements.

Tightrope to Terror (1983)

Tightrope to Terror was the last film produced by the CFF before it became the Children's Film and Television Foundation (CFTF) and took up its new funding agreement with Rank and the BBC. It had been making far fewer films over the previous three years but consequently had more to spend on each one. This is certainly evident here in the location shooting in Italy, the spectacular alpine scenery and the impressive stunts.

The story centres on two sisters, Susan (Rebecca Lacey) and Lisa (Elise Ritchie), on holiday with their father in the Italian Alps. The sisters decide to cross a mountain peak via the overhead cable cars while their father drives his car through the road tunnel to meet them on the other side. As the girls cross the breathtaking terrain they meet up with two German boys, Christian (Mark Jefferis) and Mark (Stuart Wilde), who are experienced climbers. However, things go horribly wrong when a low-flying plane causes their car to come off its main cable, leaving them dangling in the air.

The film progresses with a series of thrilling sequences as the children scramble down a rope to the ground and then make their way back to base. Mark is injured in a fall and Susan remains with him in the boys' tent while Christian and Lisa go for help. After Christian tumbles down a crevice, Lisa has to go on alone in a storm. Eventually she makes it through to find her father and bring help. The film is one of an exceptional breed of Foundation films where girls take the central roles. Here they are every bit the equal of their male friends. The tension is well managed by writer-director Bob Kellett, a long way from the sitcom spin-offs and saucy comedies with which he was more usually associated.

The film makes a gentle point about cooperation between nations but is more likely to be remembered by its young audience for some of the most convincing stuntwork in the history of the Foundation, as well as for a straightforward but gripping narrative. Just as well that a title card informs us that similar accidents can no longer happen thanks to changes in cable car technology!

Haunters of the Deep (1984)

Haunters of the Deep illustrates the efforts made by the newly formed CFTF to move away from the tried and tested formulas of the past on to more challenging subjects. It aims to accomplish this by tackling the dark history of children's involvement in mining and by upping the scare tactics considerably. However, familiar elements remain in place.

The film's opening is certainly more cinematic than usual. Our hero, Josh (Gary Simmons), is introduced riding his bike through striking Cornish coastal scenery as American, Becky (Amy Taylor) arrives in an expensive car with her dad (Bob Sherman), whose company is reopening the local tin mine. Intercut with this is an ominous scene underground that sets the tone, strange noises warning the mine workers of an impending explosion. The story feels more contemporary, with Becky's parents divorced and her father often absent; he has combined a holiday for the two of them with a business trip to the mine. The regional accents have a convincing twang and the initial friction between Becky and Josh eventually leads to friendship.

The first day of work at the mine is disrupted by a cave-in that leaves Amy's dad trapped along with Josh's older brother, Daniel (Peter Lovstrom), and an older miner. Josh has already experienced premonitions of disaster, seeing the ghostly figure of a boy beckoning him towards the mine through a fog. The old mine manager, Captain Tregellis (a suitably curmudgeonly Andrew Keir), explains the tragic history of the mine to Josh and tells him the story of his childhood friend, Billy (Philip Martin), who died in the pit. The ghostly apparition is revealed to be Billy, who then helps Josh to rescue the men trapped underground. Billy shows Josh another entrance to the mine and comes to Josh's aid at crucial moments, helping him lead the men out of the mine. They escape just in time as the sea comes crashing in. We see a final ghostly shot of Billy's smiling face superimposed over his gravestone.

The increased budget is apparent in the underground sequences, shot at Elstree, which had become the CFTF's home. Ceilings and walls collapse convincingly as water rushes through the tunnels. First-time feature director Andrew Bogle skilfully accomplishes the ghostly atmospherics, as tapping noises and whispering voices warn of the impending disaster. It is the spirits of the dead miners, known locally as spriggens, trying to help their descendants escape. The film makes the most of the beautiful Cornish scenery along the Penwith peninsula and weaves in traditional folk legends to add a distinctive flavour. A history lesson is intertwined with the story, bolstered by the Captain's reminiscences, to instruct young viewers about the terrible human cost of mining. The moral message is clear: nature, in the form of the sea, is to be respected, with human greed revealed as the true cause of catastrophe as the pit has been overmined for too long. Amy's father is quick to learn his lesson and to appreciate his own daughter. Despite occasional slow pacing and exposition, the film demonstrated the CFTF's commitment to its new remit.

Out of the Darkness (1985)

Out of the Darkness is writer-director John Krish's third and final project for the Foundation and is typical of the adventurous material tackled in its final years. The film opens in characteristic fashion. We meet Mrs Neil (Jenny Tarren), who is spending a few days in the country with her daughter, Penny (Emma Ingham), son, Mike (Michael Flowers) and his friend, Tom (Gary Halliday). They stay at a guesthouse with Mr and Mrs Barrow (Eric Mason and Charlotte Mitchell) while mum looks at the old cottage she has bought. The grim history of the house and the surrounding area is partially disclosed by Julian Reid (Michael Carter), a local historian with an interest in ghost stories. Both Tom and Penny experience strange visions of the past and repeatedly see the figure of a boy with a small bell tied around his neck. Mrs Neil leaves the children in the care of the Barrows for a few days and Mr Barrow reveals more of the local history. Further clues appear, including an old ring seemingly left by the ghostly boy. The finale brings past and present together as Tom sees a vision of what happened to the boy and is himself rescued from an isolated mountainside by the combined efforts of the villagers, whose actions lay the ghosts to rest for good.

What makes *Out of the Darkness* disturbing is the dreadful secret that emerges. This is based on real historical events that took place in the village of Eyam in Derbyshire in August 1665. The village was struck down by plague and the villagers took the decision to seal themselves off from the outside world to avoid the disease spreading. Less than a quarter of the population survived. In the film, one boy is saved when his family smuggle him out. When he arrives in the neighbouring village he is taken in by a family who all then die from the plague; this is the cottage Mrs Reid has bought. The other villagers hound him into the countryside and put the bell around his neck to identify him if he returns. As Tom discovers, their actions result in the boy's death when he is chased up the mountain and trapped inside a cave by a rockfall; the mob leave him to starve. For John Krish, it was the theme of mob violence that made the story compelling and important.[17] For a Foundation production the film is unflinching in its depiction of cruelty and cowardice. As Julian points out, ordinary people can be savages.

Krish makes excellent use of his location. As actor Michael Carter recalled for the BFI, 'the past seems to inhabit that part of Derbyshire with its strange edges and escarpments of rock, old villages and houses'[18]. The film is alarming at several points. The children's visions of the past are introduced by an unnerving effect in which the screen seems to fog and go out of focus. The melancholy figure of the boy is haunting, but this is matched by flashbacks to the tragic events as we see the villagers driving him into the hills by torchlight. Another disturbing sequence occurs when Penny goes upstairs in the cottage alone and sees men carrying a child's coffin out the front door. Other small details enhance the chilling atmosphere, as when the present-day descendants of the original mob are seen at the village shop or garage. Shock cuts like that used to first introduce Julian are neatly designed to send the audience jumping out of their seats. All of this is topped by the ending when, wandering into the woods, Tom makes his way through the fog only to find himself back on the night the boy was pursued to his death. For a children's film the results are unsettling.

If the film tells a story of persecution, its biblical qualities are also evident at its conclusion, as the modern-day villagers achieve forgiveness by uniting to rescue Tom from the mountain. In an act of atonement, they effectively reverse the selfishness of their ancestors and set the ghost boy free. As Julian concludes, Tom has helped the village get back its heart. This complex, dark and decidedly adult film remains one of the Foundation's most singular achievements.

Terry on the Fence (1985)

One of the most adult and controversial films in the Foundation's history, *Terry on the Fence* is also a candidate for one of its best features. With more than a passing resemblance to the BBC's groundbreaking *Grange Hill*, which was commissioned by future CFTF Director, Anna Home, it presents the moral ambiguities of the real world with a toughness that goes further than any previous Foundation production.

The film begins with one of the Foundation's favourite themes, the runaway. Terry (Jack McNicholl) has a row with his mother at home and when she slaps him he runs off. Wandering about, he accidently comes across a gang of rough kids led by the aggressive Les (Neville Watson). Les intimidates Terry, first by showing him the scar he has from an unspecified attack by his own mother, and then by threatening to leave him locked in the dockyard building the gang uses as a hideout. Terry is forced to take the boys to his school and show them where to find a cupboard full of radios. The next day in school suspicion falls on Terry and he confesses his part in the break-in to the head, but refuses to give up the identity of Les. Terry tracks Les down and witnesses firsthand the brutal treatment he receives from his mother. Les agrees to help Terry by retrieving the radio he has sold to a fence but the two boys are subsequently caught and wind up in juvenile court. In the end justice is done and Terry is acquitted but he is also able to speak up on behalf of Les, for whom he feels a great deal of sympathy.

Terry on the Fence (1985): the Foundation embraces realism and produces one of its finest films

Terry on the Fence is so different from the traditional CFF output in the 1950s and 1960s that it might have landed from another planet. Its grittiness and honesty are a revelation. For the first time children are heard swearing, albeit in relatively mild terms like 'bloody'. Les is in possession of a knife which he uses to break into the school and there is an underlying threat in the first scenes between Terry and the gang. Racial tensions (in a Britain hit by race riots in the 1980s) are even acknowledged when a black boy and white boy in Les's gang exchange insults. The film's frank depiction of violence led to the first real conflict between the Foundation and the British Board of Film Classification resulting in the removal of the knife threat, although the shots of Les's scar (including an eye-watering moment when he scratches it to show Terry he is in earnest) were left in. The film's action is set against superb location shooting in Southwark and Greenwich; speaking to the BFI in 2014 Neville Watson said: 'many of the locations are no longer there having been swallowed up by redevelopment ... in some ways it's a snapshot of a London that no longer exists'[19]. Performances and dialogue are unforced throughout and the film is careful to establish a sense of everyday life in its opening scenes with Terry and his family.

In addition to this, *Terry on the Fence* follows the example of other late CFTF films like *Friend or Foe* in presenting its young audience with moral quandries far removed from the certainties of the Foundation's earlier work. Terry's problems begin when his mother slaps him but this is shown to be a result of the stress she feels; and there is never any question about the bond between Terry and his mum. Les is initially a frightening figure but learning about his life means we see him in a different light. This culminates in the sequence near the end when the police catch Terry retrieving the stolen radio. Les is hiding behind a tree and when the officer asks Terry if anyone else is with him he is literally and figuratively caught on a fence, unsure whether to do the right thing according to the law or whether to protect his new friend. The issue is clouded by the affection Terry now feels for Les, a feeling shared by the audience and reinforced by Neville Watson's charismatic performance. Unlike the Foundation's early work, there is nothing reassuring or easy here. Moral decisions can be hard

Directed by Frank Godwin for Eyeline Films and adapted by him from Bernard Ashley's novel, *Terry on the Fence* shows a remarkable progression in the work of the Foundation; Ashley himself had built a reputation for his unflinching portrayals of teenage life.[20] The film indicates what might have been had its funding continued. Instead it was left to the likes of the BBC, which Ashley also worked for, to continue the tradition of hard-hitting children's drama with shows like *The Story of Tracey Beaker* (2002–11). My own daughter, being employed in her occasional capacity to test the longevity of the Foundation's films, was gripped by *Terry on the Fence* and shared Terry's sympathy for Les, an emotional engagement that still gives the film its power to move.

The BFI reissues

With the demise of the CFTF, the rights to its back-catalogue fell to the British Film Institute. The BFI embarked on a programme of remastering the films onto digital formats and then reissuing them in DVD sets for sale to the public. The technical aspects of the project are currently being overseen by Doug Weir at the BFI's London offices in Stephen Street. I visited in 2014 to ask him about the process and its challenges. He began by explaining the difference between remastering and restoring:

> Strictly speaking we are remastering the films rather than restoring them. This means that we are transferring the source elements into digital formats to help preserve them and to make it easier for them to be made available to the public. There is an element of restoration in making sure the films are in the best possible condition for transfer but it is not a full restoration as such. That would be a costly and time-consuming exercise involving working directly on the original celluloid. We don't currently have the resources to do this. If there are any wealthy benefactors out there we would love to hear from them![21]

I asked him about the sources for the film elements themselves:

> Many of the films were already in our possession within the BFI National Archive. These copies are mainly in good condition. We come across the occasional scratch or problems with mould but on the whole they have proved to be fine. If we do need to supplement the Archive copies with other materials, then it is not proving too difficult. Most of the CFF films are still held by four or five distribution companies who have their offices in central London. It's usually not hard to find copies of missing films or to source second copies to supplement our own collection. With the whole industry undergoing a process of digitisation in the last few years – hardly anyone shoots on film or projects film any more – we are finding that distribution companies are often very happy to pass on old copies on film stock to us. I tend to look for these copies to help fill in the gaps when the sources we have are weak or missing sections. So if a sequence in a film from the Archive is damaged, I'll try to source the section from a distribution company to make a composite that is of better quality overall.
>
> I try to work from something called an interpositive. When a film is shot the raw negative and the magnetic soundtrack are separate. The interpositive brings the two together and marries them. It also creates a copy which is both negative and positive. This means it can be scanned to produce digital copies and the quality remains good. I try to avoid using the duplicating negative which the CFF would have originally used to make the prints which then did the rounds of the Saturday clubs. This duplicating negative is often badly damaged due to the large number of prints which were run off from it over the years. I also try to avoid using the original negative so as to avoid causing any damage to such a precious resource. I have occasionally been forced to use the negative if there is no other source to use. Of course the negative does produce beautiful results – there are some sequence in our remastering of *The Boy Who Turned*

Yellow where the original negative was used. The interpositive produces excellent results most of the time anyway. On the whole the quality of the sources has been very good. Some of the later films from the 1980s which were made for television are shot on 16mm rather than 35mm which produces a softer visual quality. It's not that the sources themselves are damaged; it's more that the original stock being used was just not as good. A German distributor had a number of films in excellent condition too. We have licensed them to make DVD releases as well with some of the materials they have.

At present we are remastering twenty hours of footage per year. We tend to do this in batches of four hours. From this we select the material for release in DVD format. We are aiming to release two DVDs per year, each containing three feature films or the equivalent in serials or shorts. As we go along I am posting short clips on YouTube to give people a taste of what we are doing and act as teaser trailers for the releases. I reckon that about 95 per cent of the Foundation's output is available to us. One fascinating aspect of the process has been getting the sound element separately from the footage. Listening to the audio track in isolation has revealed just how effective the scores and the sound effects were. One of my personal favourites is *Sammy's Super T-Shirt* which has the most wonderful sound effects on it. It would be great to release an album of extracts taken just from the audio tracks.

I am not sure how many of the films will be released in the end but we are continuing at present to work our way through the back-catalogue remastering and reissuing the films so that they can be enjoyed again. I think anyone watching a film like *The Boy Who Turned Yellow* or any of the early black and white films can see just how well shot they really were.

Notes

1. See the Foundation's website at <cftf.org.uk> – the catalogue listed is a close approximation of the one available in the final years of the Foundation.
2. The DVD is entitled *Treasure and Trouble* and has a number of informative extra features.
3. Essay by Norman Wright in the booklet accompanying the BFI's DVD release of *Five on a Treasure Island.*
4. Michael Crawford, quoted in the booklet accompanying the BFI's DVD *The Race Is On,* which includes *Soapbox Derby.*
5. John Krish interviewed by the author, 11 February 2013.
6. See the special features on the BFI DVD release *London Tales*; the John Krish interview is part of a short documentary about the CFF from the series *Topic* (1958–9) which was made by the COI/Foreign Office to promote Britain to American audiences.
7. See the interview with Vivien Halas in the booklet for the BFI's DVD *Weird Adventures* which includes *The Monster of Highgate Pond.*

8. Anonymous review of *Go Kart Go* in the *Monthly Film Bulletin* vol. 31 no. 364 (May 1964), p. 73.
9. Essay by Norman Wright in the booklet accompanying the BFI's DVD release of *Five Have a Mystery to Solve.*
10. Anonymous review of *Cup Fever* in the *Monthly Film Bulletin* vol. 32 no. 381 (October 1965), p. 149.
11. Michael Powell, *Million-Dollar Movie* (London: Heinemann, 1992), pp. 536–9.
12. Gary Kemp, *I Know This Much* (London: 4th Estate, 2009), pp. 51–9.
13. See the interview with Harley Cokeliss in Chapter 3.
14. See the interview with John Tully in Chapter 3.
15. For details of how the effects were achieved, see the interview with Harley Cokeliss in Chapter 3.
16. See the interview with John Krish in Chapter 3.
17. Ibid.
18. Michael Carter interviewed for the booklet accompanying the BFI DVD *Scary Stories*, which features *Out of the Darkness.*
19. Neville Watson, 'Being Les', in the booklet for the BFI's DVD *Runaways* that includes *Terry on the Fence.*
20. See the interview with Bernard Ashley in Chapter 3.
21. Douglas Weir of the BFI interviewed by the author, 25 April 2014.

3 The Personnel

The Children's Film Foundation was fortunate in the remarkable team of staff who passed through its ranks over its near thirty-five years in production. It prided itself on the many talented young actors who made their debuts with the CFF and then went on to bigger things. The talent behind the camera was often just as impressive, from the leading directors and writers it managed to recruit, to the army of hardworking technicians who gave their time at minimum union rates in order to support its operation. Then there were the independent production companies who relied on the regular business that the CFF sent their way to keep them afloat.

Attempting to gather the memories of some of those involved, particularly from behind the camera where they had direct experience of how the Foundation operated, is a challenge for the researcher today. The principal difficulty is simply that so many of the key personnel, like Mary Field and Henry Geddes, are long gone. There are a handful of extant interviews and memoirs that recall the experience of working for the Foundation and these have been used in preparing this book, especially for Chapter 1. However, some of the film-makers are happily still around to provide direct testimony. The following interviews record their reflections. Here we get a sense of the limitations and frustrations entailed in operating within the CFF remit. At the same time, there is also a great sense of the opportunity, indeed privilege, of working for a rather special audience, one comprised of children.

Bernard Ashley

Bernard Ashley is one of Britain's most distinguished children's authors. Born in Woolwich, south London in 1935, he followed National Service in the RAF with a long career as a teacher, which included thirty years as a head. His first children's book, *The Trouble with Donovan Croft*, was published in 1974 and well received. Both *A Kind of Wild Justice* (1978) and *Running Scared* (1986) were shortlisted for the Carnegie Medal, which is awarded to the year's best children's book. He has developed a reputation for dealing with serious moral questions in a way children can easily relate to, as well as for the realism of his approach.

Bernard wrote his second children's novel, *Terry on the Fence*, in 1975. The CFTF acquired the film rights from his publisher and in 1985 approached the production company, Eyeline to make a seventy-minute film. The film's eventual director, the highly experienced Frank Godwin, got in touch with Bernard:

> We met at his flat. I remember that he fetched out a bottle of wine but then couldn't find a corkscrew! Frank Godwin was rather like a David Lean in his approach to film-making; he was meticulous and he was very much the man in charge. I had no real input into the script itself, which was written by Frank. However, I was consulted by him on the casting. He wanted to get a full sense of how I conceived the characters to be.[1]
>
> I was invited to attend a couple of days' location shooting in Greenwich but very much as an observer. Frank was obsessed with film as a medium, often talking about things like the grain of the shots. He filmed on 16mm, which was the format required by television, but concentrated on giving the movie strong cinematic qualities. I was particularly pleased with the score by Harry Robertson, which was really effective. I remember that the BBFC objected to a scene in which Terry is threatened with a knife; so, bizarrely, this was altered to have Terry threatened with being imprisoned and left to starve! The BBFC would not grant a 'U' certificate with the knife in the film.

Bernard's books are renowned for their tough content, so I asked him about the Foundation's reputation for gentility as against his own status as writer of gritty stories that don't condescend to children:

> I felt that the very choice of this book showed a certain attitude at the CFTF, perhaps a changed one. I would put a good deal of this down to the approach of Monica Sims, the Head at the Foundation. I think the toughness of the book was retained. I also feel that the Foundation had a strong sense of the importance of moral messages for children, which is something that I share. This is still there in the film but is reflected via a feeling of social concern, so that one of the characters who has gone off the rails is still given a second chance. The message is that unavoidable circumstances can shape youngsters' lives and that everyone deserves a second chance. The values here are more proletarian than middle class, but they are still very clear.
>
> I attended the premiere at the National Film Theatre which was an enjoyable occasion. I am still happy with the final product. Later on I screened the film to some of my own pupils in my job as a head teacher. Many years ago, when I was doing my teacher training, I remember that I was shown how to project films and then got a certificate from the Rank Organisation to say I was competent in this area. This meant that I could arrange film screenings of material from Rank at my school. Oddly enough, the screenings often included CFF films.
>
> *Terry on the Fence* was subsequently screened by the BBC on television, although I recall that they did edit out one use of the word 'bloody'. Anna Home, when she was at the BBC, had wanted me to write some original material for them but I always preferred to adapt my own novels. Working with the BBC in the 1980s was also a great experience. Their adaptations of my books were well funded and handsomely produced. This seems

> to be out of the question now for a British children's drama. I felt that Anna Home shared a commitment to socially relevant work for children. Much later on we developed another project together for the Foundation but by then they were no longer producing films. They couldn't interest the BBC in funding a children's film either by that stage. Later on again, I entered an open competition with the ITV network for a children's drama but although chosen it was later dropped due to costs.
>
> I haven't seen *Terry on the Fence* in a long time but I still have very positive feelings towards it and the CFTF.

John Krish

John Krish was one of the most gifted of the CFF directors. His work away from the Foundation shows his remarkable range covering, as it does, everything from public information films about the dangers of wandering onto railway tracks to training films for the Prison Service. He is best known for a number of remarkably sensitive documentaries, including *They Took Us to the Sea* (1961) and *I Think They Call Him John* (1964).

We began by discussing John's first film for the CFF, *The Salvage Gang*, made in 1958. The film was produced by World Wide, a company he had collaborated with on a number of documentaries:

> World Wide was approached to make the film and they asked me to direct, working from the existing script. I found the script was virtually unusable. The dialogue was particularly bad. It was unconvincing and took a quite patronising view of working-class children. I reworked it by improvising the dialogue with the cast, a technique which I didn't normally use, but needs must. Nonetheless, I felt confident working with the cast this way. I always tend to work instinctively anyway, rather than slavishly following the script.[2]

The low budget presented no problems as he was used to working with restricted funds from his background in documentaries:

> I always took the view of being pragmatic, getting on with the job, and doing the best that I could. I had no contact with the Foundation during the shoot itself. I was basically left to my own devices as long as I kept to the budget, which was all of £17,000, and stayed on schedule. There was a four-week shoot. Lots of research went into getting the locations right. Everything was tightly planned. I remember being paid £30 a week to direct. The actors were all from stage schools and from quite middle-class backgrounds, even though this wasn't really appropriate to the subject. Despite my views, Mary Field insisted on this. In my opinion, there was a case for renaming them as the 'Middle Class Children's Film Foundation' at that time. The cast was actually taken straight from an earlier CFF film about kids raising money for bonfire night. Then an actress was asked to re-voice one of the characters anyway. I never patronised the children but treated them the same way that I would an adult professional.

> I was invited to a CFF screening in Stepney. The children were shown a short film where some very middle-class children were being taken around an idyllic village in a horse-drawn cart. The children in the audience were completely bemused by the film but Mary Field loved it and seemed to think it was exactly what they should be shown. I have to say that I felt her view of childhood was out of touch with most children's lives and out of date, even in the 1950s. She wanted everything to be 'nice', but this really meant genteel in practice. I didn't find it easy to work with her. There was an element of snobbery, with an odd attitude towards children. I took a rough cut of my film to her which was marked up to show where various editing effects such as dissolves or fades would take place. She wasn't familiar with the wax markings on the film and asked for an explanation. When I described what they were for, I was told to stick to simple cuts and not to use these kinds of effects. She said that they wouldn't be understood by the 'Hammersmithites', by which I took her to mean that working-class kids would not understand such 'sophisticated' techniques.

There is evidence from the CFF archives itself to support this view. A number of internal reports in the 1960s refer to the need to update the cinematic techniques used so as to reflect the increasing visual literacy of the young audience. John delivered the film and then heard no more from the Foundation. Despite these difficulties he remains pleased with the finished film:

> It looks good and moves well. I recently went to a screening of the new, remastered version of the film and was amazed at how good it looked. A review in the *Telegraph* said that it was filmed with 'his customary monochrome elegance'. That phrase gave me a lot of pleasure.

He didn't work for the Foundation again immediately:

> James Carr, who ran World Wide, was not that keen on working with them. Before the film he said that he didn't think we would get on with them and the experience tended to confirm this. Their approach was too patronising towards their intended audience.

John recalls an idea for another film which came to nothing:

> It was for a version of Faust aimed at children and was suggested to me by Lord Birkett, the distinguished lawyer, who was a great supporter of my work. He made an introduction to Frank Wells at the Foundation about getting it made. However, Wells was not interested.

We moved on to discuss *Friend or Foe* from 1982, made for the Foundation after an interval of twenty-four years. John was contacted by Bob Kellett (formerly a director of 'saucy' comedies, then a producer-director and general 'arranger' for the CFF), who wanted to make an adaptation of Michael Morpurgo's book:

John Krish, one of the most adventurous and imaginative directors to work for the CFF

I felt a strong personal connection with the subject of the book as I had been an evacuee myself during World War II and the experience had a deep effect on me. I wrote the screenplay myself, and made some quite radical changes to the narrative structure to make it more linear. I think the audience really need to be led by the nose. I removed the original ending, which included a flash-forward which I felt over-complicated the narrative. Cinema is a different medium from a book. Some years later I found myself sitting next to Michael Morpurgo at a public screening of the film. I was rather nervous as to his reaction but I'm pleased to say that after the screening he told him me 'It's a bloody sight better than the book'. I am particularly proud of the last line of the film – 'I think war is stupid' – which conveys my own views. I feel strongly that it isn't necessary to soften a subject like this for a young audience, they are perfectly capable of responding to it and understanding it.

Elstree Productions made the film at Beaconsfield Studios and the producer was Gordon Scott, who John didn't see eye to eye with:

Scott's main aim was to reduce costs. The Foundation offered producers a bonus if films could be brought in under budget, so Scott made everyone's life a misery in his attempts to secure this. I regarded the budget as something that had already been costed as low as possible anyway. Everyone was working on minimum as a gesture of goodwill towards the Foundation as it was. Despite this, Scott tried to cut costs further all the time. On location he refused to pay for the cast and crew to have their clothing washed. Everyone was angry and the prop department threatened to walk out. I was able to persuade them not to. The film's composer was personally appointed by Scott. I asked for a simple score but this was disregarded. What I was looking for was a Kurt Weill folk style. One evening I was having dinner with the two boys playing the leads and their chaperone at the hotel where we were staying when Scott came to the table and said

> that they could only have one can of coke each. His manner was so unpleasant that he reduced the chaperone to tears.
>
> The children in the cast came from the Anna Scher Theatre School. This was an after-school drama club for children in Islington, often working with kids from troubled or underprivileged backgrounds. They saw drama as a kind of therapy, instilling loving values as well as developing acting talent. They were perfect for the film. I only had problems with one child, who wasn't an actor and kept looking at the camera during the school sequence; unfortunately, after three warnings we had to take him off the film.
>
> I focused on trying to give the film the right look. I still feel that the film is my most important work because of its antiwar message. The making of the film indicates just how much the Foundation had changed since *The Salvage Gang*. Back in the 1950s they would never have made the film. It went on to win the Ruby Slipper prize at the Los Angeles International Festival, which was the top prize, a sort of Oscar, but Stanley Taylor from the Foundation went to receive the award himself and I was only notified afterwards with a memo.

The film went on to amass a number of other awards including from the Laon Festival, France (1984) and the Neo-Youth Festival, India (1983), as well as an award from the London Evening Standard for best screenplay.

'Another memory I have is of the day I filmed the arrival of the children in the village hall and as they wait to be chosen', John recalls.

> The villagers were extras and normally they could be a disinterested bunch, often needing to be chivvied along by the first assistant, just there for a day's work hoping to be chosen to be in the same shot as one of the main actors. It can be a pain, but not this day. I have never seen them so involved, so moved. They were totally integrated in what I was reconstructing. I thanked them at the end of that day's work and told them how wonderfully they'd contributed to the scene. Then I found out why they were so splendid. It was because they were reliving their own time as evacuees. That was such a special day's shoot, for all of us.

Finally, we discussed 1985's *Out of the Darkness*. Bob Kellett was again liaising from the Foundation's end. The script started as an idea by the son of the renowned documentary film-maker Edgar Anstey:

> The original story about the plague was lumpy with no clear narrative line. The idea of using a ghost was not in the initial story; I added this. What interested me was to convey a sense of what it was actually like to live, and die, in a Derbyshire village in the seventeenth century. I visited the village of Eyam, which was the real-life basis for the story, and found a specific account regarding the local vicar who wanted to contain the plague by keeping all of the villagers together and how one local family tried to smuggle a child out. I used this in the final script.

There were difficulties in the production. I wasn't happy with the initial cut of the film and ended up re-editing it myself. There were more problems with Gordon Scott who was again in charge of the production. While on location, he caused dissent amongst the crew. He wanted the children to work day and night, which was not normally permitted. The budget was tight but I felt it was possible to handle this. I had a free hand over casting and found the children myself. It was important that they had provincial accents. I found them in a school in Manchester. I had the children do a reading and selected the three leads from a group of twenty. I think the film was liberal in its attitudes for the Foundation. A lot of this is down to the underlying influence of Monica Sims. Her attitude was progressive, and she even came to the set to reprimand the producer for his behaviour.

Working on the project became so stressful that John actually became very ill:

I was sent to the local doctor who took my blood pressure, listened to my heart and said 'You must go home at once – I cannot prescribe for you because I'm not your doctor.' I explained that leaving the film was impossible. So he organised a nurse who was by my side – telling me to sit down, taking my blood pressure – caring for me. She was special. At the end of the shoot my wife had to come to drive me home as I was too exhausted to drive myself.

The underlying theme of the film is to do with mob violence. As with *Friend or Foe*, I don't think that it would have been made under the old regime at the Foundation. Monica Sims wanted the film to be strong, not to water it down. The only change she asked for was to have four seconds trimmed out of the chase scene as she felt it was too frightening for children.

The film debuted at the London Film Festival and was subsequently screened at the National Film Theatre with John taking a Q&A session. He remains pleased with the film:

The acting is strong and the art direction striking; the forest was a piece of magic from the production designer, who constructed it in a large empty warehouse that was near. It is important to get some kind of message across within an entertainment format, to convey moral values, and I think I was able to achieve this with my films for the Foundation in an accessible way.

Iain Smith

Iain Smith, who hails originally from Glasgow, is one of the leading figures in the British film industry. He was awarded a special BAFTA in recognition of his achievements in 2006 and an OBE in 2008 for his services to film. In recent years he has been producing major feature films in Hollywood but early in his career, having graduated from the London Film School, he worked as a production manager and passed, briefly, through the ranks of the CFF. Later on he was to serve on its board of directors.

I asked Iain about his memories of working for the Foundation in the early 1970s:

I got my first job as a production manager for the Foundation in 1973, working on *The Camerons* [1974] for the producer Roger Cherrill. It was directed by Freddie Wilson, who had edited many classic British movies and was now trying his hand at directing. We shot the film up in the area around Lossiemouth in the northeast of Scotland. A couple of years later, I was production manager on *Nosey Dobson* for Mike Alexander's Pelicula Films, which we shot on the Island of Arran in Scotland. These were, regrettably, the only two productions I worked on for the Foundation.[3]

Working for the CFF was a huge pleasure. Most of us on the production side were learning the ropes and were under the care of the indomitable Henry Geddes. The Foundation staff provided us with a structure that both educated and commanded us at the same time. We were given enough freedom to experience responsibility but were also watched over, and quite often saved from our over-zealous mistakes. For me it was a crucial experience. To be able to run a feature film at that early stage of my career and to carry the responsibility on my young shoulders was to prove a huge benefit later when larger-scale opportunities presented themselves.

Budgetary constraints were ever present, of course, but in the case of both films they were entirely sensible and achievable. The value of everything was carefully assessed at every turn, as it had to be, and should always be. The rewards, as I've already said, were huge. The sense of being on your own but with a guardian angel watching our choices and decisions was wonderful and encouraged me to feel able to achieve so much more than I otherwise would have. There was also the reward of seeing our work playing in front of theatres full of rowdy kids and experiencing the real reason for telling great stories on film; the audience's pleasure and enlightenment.

Thirty years passed before Iain was to be reacquainted with the Foundation and it was a very different picture:

I was approached by the producer Simon Relph, taken by him for a nice lunch, and asked if I would consider becoming a board member of the CFTF as a bit of new blood, as it were. I agreed enthusiastically and, as a director of the company, came, of course, to understand the desperate plight the CFTF was in. The financial realities were pretty extreme by the time I got there and with so little in the kitty there was not much we could do other than continue to manage the Foundation's steady decline as intelligently and sympathetically as possible.

There were many earnest attempts to raise sponsorship and investment but the simple truth was that family entertainment had become a low priority in the wider commercial environment and the Foundation was seen as old school anyway, an image we tried hard to dispel. A great deal of attention was devoted to the archive library, which was extensive and relatively underexploited, but there was only tepid interest from various distributors who made relatively token attempts to get the material out there. It was a pity to have ended this way but the media landscape had changed so drastically by then. It was a rather sad end to my association with a great organisation.

John Tully

John Tully had a varied career as a writer for television before making his CFF debut with *The Man from Nowhere* in 1976:

The film began with an idea of my own. I must assume that Charles Barker Films, along with the other production companies used by the Foundation, had learned or been informed by the CFF that they were looking for suitable stories for filming. I worked with this company and others writing mainly documentary films, usually employing a dramatic approach to the subjects, and I also worked on fiction scripts for the BBC and others. The company would have invited me to submit an idea, which I did. The initial storyline was accepted and I wrote the script, which was also accepted, and the film went ahead.[4]

I do not remember having any direct contact with the CFF itself but I took part in location hunting with James Hill, the film's director, whom I have described as 'clever but affable' in an article I have written for the BFI.[5] I did attend the shoot from time to time, ably conducted by James for whom I had a lot of respect. He was firm in his direction, kept close to the script, but added some very distinctive touches of his own. There is a scene in a graveyard in which the script probably advised something like 'the stranger appears suddenly'. When I first saw the gloved hand whipping into view and clamping on a gravestone it made me jump.

John's next film for the Foundation was *One Hour to Zero* in 1976:

This was another idea which I submitted to the CFF via the production company and subsequently scripted. A serious problem arose with this film which had nothing to do with me directly. It concerned the casting. One of the two boys principally involved proved to be hopelessly miscast, as became painfully clear when we were on location and actually filming. I could only commiserate with everyone else concerned. In the end, his entire part was dubbed over by another young actor and the end result was acceptable. Again I had no direct connection with the CFF, nor did I attend a subsequent screening with an audience.

Mr Selkie in 1978 was a very different matter. The original story, a legendary Scottish tale, I believe, was discovered by the CFF itself and then offered to me, I suspect at Henry Geddes's instruction. The production company, this time Wadlow Grosvenor Productions, must have invited me for the job. The story is pure fantasy and not strictly my metier. I guess I take a rather practical, feet-on-the-ground approach to my work. Nevertheless, my submission was accepted and at some stage I think I must have met Henry Geddes in person. My best memory is only of a well-built guy seated behind a desk discussing very politely what was required.

> I duly wrote a full script for the film and work started in earnest. The office manager for producer Jean Wadlow, a key figure in her set-up, drove me out to the east coast of England where we spent quite some time hunting for locations, including at least two pools each with a seal available in it; fortunately one seal looks very much like another seal, except perhaps to seals. The next thing I heard was the CFF was not happy with the script. I wasn't told precisely why but I suspect my feet may have been too close to the ground. From what I have subsequently heard it would seem that others weren't too good at flying either. I have always assumed that Geddes continued to be personally involved in the operation. I don't remember ever seeing the finished film.

Although John was never involved in the Foundation's popular series *The Magnificent 6½*, he did write for the even more successful television follow-up, *Here Come the Double Deckers*, which the Foundation did not make. His reflections on this experience do, however, say a good deal about writing for children:

> This project was an outright punishment for past sins. I don't know how I contacted or was contacted by the producers but I understand they were American and it was made clear to me early in the procedure that while the story must involve the children on the double-decker bus, no child must ever be mean-spirited, vengeful, deceitful or ... anyhow, all must be little angels. To my mind this cuts out about 99.9 per cent of all possible storylines. However, I had a family to support and it seems that somehow I produced a script for them. I find a record of only one, though I thought there were two. Perhaps the second was judged too bland for production!

Harley Cokeliss

Harley Cokeliss was born in San Diego, California and raised in Chicago. He came to the UK in 1966 and studied at the London Film School. He had worked in television documentaries before making his feature debut for the Children's Film Foundation with *The Battle of Billy's Pond* in 1976. He went on to make one of the most enduringly popular of the Foundation's films with *The Glitterball* in 1977. Among his later credits, he was a second unit director on *The Empire Strikes Back* (1980) and directed *Black Moon Rising* (1986) with Tommy Lee Jones and *Inferno* (2000) with Ray Liotta. He also directed the pilot of the *Hercules* television series (1998–9) and worked on the spin-off series *Xena: Warrior Princess* (1995–2001).

We started by discussing *The Battle of Billy's Pond*. This, like his other CFF film, was developed from his own initial ideas:

> I had only recently left the London Film School and had spoken to my then agent, Jane Annakin, about taking my career forward. Jane suggested talking to Henry Geddes who was running the Foundation at the time. I worked with the writer Howard Thompson on developing a script idea I had about some kids stopping the pollution of their favourite pond. The Production Board at the Foundation agreed to the film and I brought in my

own producer, Mark Forstater, an old friend. The film was shot on 35mm.[6]

The idea was to make an ecological thriller with the kids as the heroes. I thought 'this can be a Don Siegel film for children.' The narrative included lots of action and stunts. Although professional stuntmen were used, the kids also got involved; the sense of jeopardy was very real. Sometimes it almost went too far; there was a scene with a large truck that was quite hair-raising though working with the young actors was always great fun. Coping with a low budget was not a problem. Having been at film school and having made documentaries for both the BBC and ITV, I was used to a tight schedule. Henry Geddes gave me some good advice. He told me that with an audience of children you had to convey narrative information visually, not through dialogue. I went to see a Saturday morning film club screening and found that the kids did get rowdy if they weren't interested in what was happening on the screen. It taught me that you have to grab their attention from the start and hold it. The pace needs to be fast and there has to be plenty of excitement.

The important thing is to show rather than tell. For example, there's the classic example of the story of the stolen poison pills. Someone can explain the plot in a conversation but it's better to actually show something like a dog eating a pill and keeling over. The kids get the idea straightaway. I kept the film on schedule and within budget. The focus with the Foundation was on getting it made efficiently. I had control over the edit, and we had very positive feedback subsequently from the production board, including from Michael Powell when he saw the completed film. There was never much direct contact with the Foundation, other than at the start with greenlighting the film and at the end with approving the final cut. The film was invited to a number of festivals and won prizes in Belgrade and Moscow. I think it was as a result of the positive responses we had that I was asked to make another film for the Foundation, which ended up being *The Glitterball*.

Harley recalls:

A considerable challenge on *Glitterball* was how to produce all the special effects on a very low budget; the whole film only cost £56k, so problems were overcome by thinking around them in inventive ways with many effects achieved in-camera using techniques from early cinema such as reversing the film, or speeding it up, or placing the camera upside-down. For example, the scene of the alien drinking a bowl of custard was achieved by pumping custard into a bowl through a tube in its bottom and then reversing the film to make the custard disappear. The action of the Glitterball itself was created using a variety of different balls, including a ping-pong ball, a wooden ball and a metal one, depending on the scene. The ping-pong ball could be moved around by pushing it with a jet of compressed air. Another version of the ball was made using a plastic ball from Woolworths which had glitter in it. The technicians drilled a hole in it and fitted a light bulb to create the glowing effect. Stop-frame animation was used for some sequences with Barry Leith, who worked on the children's television show *The Wombles* (1973–5), achieving some lovely effects, like the Glitterball eating all the fruit in the fruit bowl. For the outerspace effects we went to Brian Johnson, who had worked for Stanley Kubrick on *2001: A Space Odyssey* (1968) and would later work on Ridley Scott's *Alien* (1979). He was working on the television series *Space 1999* (1975–7) for Gerry Anderson while we were making *The Glitterball*, and Gerry very graciously allowed us to borrow him after hours.

Harley is particularly drawn to stories with an element of the fantastic:

It suits cinema. You can make the impossible happen. There has to be an internal story logic that the audience buys into, and then things can be as fantastical as you like. This is what is called 'ghost logic'. So there have to be rules that the audience understand and you have to stick to them; they can't be broken or it's cheating and you will lose your

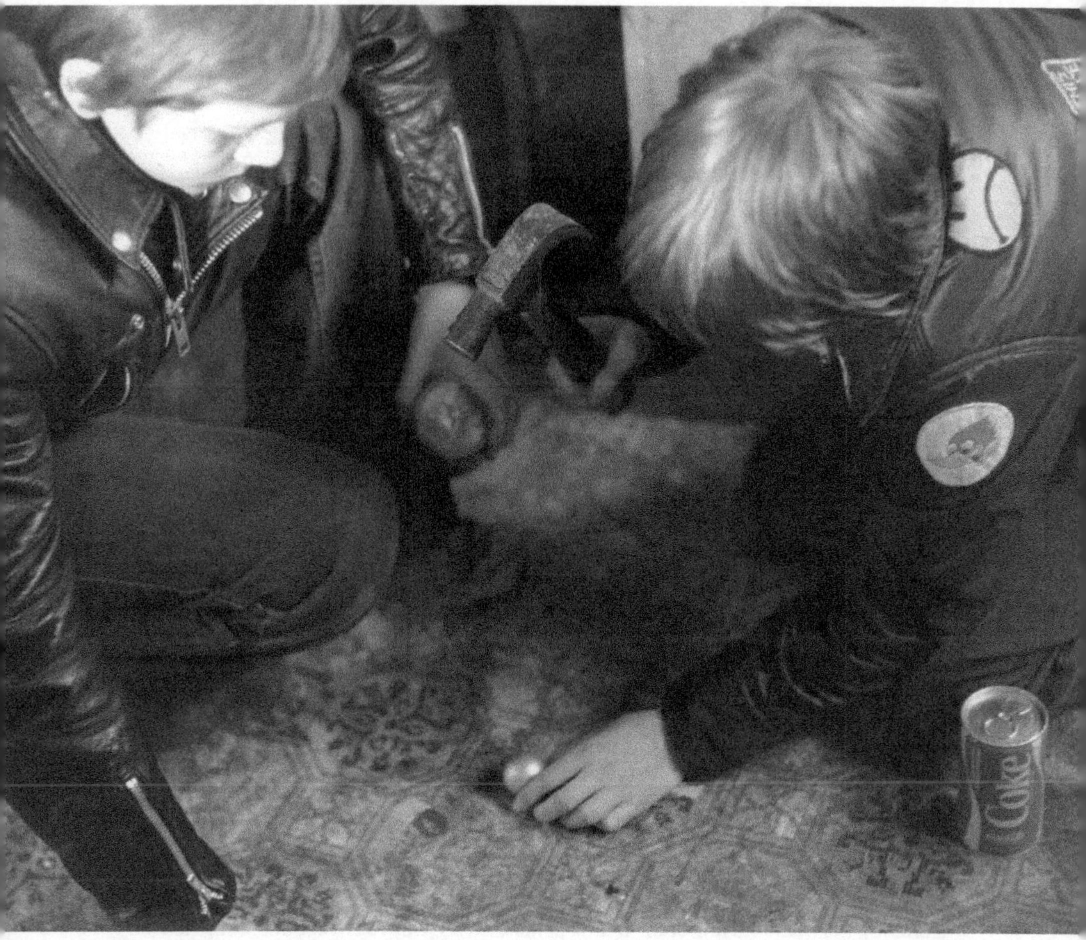

The Glitterball (1977), directed by Harley Cokeliss, surpassed its low budget and became one of the most popular of the Foundation's films

audience. It doesn't matter how strange the rules are, as long as you are consistent with them.

The Glitterball was highly successful. The BBC showed it at Christmas three years running in the 1980s, along with *The Wizard of Oz* (1939). Monica Sims selected it for a special anniversary screening for the Foundation in Leicester Square in the 1990s. It had a great reception. Later, when working on *The Empire Strikes Back*, I screened the film to cast and crew and it went down very well. There was talk of a sequel or a remake by the Foundation, but sadly it never happened.

Monica Sims approached Harley at the anniversary screening to suggest making another film: 'I headed to a bookshop and found the children's section, but it was vast.' A conversation with the children's book editor at the *Guardian*, Julia Eccleshare, took him to the writer Melvyn Burgess:

I read all of Burgess's books but settled on *An Angel for May*. The Foundation was no longer funding film productions and could only help with the script development stage. They optioned the book and commissioned an initial draft and revised scripts. The film was eventually shot on location in Yorkshire, which was important in giving a real sense of place and authenticity. We had amazingly good weather, although being near a wind farm and getting frequently blown around by high winds wasn't so easy. By this point, Anna Home had arrived at the Foundation. She was extraordinarily well connected and helped find investment from CITV for the film. A key factor was getting the actor Tom Wilkinson on board; he was keen to take part as he and his children loved the book. With his participation we were able to attract other actors who agreed to appear for what we could afford to pay them. I remember with particular affection working with Dora Bryan, who we lost recently.

The film was invited to many children's film festivals, winning eleven first prizes. For me, the key was making the film as real as possible. The book has a powerful emotional effect on me and I wanted to convey this by maintaining a strong sense of reality. When it was shown to the backers they were similarly affected by its story. The reaction was strong wherever it was shown, all over the world. I remember a screening for the hearing impaired with signing which was hugely well received. At a screening I attended in Sheffield a young girl came up to me after the Q&A session and said that she had 'cried seven times' during the screening. It remains a very special film for me.

Working with the Foundation was a terrific experience; it was a joy to make films with them. The process was simple: agree the script, then keep to the schedule and budget and deliver the film as per the script. The most important factor when making children's films is to 'Never be boring! Move the story on.' Kids want to identify quickly with a central character, preferably of their own age. These are stories about children, for children. Getting the tone right is crucial. You need to engage their imaginations. Sharing the point of view of the main character is the way to engage and hold their emotions. Really it's no different than making films for adults, the same principles apply. You just have to remember that some content isn't suitable for children.

I remember talking to a senior executive at Columbia some years later. On the wall of his huge office in Hollywood, among the photographs of all the stars, was a wooden plaque which just said 'The Five Questions'. I asked what this meant and he told me that it was something that writer Paddy Chayefsky had created. The questions are to help writers think about how the audience identifies with the lead character. First, who is he? Then, what does he want? What stops him from achieving this – this is the conflict. What do we want for him – it might not be what he thinks he wants? How does he achieve this in the end? Overall, you have to care about this character. Fairytales provide the model for most narrative structures, showing that things intended for children are actually the basis of all storytelling. I remember the work of Bruno Bettelheim. His book on fairytales, *The Uses of Enchantment: The Meaning and Importance of Fairytales*, focuses on their universal narratives and underlying ethical dimension; I still have a copy on my bookshelf.

Monica Sims

Monica Sims arrived at the CFTF in 1985 with a record in public service broadcasting that few could match. Having joined BBC Radio from the theatre in the early 1960s, she quickly became the editor of *Woman's Hour* (1946–). From there she moved on to become Head of Children's Programmes for BBC Television, a post she held from 1967 to 1978, often thought of as a golden age for children's television in Britain. She was then Controller of BBC Radio 4 until 1983. After 'retiring' from the BBC she became Vice President of the British Board of Film Classification, as well as becoming director of the Children's Film Foundation. She was later awarded an OBE.

By the time Monica arrived at the Foundation it had already become the CFTF and the writing was on the wall as far as its future was concerned:

> The Foundation had moved to offices at Elstree Studios and I would head over there for various meetings with the board. There was always paperwork to deal with and many reports to read. Our funding from the Eady Levy was cut and then went all together, so that we had very little money with which to operate. We made only a small number of films during the late 1980s with the finance we got from the deal with Rank but it was much reduced from the Foundation's heyday. Stanley Taylor was there and so was Lord Birkett and they both helped greatly in trying to keep things going.[7]
>
> My job was mainly to try to find books to adapt or original scripts which we could develop into films. We still made one or two films in-house but we mainly went to external production companies once we had a suitable screenplay. I was expected to find these subjects and bring them through the development stage but it was a difficult task without money, especially once the deal with Rank and the BBC had ended. We never had any funds from which to pay for the book rights and so we couldn't really compete for the best titles or necessarily commission the very best writers. There is a myth that children's films are cheap to make but this isn't necessarily the case and it became really hard as the 1980s went on to get films off the ground as the cost of

production soared. This is something that the BBC experienced as well. On top of that, the matinees, which had been so hugely popular, were dying out. That meant that the demand for the Foundation's films was dropping away. We had a hard task then to persuade government of the need for our existence. We were really up against it.

In my view, children are a discerning audience and demand high standards. You need good scripts and strong production values. Finding the right writers can be hard. I think my experience with the BBC was really useful here. I had a good sense of what children would like and of dealing with creative production within a quite traditional institution. One of my favourites from my time with the Foundation was definitely *Terry on the Fence*. I think it was excellent and did all the things I wanted from one of our films. I had ambitions for us to move out into other areas, such as cinema education with children, or encouraging them to make their own movies, but we were never able to do this due to the lack of funding.

Today many children's films are aimed at adults as much as they are at children, which makes for a very different kind of film. I think one of the great achievements of the Foundation was to make films that were absolutely aimed at children, putting the children foremost. That doesn't happen so much now.

Claude Gresset

Claude Gresset was one of the legion of technicians who gained a foothold in the film industry through their work with the CFF. Claude had begun his career behind the camera as a humble runner but advanced to first assistant director with the Foundation. He worked on four films for them: *Scramble!*, *Where's Johnny?* (1974), *The Hostages* (1975), and *Night Ferry*. All were made by CFF regulars Eady-Barnes. Later he became a location manager for cinema and television including the popular series *Reilly: Ace of Spies* (1983).

I began by asking Claude how he came to work for the CFF:

I had worked as a runner on a number of films since the late 1960s including *The Jokers* (1967) with Oliver Reed and Michael Crawford, which was directed by Michael Winner. I was introduced to the director David Eady in 1970. We talked and I became interested in working on the children's films he was making for the CFF. He first hired me to work on *Scramble!*. We had an enjoyable shoot on that film but I do remember that every time we set up a shot with the motorbikes running and we were ready to go, one of the bike's engines would immediately cut out and we had to start again. A young Robin Askwith played the villain in that film. He played it so well that everyone was afraid of him, including me. He wasn't like that at all off camera, he was extremely nice.[8]

Henry Geddes was in charge when I first worked with the CFF but I never met him. The person I recall was Bob Kellett, who was a lovely man. He became a good personal friend and I worked with him on a feature film called *Futtock's End* (1970), which was great fun. The Foundation films were made on very low budgets but I don't remember this ever being a problem. Scripts were written with this in mind, so it was never difficult. We didn't need any more money than we had to realise the scripts. The productions always had small crews but everyone chipped in and helped each other. The scripts for most of the films I worked on were written by Michael Barnes and they were very good. He made life easy for the director and crew. Everything you needed to know was there. You just had to shoot it. They were even written to ensure that the locations were easy to find. I remember that Michael Barnes had seven daughters and that they would sometimes visit the set when we were shooting.

There were never any problems with the child actors either. Scenes were kept short and the dialogue wasn't difficult. There were no long speeches. They tended to play characters just a couple of years younger than they were in reality, which made it easier for them. The leading children were usually more experienced than the ones playing the supporting roles but then they were only given a few words to say. Great care was always taken with them including chaperones.

I always had a happy time working for the CFF. It helped me to progress from runner to assistant director and I learned a great deal. For me it was a crucial stepping stone in my career.

Gerry O'Hara

By the time Gerry O'Hara arrived at the CFF in the early 1970s he was already a highly experienced director. His film career included nearly twenty years as an assistant director with such distinguished credits as Laurence Olivier's *Richard III* (1955) and the Oscar-winning *Tom Jones* (1963) to his name. During the 1960s he had moved into writing and directing with work for both television – *The Avengers* – and for the cinema. The latter included the popular thriller *Amsterdam Affair* (1968). He certainly qualified as the archetypal 'safe pair of hands' so often favoured by the Foundation.

His first assignment for them was *Paganini Strikes Again* in 1973, described with characteristic brevity in the CFF's catalogue as 'Young musicians become amateur detectives'. The script was by Michael Gorrell Barnes and the film was produced by Cyril Randell for Interfilm. Gerry remembers the CFF as a slightly shadowy organisation:

I didn't have any hand in the script. I was simply the out of work director for hire. I came in to shoot the screenplay as written. I oversaw the editing but I don't remember actually seeing the finished product or being invited to a public screening. The same process went for all the work I did with the Foundation. Contact with the CFF hierarchy was minimal but at least they didn't interfere. I heard later that Henry Geddes's wife, the writer Pat Latham, really liked the film and admired the directing job I had done. The shoot itself was a happy enough experience.[9]

The next thing I did for them followed straight on, probably because the first film went well, and was a series of fifteen-minute shorts called *Professor Popper's Problems*, about a mad scientist who manages to shrink himself and a group of school kids. We had to use various oversized props such as an enormous telephone to suggest the idea of them all being tiny. We had a very small budget with which to achieve this, so this

> wasn't the easiest thing in the world. Fortunately, we were shooting at Elstree Studios and we were able to borrow quite a few things to keep the costs down. Nobody minded really as it was a CFF film. The special effects were designed by Tom Howard who was really talented at making the money go a long way. Professor Popper was played by Charlie Drake, who was then towards the end of his career in films. I was asked to take particular care of him, so I would pick him up in my car from his flat near Leicester Square and take him back again at the end of the day's shooting. I went for lunch with him every day at Elstree as he didn't like to eat alone. He was a really decent chap and very professional.

Gerry's third and final assignment for the Foundation was *Blind Man's Bluff* in 1977. The producer was again Cyril Randell, who he had considerable affection for, and the script was written on this occasion by Pat Latham herself. However, on this project he found the experience less happy than before:

> The powers-that-be at the CFF were not so easy to work with this time. One incident in particular really upset me and has stuck in my mind. I cast a young black boy as one of the lead characters. I remember attending a screening of rushes early on in the production when a booming voice rang out saying 'Who cast him in the film?' It was one of the executives from the CFF. I was furious that they thought there was any problem about this casting and shouted back 'It was me!' It was a very nasty moment, even if it was an isolated one, but I stuck by my guns.

Pamela Poll

Pam Poll remembers that when she first joined the Foundation at the beginning of 1982 to work as Secretary to Stanley Taylor, the CFF's Administrator, it was a crucial time in its history as it was embroiled in major restructuring and rebranding as the Children's Film and Television Foundation. The production of new films had been substantially reduced and its back-catalogue was now undergoing a process that would lead to it appearing on television under a new contractual arrangement with the Rank Organisation. Within three years the Eady Levy, which had provided support for so many years, would be gone. These developments were overseen by Stanley Taylor, whose role was eventually to wind up the Foundation's direct production activities by 1987. She remembers an efficient, perceptive man focused on the job in hand:

> I joined the Foundation in 1982 which was not its heyday, in that it was a period of change due to the loss of the Eady Levy but I did, of course, learn a fair amount about the Foundation's operation in earlier years and there was still a small network of cinemas involved with Saturday morning matinees.[10]

The Foundation had moved from its offices at Great Portland Street in central London to Elstree Film Studios. Pam recalled that this occurred because a board member at the CFTF, the Managing Director of Elstree Studios, had been able to arrange for us to have office accommodation there at a 'peppercorn rent'. The move to Elstree had been accompanied by downsizing, which had included a substantial reduction in staff. We had become a very small operation. I had heard stories of what Great Portland Street had been like in the 1960s and 1970s when it had been a happy place and there had been a real buzz to the offices. The operation had become really modest. My first job was to prepare for posting a letter written and individually signed by Lord Birkett, the Foundation's Chairman, to all Equity members who had appeared in the CFF's films to seek their permission to release part of the back-catalogue for screening on television, something previously forbidden. The deal was agreed for ten films to go to the BBC each year for two years, followed by a further ten to ITV the following year.

By 1981 both the ABC and Odeon chains had withdrawn from the Saturday matinee screenings, leaving only a handful of independent cinemas still running the programmes. Pam remembers:

by this point the Saturday film clubs were almost extinct. A major factor in their closure had been the oil crisis, which led to a large rise in heating costs for cinemas. They didn't want to open on Saturday mornings any more. The few left seemed to be largely in the north of England or in Wales. ABC stopped their clubs, so what remained were a few independents and the last few on the Rank circuit who chose to keep the scheme going. Some cinemas were very loyal to the tradition and didn't want it to end. They still managed to keep generating audiences.

The Foundation continued to support the development of scripts and to act as an industry advisory body. Writers and producers could send in ideas. These were seen initially by Daphne Jones on her retirement from Children's Programmes at the BBC and subsequently by Monica Sims, a former Head of Children's Programmes at the BBC, who joined us in 1985. The Executive Committee of the Board sat regularly to consider any recommended script ideas. Money could then be provided for a treatment or even a full script. Money was coming in from Rank Film Distributors in respect of the new agreement with the BBC and ITV, and Rank were still running a few matinees and undertaking some overseas distribution of the Foundation's back-catalogue.

The problem was in taking the scripts through to actual production. Many good scripts never made it to the screen because production funding was so hard to come by. When Anna Home arrived later on she had tremendous dynamism, she was exhilarating to work for. However, the challenge from children's television ever since the 1970s had become enormous and was growing. The number of scripts turned into films or television programmes dwindled away. Film Council money eventually came in to support the script scheme but it was very small. They couldn't help producers get the scripts turned into films and so the releases dried up completely. Anna continued to negotiate with the arts councils to try to get improved funding but it didn't lead to anything.

Pam left the Foundation herself in 2005. Looking back she is proud of the Foundation's achievements, despite the fact that she was involved at a difficult time in its history:

> The Foundation provided healthy, uplifting material for children, as well as securing a wonderful training ground for production personnel, especially for young actors, some of whom went on to become famous. One of the great things about the Foundation is that it made films for children which reflected the national culture, something which is often lacking today with so few genuinely British films being made for children.

Notes

1. Bernard Ashley interviewed by the author, 18 January 2013.
2. John Krish interviewed by the author, 11 February 2013.
3. Iain Smith interviewed by the author, 29 January 2013.
4. John Tully interviewed by the author, 21 June 2013.
5. See the booklet accompanying the BFI's DVD release *Scary Stories.*
6. Harley Cokeliss interviewed by the author, 10 February 2015.
7. Monica Sims interviewed by the author, 11 December 2013.
8. Claude Gresset interviewed by the author, 8 October 2014.
9. Gerry O'Hara interviewed by the author, 2 December 2013.
10. Pam Poll interviewed by the author, 6 February 2013.

4 The Audience

Perhaps the most significant aspect of the CFF's work, and the element that took its impact far beyond the world of film production, was the relationship it developed with its audience. For successive generations of British youngsters from the early 1950s to the 1980s, the trip on a Saturday morning to the cinema to take part, often a very active part, in a film club was a highlight of the week. For many it was their introduction to the habit of cinema-going, or at least to a love of film. The experience was so powerful that it has yielded abiding memories, and remains the source of much nostalgia, for those children now long grown into adulthood. This was something also noted by Terry Staples in the introduction to his study *All Pals Together*.[1]

The purpose of this chapter is to gather together some of those memories in order to record and preserve them. It is also an opportunity to investigate the nature of the impact of the screenings. This is particularly relevant considering the Foundation's avowed aims, which went beyond simply providing entertainment or a baby-sitting service for pressurised parents at the weekend. The CFF meant to help shape the British citizen of tomorrow, not just into a regular cinema-goer, although that was obviously important to cinema managers, but into an active, conscientious and morally upright individual. This would be someone who would instinctively know right from wrong, who would be willing to stand up to the bullies, and who had a well-developed sense of fair play and justice. These concerns seem even more relevant today, at a time when the allegedly pernicious effect of the media on children is still the subject of daily tabloid debate. The view of the CFF was the opposite, recognising film's potential to be a constructive influence in the life of future adults.

The material gathered here is drawn from three field surveys carried out during 2013–14. The first made use of my immediate work colleagues by surveying staff and students from the University of Wales, Trinity St David across its campuses in Lampeter, Carmarthen and Swansea. Although a sizeable proportion hailed from Wales, the nature of universities meant that I had responses from individuals who originated from right across the UK, and from abroad. Although many of the students were too young to have personal memories of the Saturday screenings, mature students responded in droves and the younger ones preyed on parents, or even grandparents, to take part, which happily they did. I received close to 100 responses, two-thirds by email and the remainder in person. A basic questionnaire of five questions served as a starting point for conversation or correspondence. The questions covered simple quantitative information about when and where they saw the screenings, as well as their age at the time, and then went on to ask about their specific memories of both the films and the events themselves. In many cases the correspondence and interviews went well beyond the remit of the initial questions to take in a wide variety of recollections. The approach was always informal. The written questionnaires sometimes gleaned more information than the interviews in that respondents were able to submit their own accounts and tended to go into a great deal of detail as they recalled their memories.

The second survey involved an appeal for respondents on the letters page of two of the major newspapers for Wales, the *Western Mail* and the *South Wales Echo*, along with their website at walesonline.co.uk. The final survey used the letters page of the *Bristol Post* newspaper and its website to the same effect. Sadly these attempts only produced a total of about twenty responses, although some were highly detailed. I am afraid that I have nothing more scientific to defend my methods than that I wanted to take advantage of convenience by surveying colleagues and students, as well as focusing on the place I now live (Wales) and the one I grew up in (Bristol). I can't make claims for the empirical stringency of the survey work but it did succeed in producing what I had hoped for, in that I was inundated with a positive slew of intense memories, many of which were funny and some very touching. I believe that they do provide a real insight into the actual experience of being an audience member at the Saturday clubs and of the lasting impression they left. The entries in this section have been anonymised to protect the innocent!

In addition, I attempted to make contact with individuals who had experiences from the other side of the movie screen; that is, those who actually helped to run the Saturday clubs. This was a more difficult undertaking in that there is a crucial age difference here. A child of the early 1950s is now in their seventies and one from the 1970s generation, like me, is in their fifties. Unfortunately, someone sufficiently mature to be running such an operation in the early 1950s is now likely to be over ninety and even those involved in the 1970s might be well over seventy. They are an increasingly rare breed. Fortunately, I was able to track down a few hardy survivors with vivid recollections of being behind-the-scenes organisers of children's film clubs. Their contributions are recorded towards the end of this chapter.

The results produced by the questionnaires and interviews were fascinating and are detailed below. It was possible to extrapolate some broader themes from the individual stories. These are summarised in the chapter's conclusion. If the testimonies tend to contradict some of the assumptions the Foundation made about the susceptibility of its audience, they do attest to the power of public cinema events for children in providing a social activity of genuine significance to the development of that audience.

The CFF did not specifically organise Saturday morning children's cinema itself but rather supplied it with a regular stream of material. Some cinemas signed up to whole programmes from the Foundation, complete with shorts, serials, a feature and a structured interval. Others only took elements from the CFF programmes, usually the more popular comedy series and the features, and bulked the rest of their programmes out with other materials they sourced elsewhere. Some took none of the CFF's products at all. The Odeon, Gaumont and ABC chains, which account for the majority of the clubs, tended to use the CFF programmes as they had signed up to the CFF from the start. Although some of the memories recorded below do not relate directly to the Foundation's production work, the phenomenon of the Saturday screenings would not have existed in the form it did for thirty-five years and more without the model developed and supported by the Foundation.

The audience and their memories

One theme that emerged from a number of respondents was how their experiences were affected by their location, particularly if it was a rural one as they might attend a screening at a tiny local cinema or in a neighbouring village, or else have to make a journey to the nearest town:

> We travelled in on our own on the bus from one village to the next feeling very grown up until we got to the Palace cinema at Hirwaun, near Aberdare in South Wales. It was a flea pit really but we loved it and were devastated when it closed down.

Rural screenings tended to take place at independently run cinemas or ad hoc venues like church halls or community centres operated by enthusiasts from the local community. A number of people who lived in rural locations described how their village had a small improvised cinema but how, by the late 1970s, these had closed and film-going became a more occasional pleasure involving a bus trip to a larger town. One respondent remembered making the journey from his village in Yorkshire to the market town of Hebden Bridge:

> It only had one cinema, which is still going, called The Picture House. It would be in the late 1950s, when I was nine or ten. I can remember walking in after lunch on Saturdays to the town a mile or so away clutching my shilling for admission.

Some walked considerable distances or cycled, while others took public transport:

> It was a bit of an adventure as we lived in a village about five or six miles from Huddersfield. It was the first thing my brother and I did on our own after initially travelling into town by bus with our mother, who would go shopping. Then it was fish and chips with crinkly chips and the new 7-Up drink, it was the late 1950s. It was always a difficult choice, to go to the swimming baths or the ABC Minors.

One venue for improvised screenings was a school. An interviewee recalled monthly screenings on a Friday evening at his junior school in Norfolk in the early 1970s:

> The film club featured Children's Film Foundation movies, along with support cartoons. There were some exceptions to this including a screening of *The Wizard of Oz*. The admission price was the princely sum of five pence. The screenings were organised by our deputy head. I remember seeing some Disney films and spy movies with attractive female stars. A lot of the CFF films have stayed with me. There was *The Johnstown Monster* where the kids create a fake creature for the tourists in Ireland and *Supersonic Saucer* which was a sort of precursor to E.T. with a friendly alien. I remember *Our Magazine* [sic] which showed children with exotic lifestyles like gypsies or kids who lived on longboats. I also remember watching *Treasure at the Mill* without any sound. Their films were hit and miss. They had interesting casts with good young actors and some famous faces. They were good fun, distinctively British and not too long, but they were so kid centred. I didn't identify with films that were about groups of kids.

The latter approval contradicts one of the Foundation's guiding principles, that children prefer to watch other children on screen, although the CFF's view was borne out by the bulk of respondents I spoke to. The date of some of the films recalled here also shows how the Foundation continued to recycle its productions for years.

Another venue cited was military camps:

> At that time, 1960, we lived in army quarters at Tidworth, the army town near Andover in Hampshire. I remember being taken on a Saturday morning along with loads of other army children to a large hall in the garrison buildings for a film show. We were given squash and biscuits afterwards. We went fairly regularly, especially when our mother was on the rota for serving up the squash and biscuits. Behaviour was exemplary by all. In my own case, as a senior officer's child, it was reinforced to me at home that I had a responsibility to behave myself. In any case, there were lots of adults around, including soldiers in uniform.

Another remembered film screenings he saw as a boy in the late 1950s when his father was stationed with the armed forces in Tobruk, Libya: 'They kept showing us the same things over and over again. The commercial Arab cinemas had a much better selection of English language films.

The trip to the cinema was often made in the company of friends or siblings; it was rare indeed, if not anathema, to attend with your parents. If it was an older brother or sister, they were expected to keep their younger siblings in order. Attending with extended family such as cousins was also a common feature. Being in charge of younger children could be a chore but it often brought rewards in terms of a valued sense of responsibility: 'I felt that I was being trusted by my mum and dad to look after my younger brother, so it made me feel more grown up.' If the trip was made with friends they would meet up and then either walk in together or else go in by bus. For some, the walk from the suburbs could take as long as two hours. They might meet their friends at the cinema itself or congregate with a group from their school. A common feature before screenings was the chaos of kids running around the auditorium trying to get a

Supersonic Saucer (1956) with its friendly alien

seat with their friends. Few were driven to the cinema by parents in a car until the 1980s. Rivalry between school groups was common, generally manifested in reasonably good-humoured taunts. The clubs could also be the venue for burgeoning romance, usually of the most innocent kind, as one gentleman recalled: 'We were too busy swapping seats until I took Elaine, a girl in my class, and we sat next to each other in the balcony, quietly ... well, I was only eight!' Along similar lines was this comment from a female respondent: 'Some of the time was spent watching the film but most of the time, I'm afraid to say, was to look at the boys. What a confession!' Most of those who replied remembered the programmes starting at about 10 or 10.30 on a Saturday morning and running for roughly two hours, to finish around midday. A few people recalled attending afternoon screenings that started about 1pm and finished by 4pm to allow time for the evening programme to be set up. The term 'matinee' was often used to describe the screenings whether they were in the afternoon or morning. One individual recalled showings on a Wednesday afternoon during school holidays, this at a period when most shops closed for the afternoon on Wednesdays.

The admission charge was kept low, to maintain the appeal to a young audience. Many recalled the exact price: 'Six old pence got us into the pictures and bought us a bag of chips on the way home.' The latter was also an activity shared by many and sometimes supplemented with other food treats such as ice cream or, in one case, crackling from the chippy. Seats upstairs in the balcony typically cost three pence more and this elevated price sometimes extended to the back rows of the stalls, a policy which, according to one email, was designed to separate the better behaved children from the rough 'estate kids'. Another recalled even more specific price differentiation:

> There were three levels of seating, with one shilling for the wooden benches at the front, one shilling and nine pence for the individual seats in the middle, and two shillings and four pence for the posh seats at the rear.

Many parents provided a few pence more than the admission price to allow for the purchase of sweets or other goodies either during the film from the usherettes during the film or before heading in:

> We would go to Woolworths to buy either mints or broken biscuits to take with us. There was always an interval where the lights went up and the usherettes came down the aisles and stood in front of the screen with their trays of ice cream but we could rarely afford those.

Another remembered buying imitation 'sweet tobacco and sweet cigarettes, not the candy ones, we had to have the chocolate ones to "smoke"'. Children quickly learned to manage the money they were given: 'Mum gave me enough money to cover the entrance and my bus fare. If I wanted to buy sweets, it meant walking home.'

In relation to the specific programmes that were seen, many recalled what they described as B movies, along with serials and cartoons. Both the B features and the serials were dominated by two genres: the cowboy film and science fiction adventures. Comedy was also to the fore with the short films including Laurel and Hardy, the Three Stooges, Charlie Chaplin, Harold Lloyd, Abbott and Costello and the Keystone Cops. The vintage of these two-reel slapstick films, many from the silent period, indicates their abiding appeal (and low rental cost). Many dated from the 1920s and 1930s and would have been making their way around the circuits for the umpteenth time, hence the poor condition of so many of the prints, which had to be repaired repeatedly by cinema projectionists before screening. Nonetheless, they proved immensely popular with audiences of children and often led to a lifelong appreciation of silent comedy. British comedy features from the early sound period were also brought out of the vaults, such as Will Hay vehicles and Old Mother Riley films, and later the St Trinian's films.

The science fiction features retrieved from the archives of distributors included rarities such as the obscure *Tobor the Great* (1954), a spin-off feature film from an American TV series called *Captain Video and His Video Rangers* (1949–54), which one respondent from Epsom remembered seeing in the late 1950s because 'it was so scary, although he turned out to be a good robot in the end'. Some had memories of *Buck Rogers*, originally released as a twelve-part film series by Universal in 1939. Among the science fiction series, *Flash Gordon* is one mentioned by many. Some remembered seeing the version originally broadcast on American TV between 1954 and 1955 and made as a co-production with Universal in Hollywood and West German and French partners; the first twenty-six episodes were shot in Germany and the last thirteen in France. Others specifically recalled seeing Buster Crabbe as Flash Gordon, which means that they were watching the film series produced over thirteen episodes back in 1936 by Universal, which again gives an indication of just how old some of the material circulating at the children's cinema clubs was. One spoke of seeing the Buster Crabbe version in the late 1970s. One person's whole memory of the kids' screenings is fixed around *Flash Gordon*:

> If anyone mentions Saturday morning pictures to me, a frame from *Flash Gordon* always pops into my mind. This consists of a space rocket, a bit like a silver cigar with a sparkler at its back, flying across a mountainous landscape. I suppose by modern standards the effects were pathetic as the rocket was obviously being pulled along a wire accompanied by some rudimentary pyrotechnics, but the imagination fills in the gaps.

Another talked with affection of *King of the Rocket Men*, a twelve-part series produced by Republic in 1949 and featuring a villain called Dr Vulcan: 'This was the best thing ever. I particularly liked the panel on the front of the rocket suit which only had two or three controls. They were pleasingly simple saying "Up/Down" and "Fast/Slow".' Other superheroes to make the Saturday morning screen in the early 1950s included Superman, in a film series dating from 1948, and Batman, who appeared in two series both dating from the 1940s. In a similar vein was the female Tarzan, *Jungle Girl* (1942). One respondent recalled that these already seemed quite 'old' even at the time.

Rivalling science fiction were the Western features and series. Among the latter a firm favourite was *Champion the Wonder Horse*, originally broadcast by CBS on American TV for twenty-six episodes in 1956–7. It subsequently became a regular on the BBC. In a similar vein was *Casey Jones*, with thirty-two episodes originally broadcast in the States during 1957–8 and again shown later by the BBC. *The Lone Ranger* was another staple. Initially made and broadcast by ABC in America between 1949 and 1956, it provided more than 200 episodes to draw upon. Another favourite was *Hopalong Cassidy*. This had started as a series of B movies beginning in 1935 running to sixty-six entries. Subsequently, NBC re-edited the films to a suitable length for shorter television slots and in 1949 Hopalong became the first television cowboy hero. It is these shorter versions that were used by British children's film clubs. The long-running sequence of Roy Rogers films also featured. One of the more obscure Western stars remembered was the wonderfully named Lash LaRue, who starred in a number of B Westerns during the 1940s and 1950s; he was reputed to have taught Harrison Ford how to use a bullwhip for the Indiana Jones films. One person recalled seeing the Disney-produced film miniseries *The Tenderfoot* (1964) in the late 1960s. Both the Westerns and the science fiction films were targeted towards boys, a fact that didn't escape the girls. One, who attended the ABC in Blackley, Manchester commented: 'The one thing that sticks in my mind the most is that all the content was more suited to boys – lots of guns, etc.'

The cartoons shown were almost exclusively American and included the back-catalogue of shorts from Warner Bros. featuring Bugs Bunny, Porky Pig, Daffy Duck and other popular characters in the *Merrie Melodies* (1931–69) and *Looney Tunes* (1930–69) series. Other cartoons cited include *Woody Woodpecker* (1940–72) made by Walter Lantz for Universal. Most of these cartoons dated from the 1930s through to the 1950s when they began to appear more regularly on TV than in cinemas. One of the pleasures for British children at Saturday screenings up until the early 1970s would have been the chance to see these cartoons in colour as most households still had black-and-white televisions. The back-catalogue of MGM was also sourced for perennial favourites like *Tom and Jerry* (1940–57). Reruns of Disney animated features in the Saturday clubs were rarer but did occasionally occur. One unusual memory was of *Felix the Cat*, the 1950s American television version rather than the original film animations from the silent era.

Other material from the programmes mentioned by respondents includes *Belle and Sebastian*, a series made for French television in 1965 and first shown by the BBC in 1968, with many subsequent reruns, especially over school summer holiday periods. The show was set in the French Alps and centred on the relationship between a boy and his dog. An unusual one was *Circus Boy*, an American series of shorts originally made for television and broadcast between 1956 and 1958. It featured Mickey Dolenz, later of The Monkees, as an orphan adopted by circus performers. Newsreels and documentary magazine series often figured in the memories, including those produced by British-Pathé, with the selection geared towards items that featured children. There were film versions of Tarzan, the Lassie films and various film and TV versions of Zorro:

> We used to have navy blue gabardine macs for school and when we came out of the cinema into the bright sunlight we went into the hilly fields behind the cinema and we ran up and down pretending to be Zorro, using our macs fastened with one button to be the cape.

Many people recalled the use of cliff-hanger endings which were highly effective in bringing kids back week after week. One interviewee from the Wirral remembered how

> the film ended with its hero in an almost impossible physical situation. The audience knew that the hero would survive and appear in the next episode. The main topic of conversation was how he would escape his present predicament!

It was a tactic adopted in many of the Foundation's own serials.

Many of the films offered a tantalising glimpse of another life:

> The American origin and production of much of the material gave my dad and his peers a glimpse of a way of life which seemed hugely desirable. He commented to me on the colourful cars with white rimmed tyres which contrasted with cars in Britain at the time.

> Dress and hairstyles were also markedly different from what was familiar to him. Young men in the movies often had crew-cuts, for instance. The American way of life seemed to him and his mates hugely desirable from within a postwar, grey Britain.

Memory can be a slippery, deceptive thing. The films and series remembered by one or two respondents certainly raise at least a question mark over their accuracy, particularly those from the 1970s when Saturday morning children's TV came into operation fully. Occasionally there is a blurring between this and the film clubs in the recollections. One account suggested that they had seen the science fiction series *Star Maidens* at a cinema screening in the late 1970s. The series was originally made for television and shown by the ITV network in 1976. It was rather topical, having taken on board the Women's Movement to present a gender-reversal scenario on a planet where women dominate and men are subservient, but it's unlikely that it would have transferred to a UK cinema screening so quickly. Another said she had seen *The Perils of Pauline*, a silent serial from 1914, which, if correct, reveals a startling ability by the cinema manager concerned to excavate archive materials. One interviewee claimed to have seen the parody *Batman* (1966–8) television series of the 1960s in a cinema five years before it had been made. A major challenge for organisers of the children's screenings from the late 1960s onwards arose from the fact that much of the imported television material used in their programmes now started to be shown on TV on a regular basis, by both BBC and ITV. In addition, television ownership increased substantially. This meant that much-loved series that were film club staples were now more easily watched at home.

The films actually made by the Children's Film Foundation don't always seem to have had the impact they would have wanted. Some respondents were less than kind about the CFF's output, one describing them as 'complete rubbish compared to the cartoons and US action stuff', although this was in reference to the late 1950s and early 1960s. Another said:

> I remember *Young Robin Hood* [sic] with Keith Chegwin but they were often dreadful with bad acting and poor production values. They were very middle class in their values and the kind of performers they used. They seemed to have the same locations each week, usually London or some country house, and the same plots where the kids discover a gang of smugglers, a runaway or treasure.

The need to improve the film's technical quality was, of course, something that Henry Geddes identified and attempted to respond to. Others recalled the number of stories that featured ghosts or some kind of sporting contest. A number could recall having seen them but only vaguely. Some of the young stars made an impact, with specific recollections of seeing Dennis Waterman (*Go Kart Go*), as did the established character actors like Bernard Cribbins and Roy Kinnear, who were popular. Celebrity cameos such as Roger Daltrey of The Who (*Pop Pirates*) were also memorable. Even if the CFF itself wasn't always directly identified, a description of the content betrays the film's origin: 'I remember weekly serialised children's dramas. These conjure up images of

Another star in the making: Keith Chegwin in *Robin Hood Junior* (1975)

lank-haired kids in snorkel parkas, Raleigh Chopper bikes, and petty criminals operating from a disused gasworks.' The impression left seems to differ depending on the period in which individuals attended, so that the image of country houses, hidden treasure and children with cut-glass accents dominates in the 1950s, while flares, tank tops and council estates are the prevalent memory from the 1970s. The CFF's Famous Five films do seem to have left a lasting impression and a number of people seemed to specifically associate them with the Foundation's output, especially if they had attended in the first half of the 1960s. Comedy series like *The Magnificent 6½* also left an impression in later years. One person recalled that 'the adults were usually portrayed as being silly in comparison with the kids and were played by comedians'. The sixty-minute features were remembered by many as a key part of the programme, if not always in detail in terms of individual films. The formulaic aspect of the Foundation's output may have been a factor here. Specific titles recalled with considerable affection included *The Glitterball*. However, as we will see with a number of the following recollections, the impact of the CFF films could also be positive.

The gradual decline of the Saturday morning screenings is evidenced by those whose recollections date from the late 1970s onwards. By this time the screenings sometimes consisted of little more than reruns of commercial feature films from the previous ten years with no content designed specifically for children. There are memories here of seeing the *Star Wars* films (1977–83) and the animated version of *The Lord of the Rings* (1978), which would not have been long out of their initial theatrical first runs. Occasionally the films shown were of slightly older vintage, going back into the earlier 1970s for titles like *Escape from the Planet of the Apes* (1971) and *The Phantom Tollbooth* (1970). Disney reruns such as *The Aristocats* (1970) and *Freaky Friday* (1976) were increasingly commonplace at this time. Ironically, there is little doubt that these screenings were a largely pragmatic attempt to extract the last few pounds out of the Saturday clubs by rerunning films that were past their sell-by date or by providing a second outing for recently seen films; this was exactly the kind of practice that had proliferated in the pre-CFF era and that the Foundation was partly created to bring to an end.

A recurring memory for many is the sheer noise generated by the audience of children: 'It was always LOUD compared to when we went as a family to normal film shows when it was quiet and calm.' A respondent from Yorkshire remembered the cinema manager having to come out regularly to quieten the audience. Frequently the films were drowned out by the sheer racket being made. A good deal of the shouting was directed at the screen itself, with the kids providing a commentary on the action, cheering or booing for the parts or characters they enjoyed or didn't. The start of the programme, heralded by the curtains parting, was usually greeted with wild cheering. Any romantic elements (rare in CFF films) provoked a sound booing, particularly from the boys. To add to the din, staff often encouraged the kids to shout and stamp their feet prior to the start of the screening, and then frequently found it difficult to quieten them again. The high numbers in attendance were obviously a factor here, with one person remembering children being crammed in two to a seat. Sometimes the noise was so great the theatre manager would have to call a temporary halt to proceedings.

If there was noise, then things could also get lively indeed in terms of behaviour. One interviewee remembered visiting the Odeon in Ashburner Street, Bolton:

> It was a bit of a free for all at times with the local town lads ruling it over everybody else who'd rolled in from the moors; lots of free-flying toffees and crisps. I remember at least one pitched battle like a snowball fight with sweets for ammo (Opal Fruits, Spangles, Refreshers, etc.), using the seating like trenches and redoubts; all remarkably good humoured though, no actual real aggro. I'm sure there were usherettes about but I only ever noted them appearing at the end or to haul someone out if it looked like they were going to damage the seating. Loads of fun!

Similar stories abound, such as this one from someone who grew up in Southsea:

> The events were very well attended and utterly chaotic. It was anarchy that subsided to some degree when the cartoons and films started but mostly there were kids running up and down the aisles, climbing over the seats, arguing, bickering, fighting, screaming, laughing and throwing things. I remember my mum made me a chocolate spread sandwich to eat at one of the showings. I ate half of it, separated the slices of the other half so that the chocolate spread was exposed, and launched them into the air behind me to land wherever the gods of childhood abandon decided.

Another popular pastime was getting in front of the projector beam so as to make silhouettes on the screen.

A favourite spot from which to start a sweet bombardment was the circle, from which items could be rained down over the balcony on the unfortunates in the seats below. One interviewee made a confession:

> My journey took me through Walpole Park. I remember on one occasion we gathered conkers en route and hid them in our pockets. We then randomly tossed them over the balcony at the children below along with the odd lollipop stick to see what reaction there would be. I don't remember anything more than the odd glance or shout upwards from someone below wondering what had fallen in their lap or hit them on the head. This bit of mischief was done just as the lights dimmed after the interval.

Along similar lines was this memory of film-going in Swansea:

> The boys went for the balcony and it was, I remember, prudent to avoid sitting in the five or six rows in front and below that. They spat and dropped things. There was smoking too at the back in the balcony. I never did but an older cousin who took me liked to sit there.

The interval was often a favourite time for action, as another respondent from Nottingham related: 'During the breaks all mayhem let rip. Things were thrown everywhere and I had to keep hold of my handbag!' Another confessed to buying small 'bombs' from a newsagent, which could then be propelled across the auditorium with an elastic-band catapult. A contender for naughtiest memory must be the shamefaced individual who admitted capturing two birds, smuggling them into the cinema and then releasing them: 'I watched them fly up into the projector beam.' Attendance doesn't appear to have been adversely affected by the near riots, in fact quite the opposite, as most described packed auditoriums and having to queue around the block just to get in. However, by the mid-1970s it was different: 'I felt safer at home with *Multi-Coloured Swap Shop*. Television was easier and more comfortable.'

The role of the usherettes was essential in maintaining order:

> I remember that when the lights dimmed, the usherettes used to walk round with their torches shining them on anyone being noisy or not settling down to watch the show. They would hush any noisy children. In those days we were actually frightened of a telling off!

Another interview revealed a more sympathetic memory of those at the Swansea Odeon:

> They tried to keep order but generally failed due to being outnumbered. They must have hated having to run them, to be honest. The main memory I have is some kid

> would always end up being sick through gorging on sweets and hotdogs and then start crying before being led out of the place by a long-suffering usherette.

Another recalled visiting a particularly basic venue where the seats were reused church pews and where the usherettes 'used brushes to check under them to make sure we had left'! A formidable brand of cinema manager was often in evidence at the screenings too:

> There was occasional bad behaviour by some of the older boys but the cinema manager, who dressed in a dark suit and wore crepe-soled shoes, widely known as Creeping Jesus, crept down the aisles in the dark and pounced on them, yanking them out by their ears, sometimes to cheers.

Another remembered the manager at the Gaumont in Leytonstone who became something of a local hero, helping to organise community events including celebrations for the Coronation.

For those who were members of the official clubs organised by the ABC chain or by Rank, sing-alongs were a regular feature with the audience encouraged to take part by following the lyrics on the screen, with the additional aid of a 'bouncing ball' to help them keep up; it moved from word to word in time with the melody. One interviewee remembered singing the popular German song 'Valerie, Valera', also known as 'The Happy Wanderer', a choral verion of which had charted in the UK in 1954. Of course, both the Odeon clubs and the ABC Minors had their own club songs and many were keen to recite the words for me, or even to sing them! After all these years the memory of the songs and of the massed ranks of children booming them out in the darkened theatre remained vivid and joyful. Another feature in larger cinemas was mentioned by someone who attended the Astoria, Brighton as an ABC Minor:

> There was a guy playing an organ and we all used to sing. We were rubbish! My dad told me that originally there was a big, lit-up organ that came out of the floor, but that was not there in the 1960s.

Similarly, an interviewee from Cardiff recalled: 'There was an organist who played before the curtain went up! Sweeping red curtains acted like another player in the proceedings.' Another memory from Richmond upon Thames is of the organist achieving some extraordinary sound effects: 'There were noises of a dog being run over and other things – sounds a bit gory!

Competitions were a popular aspect of the Saturday clubs. One respondent told me of her experiences from the late 1950s:

> The competition I remember was a musical contest for the kids. There were various entries, of which I remember a skiffle group performing a Lonnie Donegan song and a couple of lads who sang Flanders and Swann's 'Mud, Mud, Glorious Mud', but I probably

> remember it so vividly because a schoolfriend of mine won. I think some of her brothers had entered and she was not to be outdone. She was about seven years old and sang 'Around the World I Searched for You', a small girl, all alone on the huge stage. Audience applause was the decider. My friend won a Raleigh bicycle and Vera Lynn came to present the prize.

Mini talent shows of various kinds were not uncommon. There were also general knowledge quizzes with prizes. One of the most curious recollections in this area came from an audience member in Llanelli who recalled 'being asked up on stage to play on a large *Connect Four*-style board game'. Another unusual memory was of when

> the Army visited the Saturday Club and set an art competition. My sister and I came joint first. The first prize was a ride in an army tank. There was an armed forces event at People's Park (Llanelli) and we were told that there was no such prize! However, after much disagreement, they allowed us to have our ride in the tank. When we returned there was a long queue of expectant children, but nobody else was allowed to have a go. We felt very special and loved every minute of it.

One competition specifically related to the CFF was to make a glitterball in the style of its film of the same name. I was also told that a spotlight would circulate slowly around the audience and whoever it stopped on would win a prize: 'I remember that getting up on to the stage was a pretty unpleasant experience with the whole audience baying and shouting insults.'

Christmas could be the occasion for special events, often free, with goodie bags full of sweets and gifts for the children. A compere featured at a number of cinemas. One person recounted:

> there was a compere who came on at the end of the first half. He would do a little bit of children's comedy and then announce if it was your birthday. You would then go up on stage and everyone would sing 'Happy Birthday' and you were given an orange.

Another individual (who will remain anonymous) recalled that some of her friends would pretend it was their birthday just so that they could go up on the stage. The singing of 'Happy Birthday' could be hazardous for other reasons, as someone from Weston-super-Mare told me: 'You had to stand on your seat while everyone sang accompanied by the organ and everyone pelted you with peanuts and popcorn.' Celebrity appearances weren't unknown, although they could have their mysterious side:

> My memories include John Travolta being introduced onto the stage in the late 1970s. Much later on I began to doubt that he actually was really John Travolta and asked my dad, who told me that Travolta had actually been in Plymouth in connection with filming, so perhaps it was true.

One person recalled the yo-yo champion of America turning up to demonstrate their skills.

For some respondents the process of thinking back to their childhood cinema visits triggered intensely detailed recollections. An account from Glasgow describes beautifully the anarchic spirit of the audience and the faded charm of the venues in the early 1960s:

> This was Glasgow at Shawlands Cross, about three miles south from the city centre. There were three cinemas almost next to one another: Elephant, Embassy and Waverley. The children's screenings were mostly in the Elephant, a big cinema, rough and rundown, possibly a former music hall. I can remember a wide cinema with three aisles and between the side aisles and the walls were pairs of seats for couples. The screen was constructed on top of what looked like a high stage, all painted in worn-out black mahogany, perhaps double the height of the usherettes selling ice cream at the front during the intervals. By the late 1960s the Elephant had been demolished and the site redeveloped.
>
> I can't remember the names of any of the films but I have lots of recollections of Westerns. There were cowboys on horseback, cattle-droving, fast galloping horse rides, shootouts in bars, and campfires at night with someone strumming a guitar. And Indians in feathered headgear, nimble and fast on foot, up mountains ambushing cowboys in narrow gorges with only bows and arrows. And someone at some point saying 'Me Big Chief' and we all shouted it back banging our chests King Kong-style.
>
> The screenings were generally well attended; the cinema was about two-thirds full. I think there were two usherettes on duty. They were strict and allowed no nonsense. If anyone was larking about or out of their seats they were given a warning. If it happened again, the manager was sent for and he marched them out. I can remember people flying paper darts up into the projector beam. There would be a big roar when one made it up high, and the usherettes came straight down the aisle to catch the culprits. But they never did. On winter days the cinema filled up with fog and as it got worse outside, you could tell inside the cinema.
>
> My strongest memory is of trying to get in without paying. The Elephant had an emergency exit in the gents' toilet. One of us would buy a ticket and take a seat, then after a few minutes would visit the gents and open the emergency door and we all trooped in. Then one by one, at intervals, we would try to slip into the cinema. What we didn't realise was the manager and usherettes were wise to this and kept a lookout. They could see the bright light every time the toilet door opened and a little head peeping out into the darkness to see if the coast was clear. It was cat and mouse, with usherettes waiting to pounce. If we were lucky we spent the money on ice cream and shared it around. The ethics didn't bother us too much. We reckoned the cinema ice cream cost more than in the newsagents and either way the cinema got all our pocket money.

The memories of another respondent from Bristol also provide an evocative picture of the whole experience of the Saturday clubs that is worth recording in full:

> My mother would give me sixpence (a tanner) to go to our local cinema, the Ritz in Brislington. It was over a mile away and I would save my penny bus fare and walk so that I could buy some Black Jacks in a busy sweetshop full of kids. It was called The Black Cat and was under the cinema. Once inside the grand art deco Ritz it was bedlam, full of noisy kids sitting on upturned seats and moving from seat to seat. A portly man with grey hair and a large moustache was trying to keep order, walking up and down with kids flicking their bus tickets and sweet wrappers with an elastic band. As the lights softly dimmed, quietness and order was restored as the luxurious curtains opened and the kids cheered.
>
> The titles came onto the screen and the children waited nervously to see if their hero had survived from last week's episode with the indians (boooh!) chasing the stagecoach and the wheel coming loose and the stagecoach going over the cliff. But wait, the hero had survived (hooray!), he had managed to grab a small bush. But wait, the roots of the bush were coming loose. By now the children were on the edge of their seats. But the hero would scrabble up and whistle for his horse. We would have to wait for next week and I would have to ask mum for money as it was a very tight budget for her and I would hate asking but she would find it somehow to let me go and see my heroes.

On a rather melancholy note, many who got in touch mentioned the fact that the cinemas they attended as children had subsequently been demolished, often following a period in which they had been adapted for other uses such as bingo halls. Those that escaped demolition frequently ended up becoming a shop, nightclub or pub on a permanent basis. This process seemed to be a source of genuine regret for most. The UK version of the YouTube website contains many videos shot by enthusiasts to commemorate such cinemas, including the Odeon Bolton, the ABC Mansfield, the Kensington Ritz and various sites in Liverpool. Among many other cinemas remembered with affection were several Odeons including those in Balham Hill in London, at Romford, Southsea, Worthing and the Kingsway, Swansea. Those from the ABC chain listed included the Regal in Kingston upon Thames, the Curzon and the Strand in Belfast and the Ritz in Edinburgh. Then there was the Essoldo in Nottingham, the Lido in Swansea and the Gaiety, Cardiff. Other London cinemas remembered were the Empire at Ealing Broadway, the ABC in Hammersmith and the Wandsworth Palace (a list of all the cinemas named by the survey respondents is included as an appendix at the back of this book). The sheer number of cinemas taking part in the Saturday clubs within any given town could provide the average child with a bewildering selection from which to choose. One person recalled Barrow-in-Furness having a Ritz (ABC), a Coliseum (Rank), the Astra, the Classic and the Palace. Another reminisced about the wonders of the Regal, Norris Green, in the Liverpool suburbs:

> The cinema was very plush. It had recently been painted and done up. Most places were being spruced up at that time or were new builds, especially on bombsites. (This was the late 1940s, early 1950s). My uncle got a temporary job painting the outside of the cinema. The front got jazzed up, extra lights and so on, to attract more customers.

Many recalled the sheer pleasure of entering the typical auditorium with its thick carpets and the evocative smell of hot dogs.

Two accounts of visits to the same cinema indicate the kind of class divide that could exist within the audience. The cinema in question was the Drake in Plymouth and the period was the late 1960s. The first account is striking:

> The screenings included a main film and lots of cartoons, the content of which I cannot recall, mainly due to the activities that were going on within the auditorium! There was much opportunity to purchase sweets and other goodies from the stalls at the front of the building and at that time there were hostesses who wandered around with trays around their necks selling ice creams and drinks. I hate to think how high we all were on sugar!! I doubt very much that what was happening on screen was taken much notice of as there was a lot of food and sweets being used as missiles, much noise and mayhem, and no apparent control anywhere. I dread to think what mess was left behind each week if this was normal behaviour. I recall going with a small group of friends and although we very much joined in with the chaos that ensued, in fact if we hadn't I think we may have suffered somewhat, none of us ever returned for a repeat experience. I was so traumatised by it that I never went again.

Contrast this with the experience of a contemporary at the same cinema:

> I grew up in a council estate very close to the red light area of Plymouth, at the time still surrounded by bombsites left from wartime air raids. We would all troop off from the flats to the local cinema and have a great time escaping from our quite poor lives. We would all boo the baddies and cheer the goodies; most of the time was spent shouting at the screen, joining in with the story. We became part of the show. Morality never came into it. We wanted fun and the film show provided it. In our council flats very few people had TVs, there was only one car, there was no other way out, except through these film shows. Most of our parents had fought or lived through the Second World War, times were hard, but at least children had this short time to escape from their daily lives. I couldn't wait for the following Saturday to find out how the hero would win the day.

Although some hard-pressed parents clearly viewed the screenings as a form of cheap childminding, this seems to have made little difference to the experience of the kids themselves. Overwhelmingly respondents pointed to the social aspect of attending the Saturday morning screenings as being their most important feature: 'The best thing was the sheer excitement of the event itself, just being out of the house for a start.' This tended to overshadow significantly the impact of the films being screened: 'It was just such a pleasure to be with hundreds of other kids without our mums. It was a social highlight.' A key part of this was to be outside parental control, where comparative freedom allowed boundaries to be tested:

> Saturday morning pictures were a parent free zone. In those days we all walked the mile there and back together in small groups with children our own age and not a mum or dad in sight. Happy carefree days of children growing up and learning about the world.

Such experiences played their part in the process of growing up and becoming independent:

> My sister would abandon me as soon as she saw her older friends and I was always a bit anxious I might get picked on by older boys. It never happened and we always managed to arrive back home together, so mum never knew and I learned to be independent.

In a similar vein, another interviewee said: 'I remember feeling very grown up because I was out without my parents. I always felt safe; there was never any trouble, just lots of enthusiasm and laughing.'

If the moral tone of the films frequently went unheeded, it was at least recognised. This was especially true for the audience of the more immediate postwar period:

> We imbibed the sense of adventure, the battle between right and wrong, adversity overcome and virtue rewarded. Nearly every film had a noble character who epitomised the virtues. An alternative is the bad guy, or the selfish rotter who has a conversion and comes out on the right side in the end. Perhaps being the generation just after World War II made us identify with the fight for things that were right.

Another account echoed this, saying: 'I think the 1950s generation felt that rules were there to be obeyed and that the authority of adults should be unquestioned. The behaviour when I attended was always immaculate.' If things were more unruly for later audiences, with rather less respect for the status quo, there was still a recognition of the clear moral distinctions drawn in the CFF films: 'It was always noisy, especially when the baddy did something horrible. Children are so judgmental, right and wrong are black and white, no grey!'

One of the most positive aspects of the surveys was the number of respondents who attributed their love of films, if not always cinema-going itself, to the experience of attending the Saturday clubs. Many pointed to an affection for specific genres, like Westerns or science fiction, or for particular stars like Laurel and Hardy, as stemming directly from the experience. These feelings had remained with them afterwards and, in certain cases, for a remarkable length of time.

Behind the screen

Attending the Saturday clubs was a pleasurable and formative experience for generations of children, but the job of actually organising and managing these events could entail all kinds of challenges. It also called for a singular type of individual, one who was often willing to go well beyond the normal job specification for working in or managing a cinema. The following accounts from those who were positioned behind the scenes, and the screens, for the clubs reveals a different viewpoint but one that frequently conveys a similar sense of excitement and energy.

Denys Chamberlain from Bristol recounted his involvement in the Saturday clubs:

> My family owned and operated a number of cinemas in Bristol between 1918 and 1987 when I retired. My first memory of a children's matinee was probably in about 1931–2 when I was five or six years of age and my father owned a cinema called the Knowle Picture House. I would hold a tin in which my father placed the money (probably one old penny) and we would stand at the rear entrance to the cinema. On one occasion we were showing a film called *Alf's Button Afloat* (1938) and as a publicity stunt each child was given a button! I don't think the film ever won an Oscar.[2]
>
> From 1936 we also operated a cinema called The Broadway in Filwood Park, Bristol where Saturday morning matinees were held. The cinema seated 1100 and was usually filled. The noise was unbelievable and four male attendants plus usherettes were needed in an attempt to keep order whilst the films were being shown. An early story concerned a manager who very kindly lent three old pence to a child who had forgotten his money. On the following Saturday there were two queues, one with children who had their money and one for those who had forgotten it. During the show other attractions were also shown including demonstrations of yo-yo tricks, etc. and different competitions. I was responsible for the booking of the films and whilst we showed many Westerns and short comedies and cartoons of the times, the most popular were those produced by the Children's Film Foundation – there were never enough of them and a new production was eagerly awaited. They were probably one of the few feature films that actually really held the attention of the audience.

Michael Fisher's memories of organising Saturday clubs are more mixed:

> I started my career as Assistant Manager at the Odeon, Lewisham in south east London and ran the Saturday clubs prior to their demise around 1978–81 when they were killed off by Noel Edmonds's *Swap Shop*. I went on to be manager TIC at the Odeon, Lewisham and then I worked my way through the ranks, eventually becoming the National Recruitment and Training Executive. Odeon's efforts were called the Super Saturday Club. They were regarded as a chore by staff as only token payments were made. The kiosk staff got just thirty pence for a morning's work. As I recall, I think management and projectionists got £2. The projectionist had to make up the film and break it down. The film cans would have graffiti on them such as 'If you're showing this you should be out of business.' Eventually Head Office put out a circular telling projectionists not to write obscenities on the cans. The print copies were sometimes poor and scratched.[3]
>
> Efforts were made to do dancing and other competitions on the stage. I suppose the dancing competitions were reasonably popular. The children danced to some pop record on the stage and then a member of staff would walk down the line and the audience would cheer the best one. The projectionist did not like the stage shows as he

had to work the spots and it meant his lunch was shorter. A later, very good managing director at Odeon named James Whittell used to round off the annual conference by getting all the managers to sing the Saturday Morning Picture Song. He said his kids couldn't believe they used to do community sing-songs. We never did any community singing, but I can remember some older managers telling me they had to do this in their training; 'Three wheels on my wagon' was a particular favourite.

Attendances were usually around 200. In an auditorium of 2,858 seats this looked pretty sparse – Lewisham Odeon at that time was a rockshow venue rather like the Hammersmith Odeon. I hardly saw a CFF film, or in fact any film. Managers rarely have the time to watch films. I do recall seeing one about hidden treasure. At the time, I regarded the films shown as rather dull and worthy. I do recall serials; they were not of the quality that I remember when I was a member of the ABC Minors myself. Odeon used to distribute a quarterly magazine internally showing efforts made by managers to promote films. By far the most coverage was for the main releases, but there was occasionally some coverage of Saturday clubs. I think Plymouth and Newcastle ran quite successful ones.

Alex Jones built a reputation as one of the most committed and inventive cinema managers working in South Wales in the 1980s. His experiences are testimony to a devotion that kept his Saturday clubs running well past the demise of most of the others in the UK. His career began with a Saturday job at the Windsor, Neath. The cinema had been shut down due to falling audiences near the end of the 1970s. A new developer wanted to turn it into a nightclub but the local council insisted that at least part of the building should continue to be run as a cinema, which they did in the former Circle. On Saturday mornings they ran a disco for kids and alternated it with a film club. He remembers:

The first club screening attracted just three people. The manager of the previous cinema on the site told me that when they ran a club it had attracted 1,000. It had apparently gone into decline during the 1970s and was then seriously affected by the opening of a new swimming pool in the town; film-going was going out of fashion. After six weeks we shut down the club. Things weren't helped by the poor state of some of the packages from the CFF, which were not sent in sequence, so that serials were shown in the wrong order.[4]

Two years later Alex became manager of the entire venue. He split the cinema operation away from the nightclub and relaunched the kids' film club. He backed this with a publicity campaign in the local press and got the attendance figures to between sixty and seventy:

Things were helped by the improvement in the quality of the CFF films that had been made during the 1970s as they started to circulate around to us. They often had a strong slapstick element. They also resembled popular children's television in their style. I remember *Sky Pirates* being particularly successful.

Alex then left to open his own independent cinema, the Plaza in Port Talbot. Taking the successful Monico cinema in Cardiff as inspiration, he planned some publicity stunts for the new children's film club:

> The manager at the Monico had set up the answerphone message so that it promoted their children's club first before giving details of their current feature film screenings. They also had an MC. I spoke to him on the phone and came to the conclusion that stage-work was key to making the new club a success.[5]

By now it was the mid-1980s and the CFF had become the CFTF. Most of its circuit of clubs had already closed but Alex had no intention of falling in with this trend:

> To launch the club I screened *Raising the Roof* and the serial *The Boy with Two Heads*. I recall that the opening credits for this were always greeted with shouts of approval. I took out a full-page advert in the local paper saying that anyone attending would be given a free ticket to see *Karate Kid 2* (1986), which was then on general release. Nine hundred people attended the screening. Subsequently attendance settled down at around 500. In my view, attendance was aided by having just one auditorium. I hired an artist from Swansea to make special posters for the club which were parodies of current commercial feature releases. For example, we did one which was a send-up of *Little Shop of Horrors* (1986) which became 'Little Show for Horrors'. We also made sure that we kept the admission price low at fifty pence.

He attributes much of the success to stage business, which the children adored, with Alex acting as MC:

> Many of the stunts were related to feature films on current release, so that when *Jaws: The Revenge* (1987) was screening I had a cutout fin moving around in the balcony. At another screening, balloons were dropped onto the audience from the balcony (which was shut to matinee audiences). At Christmas Santa appeared and threw sweets to the audience. There were regular competitions and raffles, with children on stage to collect their prizes during the intermission. There was a fancy dress competition and I remember vividly looking at the kids queuing up outside in their outfits. Pop music was used as another topical reference, so we had 'Walk like an Egyptian' by The Bangles playing and all the children were ordered to walk around like Egyptians for the rest of the day. Everything was designed to make the programme as much fun as possible. The children loved it. They also made an incredible mess. The noise was so loud it made clouds of dust fall from the ceiling.
>
> The most popular gag was based on the character of the Phantom Flan Flinger who appeared in ITV's *Tiswas*. During a CFTF programme the house lights would flash on and off, followed by eerie music and the appearance of our very own Phantom, who would pelt someone in the audience with cream pie. I recall on one occasion standing on stage during the intermission, having arranged for the Phantom to attack me.

> This was partly planned to demonstrate that I wasn't the Phantom. When the light flickered and the music came on I saw just how strong the children's reaction was. Even Santa was attacked by the Phantom and dragged from the stage, never to be seen again. Parents waiting in the foyer for their children were also targeted. A story was released to the local press that the Phantom lived in the attic of the cinema and came out because he was so annoyed by the noise the children made. All of this made me into something of a local celebrity and I started to be recognised by children in the street who would point me out to their parents.

The programmes ran for five years but gradually went into a decline. The venue was obliged to go multiscreen and the breadth of choice affected attendance:

> The CFTF films were becoming very worn out with sections missing, including endings. There were no new films and some of the old ones brought out of retirement arrived in cans that were so rusted they were hard to open. Gradually I substituted commercial feature films on rerun into the programmes, cutting them in half to fit the format and using the CFTF's own 'come back next week to see what happens' title card to link the two halves. I even did this for a screening of *Star Wars*.
>
> Video rental certainly played a part in the decline of cinema-going. Ironically, I now see a huge decline in DVD rentals from the shop in the entertainment complex I currently run, while cinema attendance has steadily increased. I remember there being nine or ten cinemas in Port Talbot but by the time I managed the Plaza it was the only one left. Multiplexes were also a culprit. I think the Plaza bucked this trend because the children's club encouraged kids into the habit of film-going, which then remained into adulthood. The cinema thrived at a time of wider economic and social decline in Port Talbot itself, against all the odds. The club succeeded in running longer than almost anywhere in Wales, with the possible exception of the cinema in Llanelli. I don't believe that the more recent revival of Saturday children's screenings is comparable. This is just a way of packaging up slightly out-of-date films for a second run and using them to sell food, which is where the profits lie. They don't have the feel of the old clubs.
>
> The Plaza at its height was the busiest independent cinema in Wales. On one Saturday in 1989 we had over 5,000 people attend. The children's club was crucial to this success. I have enormously fond memories of CFF programmes at my cinemas, and how I did everything I could to use them to re-attract young audiences back at a time when cinema-going was very unfashionable to the young. I look back at my time at the Plaza as the happiest of my whole career. It was fantastically hard work but I was young and energised. The whole period was full of joy and I would happily go back to that time.

The Plaza is currently the subject of a feasibility study by the local council to look into possibilities for its refurbishment; Alex is managing independent cinemas in Cornwall.

James Taylor-Godard's love affair with the Foundation began at a young age and took him on a journey from being part of the audience to a role behind the screen, and then into his future career. James sets the context for the children's film club in

Llanelli, and his involvement with it, by telling me about the history of the cinema that hosted it. This was originally built as a flagship theatre of the Odeon chain but was subsequently renamed as the Classic in 1967:

> It was an impressive picture palace with a single auditorium seating 1,500. Then Classic Cinemas converted it from one screen to three in 1971; it was the first venture of its kind for the company. They also renamed it as the Classic Entertainment Centre. It was then taken over by the borough council in 1978, keeping the same staff and retaining the existing children's film club. The old balcony provided the largest space and was initially the home for the children's film club. It was converted into a hybrid cinema-theatre auditorium, with the two other spaces still designated as purely film screens; the film club eventually moved to one of these, which was middle-sized. The council renamed the whole venue as the Llanelli Entertainment Centre. The main space continued to be called Theatre 1 but was later renamed Theatr Elli in 1984, with the other two screens retaining the names Theatre 2 and 3 respectively.[6]
>
> I started attending the children's screenings when I was about eight or nine and kept going until I was roughly fourteen. Most of my friends had stopped going by then; it wasn't a cool thing to do when you reached secondary school, but I loved the programmes. Previously I had gone with a small group of schoolfriends. On one occasion I organised a class outing, which led to a large group attending. They were very badly behaved and I got the blame, which nearly resulted in me getting a ban. Later on I started to talk to the staff and became a volunteer, helping out. This gave me a legitimate excuse to carry on attending. There was no pay for my services but the screenings were free; entry was normally 50p, which was really cheap anyway.
>
> The typical content of a Foundation 'package' included:
>
> - Cartoons, usually *Looney Toons* or Walter Lantz;
> - Shorts like *The Chiffy Kids* or *The Magnificent 6½* but also ones that were in the form of adverts for forthcoming CFTF attractions. One of these featured Leslie Crowther as Lord Nelson on top of his column in Trafalgar Square from where he could spy new CFTF films with his telescope. Sometimes David Lodge would make an appearance as a cleaner perched on top of a ladder. Others featured Ed Stewart or Rolf Harris, and even Rod Hull and Emu who were always getting into fights in a projection booth;
> - A CFTF serial;
> - A longer clip from next week's feature film used as a trailer, usually cut short with a caption saying that if you wanted to find out the outcome you would have to return in a week; The break, which would include a raffle, the ritual throwing of sweets from the stage into the front rows, perhaps a guest appearance from someone in the show at the theatre, or from the panto or Santa if it was Christmas;
>
> Then, finally, the feature from the CFTF.

To be honest, many of the features were mediocre. Some could hold the attention but the audience was often tired by the time the main feature came on. Good features that I remember included *The Boy Who Turned Yellow*, *The Glitterball*, *Raising the Roof*, which was set in a cinema with one gang of 'good' kids and one gang of 'bad' kids involved in a competition organised by the cinema about who had the most unusual pets, and *Break Out*. This one had strong content; the Foundation sometimes depicted villains sympathetically or as antiheroes in the later films. Some films appeared to be foreign imports that were dubbed over, such as *Fly without Wings*, which was Dutch. This was an enjoyable film which dealt with disability in a progressive way and was ahead of its time. *The Johnstown Monster* had a good story but was let down by poor effects, particularly when the monster was finally seen at the end and turned out to be a small lizard photographed in close-up. The story played on the legend of the Loch Ness monster. *Mr Horatio Knibbles* was about a girl with a giant rabbit as a friend. This one was quite trippy, as were one or two of the 1960s films.

As far as the cartoons go, in addition to Walter Lantz or *Looney Toons* there were also dialogue-free foreign imports with the CFF ident at the start, either standard animation or sometimes stop-motion. They were usually one-off productions but there was a series of cartoons made about a bespectacled boy called Peter and his adventures with an eccentric inventor. They were fairly amusing but had only music and no dialogue.

When the Foundation became the CFTF and licensed some of its films to television these films were withdrawn from the packages and replaced by older, black-and-white films. The later films, from the end of the 1970s, were increasingly serious. *Terry on the Fence* was in the catalogue but I don't remember it being released to us. I suspect this was because its content was considered too dark. Some of the films became quite adult in their content, such as *Hide and Seek* which was about a boy running away from home to find his estranged father, who turns out to be uninterested in him as he is a criminal planning a robbery. *Haunters of the Deep* and *The Man from Nowhere* were genuinely scary and intense, or even disturbingly ambiguous. They sometimes had ghostly figures but these were dealt with seriously, whereas in the past films with ghosts were usually comic. However, a number of these films were let down by weak endings. I recall that Gary Simmons, who appeared in *Haunters*, became a member of a Bee Gees tribute band called 'Taste of Honey'.

If the feature was poor, the kids tended to play up more. On occasions it was nearly a riot, with drinks cans thrown at the screen. Kids regularly ran about the auditorium. Staff would take badly behaved children outside into the foyer to wait for the return of their parents. The screenings were always noisy, with much reaction to what was happening on screen. The marshal was quite a rough-looking guy who turned up in his football shirt and jeans. When he was on duty the children behaved. When he left at 11.30am, to fetch chips for his grandfather's lunch, the riot would commence; the screenings were usually 10am–12 noon.

I also remember a lot of serials and the series of shorts, especially *The Magnificent 6½*. The first two series were tremendously popular but the cast was changed for the

Hide and Seek (1972): a new, 'increasingly serious' CFF

third and it had less audience appeal. A crucial factor in its popularity was the fact that the kids were so ordinary and unglamorous, they were down-to-earth. This also applied to *The Chiffy Kids* and *The Trouble with 2B*, which was set in a school; they were both quite enjoyable. Some items such as *Ali and the Camel* were un-PC in their content and could never be shown now, in my view. Other series featured animals, such as *Chimpmates*. They seemed funny at the time but became dated and are also un-PC by today's standards. *The Adventures of Rex* was in this vein. *The Unbroken Arrow* was a serial which followed on from a single feature called *Young Robin Hood* [sic]; the Foundation was always trying to keep their audience hooked with cliff-hangers.

The children's film club in Llanelli continued in operation until 1998. It was one of the last official clubs in the UK, although I am aware that one was still operating quite late in Fishguard and that the Plaza in Port Talbot also continued to a late date. Llanelli took the entire weekly CFTF package, which was by then distributed by

> Glenbuck Films, for a long time, although other cinemas still running clubs tended to cherry-pick elements. From 1989 all the cartoons and the main feature were always in colour. This was also when the features that had been withdrawn for TV were reinstated and marked the last rearranging of the packages. Other material continued in black and white; *Danny the Dragon*, which was on the last Foundation package we ever showed in 1996, remained as the only black-and-white serial until the end and among the shorts a few Rex adventures remained in, as well as a couple of the Peter Butterworth shorts from the 1950s. Towards the end we stopped using the CFTF packages and continued the children's club using a discounted morning screening of a current commercially released children's film, or one from the recent past. That took us from 1996 to 1998. The audience had fallen away badly from its height when we had hundreds each week, dropping to around seventy-five in the early 1990s, and then about forty at the end. I think this was a result of the arrival of the multiplex, the rise of Saturday morning kid's TV and the new blockbuster Hollywood productions. The ticket price had risen to 70p and kids complained that they had already seen the older films on TV or video. I also feel that the screenings became a sort of dumping ground for busy parents to offload their children for a couple of hours.
>
> The original appeal was that CFF films were exclusive to the Saturday kids' clubs and couldn't be seen anywhere else. Kids at that time played in the street, acting out their own imaginative adventure stories. The attraction of the Foundation films was that they seemed to make these fantasies real. It was like seeing your own daydreams of adventure come alive. As a kid I wanted to be in the films, to do what the characters in the stories did. Also, the casts were led by children, making for stronger identification. The kids had named billing, whereas the adults were occasionally only named as ensembles, even when there were quite big stars involved.

Interestingly, my surveys of former audience members brought up four respondents who actually attended the Entertainment Centre in Llanelli during the late 1970s and early 1980s. The first recalled seeing mainly CFF films including *Black Island* and *Break Out*, as well as the serial *The Boy with Two Heads*, which he saw under its alternative title *Chico the Rainmaker*.[7] He reported that

> there were always two staff that kept order, and always the manager. The memories that stand out are the films themselves and also the midway break. They used to have a thing called 'Breakfast' where the staff would go on stage and throw sweets to the kids in the space between the front seats and the stage. The ensuing mêlée was always very chaotic, but I don't remember anyone getting hurt. Later, in the early 1980s, and much to my dismay, I had to take my younger sister along with me, so I could not join in the sweet mêlée in the front. She tells me I still hold a grudge against her to this day.

Another told me that

> in the depths of my memory I seem to recall they were never full, around half maybe. There were a couple of people who appeared before the film to announce birthdays and throw sweets into the audience. There was always a smattering of adults as well, parents and grandparents. They were cheaper than normal for the cinema. To be honest, if they updated it and brought it back I'd probably take my own children as we never really cared about what was shown, it was somewhere cheap and cheerful to go.

One had less than flattering memories of some of the assistants:

> They used to have helpers which served in a sort of school prefect role. The power seemed to go a bit to their heads and they would try to boss the children around. One Saturday they made us sit in the seats they wanted us to be in, which meant that we could not sit near our friends who had arrived earlier. I think it was done to save cleaning the unused areas!

Another provided a remarkably detailed account of her time attending when it was still the Odeon:

> I was an avid fan of the Saturday club. It was an integral part of my social life when I was in primary school and was something to look forward to each week. The format was always the same and included cartoons, a Western (although I am ashamed at the way the Native Americans were portrayed as the baddies) and the serial, which ended the presentation and always with a cliff-hanger. One episode was so exciting I inadvertently chewed my return bus ticket and had to hang around the terminus until my mother finished her shopping in town and paid my bus fare again.
>
> The day before I left primary school we moved to Llanelli itself, two blocks away from the Odeon but by then my interests had changed, so I stopped going to the club. Llanelli boasted six cinemas in those days but the Odeon was by far the most salubrious. It eventually became a multiscreen cinema and theatre and was called the Llanelli Entertainment Centre. All the other cinemas were either pulled down or became restaurants. It was a fine art deco building and its change of use destroyed much of its interior but externally it looked the same. I have very happy memories of the full and carefree life I spent in Llanelli and the Odeon club was an integral part of that life. My husband is also a 'Sospan' (a native of Llanelli) but he wasn't allowed to go to the Club because his mother thought it would be a bad influence on him!

Today the Llanelli Odeon is closed and swathed in scaffolding. It is home only to the ghosts of former audiences. The town has an Odeon multiplex at a different site and a new theatre called the Ffwrnes which occasionally screens art house movies or revivals. One of its senior technicians is James Taylor-Godard.

Reflections

A number of patterns emerge from the overall response to the surveys. In terms of gender, the audience seems to have been quite evenly divided between girls and boys. Girls were sometimes irritated by what they saw as the male orientation of the programmes but seem to have enjoyed them despite this. Two specific age groups appear to have attended, those between six and ten years of age and those from eleven to about fourteen. They can be divided into two groups as this is the way they tend to identify themselves. The younger group often went with their elder siblings and the two groups have distinctively different memories. For the older group the task of looking after younger siblings was sometimes an embarrassing hindrance, which prevented them from being with their friends, but just as often it brought a sense of adult responsibility that left a lasting positive impression. The CFF often recognised in its internal reports the challenge of providing material with diverse enough appeal for these different age groups, particularly as the older the viewers got, the more distanced they became from material that appealed to primary school-age children. The focus of their work seems to have shifted towards this early teens group during the 1970s in an attempt to win them back.

At about fourteen attendance peters out, as the children seem to identify the activity as something intended for younger kids. After this age the attraction of shops, music, sports and the opposite sex often takes over: 'In my teenage years we went to a local nightclub that held Saturday morning discos for children, we felt that was much more grown up for us. The girls danced and the boys watched.' Another factor in the decline in attendance from the late 1960s onwards was the competing attraction of TV, with many respondents recalling the arrival at home of their first family television set, followed by their first colour set. The decision by the BBC and then ITV to invest in their Saturday morning provision also had an impact. In the 1950s and 1960s there is a distinct impression that the Saturday clubs filled a yawning gap in terms of the entertainment available to children. From the 1970s it found itself in an increasingly competitive marketplace.

In terms of geography, the respondents came from all over England and Wales, with fewer from Scotland and Northern Ireland, but this could be attributable to the locations used for the survey. The attendance time period covered was from the late 1950s until the late 1970s, with only one or two appearing from before or after that period. One recalled attending screenings for children during World War II at the Coronation cinema, an ABC in London: 'Entry was certainly cheap, two old pence, and was known by us as the tuppeny rush – and what a rush it was, hordes of us would cram into the cinema as this was our only entertainment.' Prewar memories were rare indeed. Conversely, there were also a few, especially in Wales, who attended well into the 1980s.

The clubs were immensely popular, with few negative comments recorded. The films themselves played their part, as the audience reacted positively to the simplicity of the narratives and the clear outcomes presented. The excitement of fast-paced action and the humour of slapstick comedy were greatly appreciated. The Foundation was probably wrong to think that the films screened could really shape the moral outlook of its young audience; their interaction with their peers seems to have had much more impact on their attitudes. However, the films did help to establish for them an awareness of the values deemed significant by adults in their society and therefore form part of a wider ethical framework. The CFF films seem to have had a mixed response. Many preferred the American films and serials on offer to the homemade products of the Foundation. The higher production values and slick professionalism were differences often noted. The early CFF films were criticised for their middle-class metropolitan bias and stiff acting but the later films were often appreciated for their increasingly gritty realism and relevance. The opportunity to see a film on the big screen in which the characters and setting were close to your own experiences was crucial here. Despite some indifference, there were also many who became devoted fans of the Foundation's work and who have retained great affection for its films ever since. A love of cinema in general has certainly been one of the legacies of the clubs. The additional attractions of the screenings, including the competitions and songs, seem to have been a great success too.

Overshadowing the films themselves was the attraction of the clubs as a social event. Even if the details of some of the films have faded from the memory, the actual experience of being in the auditorium remains vivid. The pleasures of being out of the home, away from parents and having a safe place to go with friends was of huge importance and central to this was the freedom to gently misbehave, within recognised boundaries. The chance to make a noise, move about freely, throw things (relatively harmlessly) and gently test the rules and authority figures was massively appealing and seemingly beneficial. While recognising that the films shown often decried badly behaved children, the kids in the audience actually enjoyed a degree of bad behaviour and adjudged it to be morally insignificant; adult attempts at correction were viewed as a challenge to be circumvented. A healthy disregard for unnecessary rules was combined with an awareness of where the line should be drawn. Real harm or aggression were almost totally absent.

These clubs represented a rare opportunity to escape the sphere of parental control; for many this helped to build a taste for independence and developed self-confidence. Far from undermining relationships with their parents, it seems to have strengthened them as many remembered thinking that it was a good thing for their parents to have time without them. Many also appreciated the sacrifices of parents who struggled to find even the little money needed to send them to the clubs. On a less positive note, the Britain that emerges from the recollections is one that is often divided along gender and class lines, with a keen sense of financial and social differences; one respondent told me of her own happy memories of attending the clubs in the East End of London but also commented that her husband, from a more middle-class area, was forbidden from attending by his parents. This trend didn't seem to abate between the 1950s and the 1970s. Nonetheless, the overall experience seems to be one that left an enduring, positive impression on those that attended.

Intense nostalgia, both for the clubs themselves and for childhood pleasures, is revealed in many of the responses. As one person put it: 'It was so much fun. I loved those days. This brings back my childhood, thank you.' For many, thinking of those times made the sheer excitement palpable again:

> Saturday morning; squeals of delight as the light penetrates the bedroom. Not just because school was over for another two days but it was that time of the week when joy knew no bounds. We would soon be off to the pictures and escape to a fantasy land of all manner of heroes and monsters. The joy brought about from these Saturday morning excursions to the local cinema is as tangible now as it was fifty years ago.

This nostalgia has undoubtedly fed into the success of the BFI's reissue of the CFF films on DVD. The whole topic of nostalgia in and about cinema has now become the subject of wider academic study.[8]

One fascinating recent development has been the reappearance of special screenings for children in multiplex cinemas. These usually take place, appropriately enough, on a Saturday morning or on mornings during school holidays. However, rather like the later club screenings of the 1980s, they tend to be based around a second run of a fairly recent feature film, usually American. The screenings do borrow the lower ticket pricing from the classic days and sometimes the main feature is supplemented by cartoons. A further change is that cinemas frequently require that younger children are accompanied by an adult. The development of digital technology has also led to something of a resurgence in ad hoc screenings in local community halls at children's themed events. These indicate a refreshing willingness of small communities to embrace cinema as a positive way to bring people, and particularly children, together socially. However, none of this quite replicates the sort of ethos advocated by the CFF, which belongs to another era. Neither have these changes led to an increased output in the production of children's films in the UK. This latter point is an issue taken up in the final chapter of this book in relation to the work of the Foundation's successor, the Children's Media Foundation.

Notes

1. Terry Staples, *All Pals Together: The Story of Children's Cinema* (Edinburgh: Edinburgh University Press, 1997), pp. xv–xvi.
2. Denys Chamberlain interviewed by the author, 13 and 15 August 2013.
3. Michael Fisher interviewed by the author, 12 and 13 August 2013.
4. Alex Jones interviewed by the author, 15 March and 21 March 2013.
5. As at January 2014 YouTube contains a number of posts relating to the Plaza, including home movie footage of the venue, excerpts from programmes made by ITV and BBC Radio Wales on the subject, and details of the campaign to save it from demolition.
6. James Taylor-Godard interviewed by the author, 6 March 2013.
7. This was the title used for the 1974 television broadcast of the series in the USA by PBS, suggesting that when my respondent saw this in a British cinema some years afterwards, they saw the US prints.
8. See Pam Cook's *Screening the Past: Memory and Nostalgia in Cinema* (London and New York: Routledge, 2005).

5 The Legacy
The Children's Media Foundation

In the early 1970s, when Iain Smith first worked for the Children's Film Foundation as a production manager on *The Camerons*, it was thriving, making six or more hour-long feature films a year, alongside a sprinkling of shorter offerings. It was supplying films to two integrated national cinema chains, Rank and ABC, along with a large number of independent cinemas, which were all running popular Saturday morning film clubs. Not far short of half a million children a week were watching CFF output. By the time he returned as a member of the CFTF's Board of Directors thirty years later, now with a wealth of international industry experience behind him, the picture was entirely transformed:

> The truth was that the whole idea of children's entertainment had been completely swamped by the technological revolution hitting the industry as a whole. In the new multiple-choice, video on demand world, children's entertainment was a much more muscular, young-adult thing than it had ever been in the heyday of the Foundation. Our films were already heritage rather than entertainment. We explored the idea that the Foundation could become the agency for making creative and commercial choices on behalf of other funds but that didn't get very far either. My role was to assist and advise in these endeavours and in particular to represent the interests of children's cinema at the UK Film Council where I was also a board member. I also brought an industry perspective to the table with my knowledge of Hollywood and the larger production environment.[1]

By this stage Anna Home was heading what remained of the Foundation. She endorses Iain Smith's assessment:

> When I became CEO of the CFTF it had ceased to directly produce or commission films or television programmes for children but was hoping to continue in the role of script development. A scheme was launched along these lines with the support of the Film Council and the BBC but nothing concrete came of this. Effectively my remit became one of winding up the operations of the CFTF. The Foundation no longer drew down any statutory funds. It really existed in name only and in terms of its heritage. The Foundation's paper archives were in a cupboard at Elstree Studios in a pile of boxes.

> Funding was obtained to catalogue all the material and produce an index. This was completed and the materials were then handed into the care of the BFI. The films themselves were scattered in labs all over London. They are now under the auspices of the BFI as well and are being lovingly remastered and re-released on DVD.[2]

There is little denying the decline in the Foundation's fortunes. From 1977 to 1983 its release rate slowly fell from six to two films per year as production costs rose and its grant failed to keep pace. With reconfiguration into the CFTF in 1983, and the loss of direct public subsidy, the number of features made fell to just seven in three years. From 1988 onwards the CFTF no longer made films itself but just funded the development of scripts. This resulted in the production of just four features and five serials by 2002. Its role from this point onwards was largely advisory and as custodian of the back-catalogue. The arrival of Lottery funding early in the new millennium heralded a burst of optimism but this was shortlived; funding of script development on several projects failed to lead to any production work. The July 2010 announcement of the axing of the Film Council by David Cameron's coalition government was the final nail in the coffin of the Foundation. The last act was effectively the handing over of the back-catalogue and archive materials to the BFI in June 2012.

However, the Foundation has not yet disappeared altogether. Anybody accessing its website today will find a digital copy of the back-catalogue, a potted history and a contact address for Anna Home at an organisation called The Children's Media Foundation (CMF), a body that continues to uphold the traditions and legacy of the CFTF by campaigning for high standards across all forms of media targeting children in the UK. As she puts it:

> The CMF was created out of a sense of anxiety at the low priority currently given to children's media by state-funded bodies, and as a response to the ever increasing commercial pressures in the sector which have been brought about by deregulation.

The CMF owes a great deal to the legacy of the Foundation but it also built on work undertaken by the campaign group Save Kids' TV (SKTV). This was established in September 2006 at the Showcomotion Children's Media Conference in Sheffield and brought together a network of parents, educators and industry personnel who were concerned about a possible decline in the quality of broadcast media for children alongside the gradual erosion of the production base in the UK. SKTV was successful in gaining the support of many media institutions including BAFTA, as well as from the majority of the industry unions and guilds. Its credo was:

> our children need and deserve a media diet as rich and stimulating as previous generations enjoyed – and should be able to see content which reflects their everyday lives and the culture of the country they live in. Children need to hear their own voices, experience their own stories and see the places they live, if they are to become rounded, engaged citizens.[3]

This statement sounds remarkably close to the principles that had inspired the genesis of the CFF half a century earlier.

The initial impetus for SKTV was ITV's decision to close down its children's television operation. SKTV took further ammunition from an Ofcom report published in 2007 which found that only 1 per cent of TV content watched by UK children was actually newly made in Britain; the remainder consisted either of repeats or imported material.[4] The report also pointed to a 14 per cent decline in the amount of original children's material produced by UK broadcasters over the preceding eight years and recorded that the amount created within the commercial sector (including ITV, C4 and Channel Five) had halved in the same period. The authors of the report noted the increasing pressure placed on the BBC to fill the gaps left by this decline and questioned its commitment to do this.

SKTV issued a statement in response to the Ofcom report that offered a possible way forward for children's media in the UK. It proposed:

> A new public service online destination for children is required. This destination would be a beacon, attracting to it high quality content from a rich mix of sources. Such a destination would address a significant market failure because no such mainstream service currently exists – the children's broadcasters' web services are mainly online extensions for their on-air content. Our proposed new online destination will have a strongly public service feel: fun but not exploitative, entertaining but constructive, educative and safe.
>
> Crucially we propose that this service is audience-driven. So, rather than representing adults' views of what children might want to do and see, it will be shaped and produced for and by its audience.[5]

The paper was signed by Anna Home and Greg Childs. The response of the Department for Culture, Media and Sport was to ask SKTV for a more detailed plan, which it supplied in April 2009. This second document argued for

> a new public service for children ... one which makes a range of programming and functionalities available to children in the forms they want, when they want them, on the platforms they use. Our proposal for a multi-functional service delivered online would feature video, audio and interactive content, and a safe, secure social networking space.[6]

However, despite further lobbying of politicians over the next year, the best that could be achieved was a promise from then Culture Secretary, Ben Bradshaw, that the issue of children's media would be addressed in a forthcoming Digital Economy Bill. By the following year the Labour government was out of office.

With the Conservative–Liberal Democrat coalition in office, SKTV succeeded in June 2011 in establishing the first All Party Parliamentary Group on children's media, chaired by former children's TV presenter Floella Benjamin, now Baroness Benjamin.

It presented a further report to the Broadcasting Minister, Ed Vaizey, in April 2011. As its website subsequently reported, the Minister conceded that children's culture in the UK needed support but said that no funding would be forthcoming for an alternative commissioning body to counterbalance and support the BBC. In December 2011 SKTV merged with what remained of the CFTF to create the Children's Media Foundation and took the campaign forward again.

Anna Home sees the CMF as:

> A voice for children and a watchdog on continuing developments which affect the type of media available to children in the UK. We see ourselves as a critical friend to the BBC, supporting their public service role and acknowledging the good work they do, but also keeping an eye on their commitment to children's services. We are concerned at the apparent failure of C4 to live up to its original remit on older children's provision. Channel Five commissions a very small amount of original content; this is obviously regrettable, particularly in light of the very positive contributions they previously made to children's broadcasting.

Anna believes that the new Foundation can contribute positively in a number of areas:

> I believe there is a real need for proper academic research into children as an audience and as media users. What is their experience? How does it affect their development? Is there a role for standards? What is the long term impact? The funding of this kind of research is a key priority. Too much discussion of the subject currently lacks any foundation or substance.

Another area of focus is the effect of global commercialisation:

> We are concerned about American-funded media steering the agenda for all media production for children in Britain. The lack of a strong indigenous infrastructure producing distinctively British work is very worrying. Creative work needs to be produced which genuinely reflects the real world of children today, their feelings, anxieties, and concerns, without patronising or talking down to them. This work needs to be brave, controversial if necessary, and willing to talk to children on their own terms, willing to tackle tough issues.
>
> Deregulation has removed a public service remit from much of children's media production, leaving it (apart from the BBC) almost entirely at the mercy of commercial interests, with tie-ins to the toy market and other products aimed at children. There is so little work being made which addresses children in a positive, concerned manner with a regard for them as citizens and individuals, and which speaks to their needs. Too much work is dominated by commercial imperatives. Children are often low on the agenda of programme-makers today.

> Hopefully the tax break for children's live action content announced in the 2014 autumn statement, which CMF lobbied for, will have a positive impact on the nature of the children's market, encouraging broadcasters other than the BBC to start commissioning children's content. However the BBC is likely to continue to be the major provider of original children's content and it has problems of its own; cuts over the last few years, with more to come, have impacted on the amount of new indigenous content commissioned. The decision to move all children's content off the main channels to the dedicated digital channels (CBeebies and CBBC) was logical because that is where the target audience is, and increasingly on the iPlayer. However, it means there is less general awareness of the output and there is a danger that the genre becomes out of sight and out of mind for mainstream executives, politicians, etc. It is very important that children's services remain a high priority in the upcoming discussions about the new Charter and licence fee. The CMF will be making this a priority in 2015–16.

Anna's philosophy for children's media is evident in the introduction to her book, *Into the Box of Delights: A History of Children's Television.* Here she says that television (and by implication the wider media) is 'an important influence in children's lives, one that helps to determine their taste, attitudes and knowledge of the world'[7]. The book's analysis of the impending threats to children's television from overcommercialisation and deregulation, although written twenty years ago, has proved prescient: 'Will it still exist in its present form or will it, as in many other countries, have been reduced to wall-to-wall cartoons and so-called family drama?'[8] In her chapter on storytelling, her defence of Rik Mayall's reading of Roald Dahl's *George's Marvellous Medicine* on the BBC's *Jackanory* (1965–96) slot, a series which she helped bring into existence, reveals much about her approach.[9] She argues that it pleased children by recognising their desire to be 'anarchic and anti-adult' while also acting as a positive influence in encouraging them to read. Her book concludes by defending the model of children's broadcasting that she helped develop at the BBC:

> Children's television of the type that Britain has had in the past is never going to be hugely profitable. But the appetite for it continues, and it is important that the new generation of children should have the opportunities their parents had.[10]

She might equally well have been talking about the CFF.

Iain Smith echoes these concerns:

> As far as children's media is concerned I think we are at a very sorry pass. The CFF existed at a time when childhood was an actual period of one's life – between infancy and teenage. Now there is barely any childhood in media terms. Children growing up seem to go from pre-school to early teens in one leap. In the face of more enticing fare, the wonderful age of being innocent does not interest them any more, or so it seems.

> I am, however, sure that there is a latent need and perhaps even a demand on the part of mindful parents to see better quality entertainment choices available for their kids. The problem is that in a savagely diminished British investment environment, children's or family entertainment is seen as high risk, or even unnecessary, especially when it is so difficult to measure and quantify demand. This is particularly the case in the face of the huge blockbuster movies coming out of Pixar, etc. Theoretically, disruptive technology and the merging of film and television into media content should present all of us with possibilities for satisfying a more variegated cultural appetite, including more intelligent and targeted children's entertainment. This raises the currently unpopular idea at the heart of the work of the Foundation, that films should not only be entertaining but should also be morally uplifting. The current lack of any serious provision of morally intelligent media for British children above the age of five and below the age of thirteen is a potential social problem the effect of which has yet to be felt.

Despite this gloomy evaluation, the CMF has already established itself as central to the burgeoning debate about the condition of children's media in Britain. During 2013 it contributed its views to the review of the BBC Trust; continued to develop the All Party Parliamentary Group, which now has eighty members and a regular newsletter; and organised discussion events around themes such as gender representation in children's media. It has staged several talks enabling the public to hear from key industry personnel on issues relating to children's media; has established a distinguished board, including a number of high-profile supporters (such as the children's novelist Philip Pullman); and launched its own website.

The CMF's Director is Greg Childs, who started his career as a producer at the BBC before becoming a leading consultant in children's media:

> After university I had a summer job at the BBC which then led to an apprenticeship as an assistant floor manager. I worked as a researcher in entertainment and then moved to children's programmes. I then joined a scheme for trainee producers, also with children's programming. I started in the area of pre-school and spent a number of years in the team on *Play School* [1964–88]. I learnt a great deal about children as an audience here. Part of my job was to go out and observe children watching programmes to get a sense of their reactions. I talked to nursery staff and other professionals, as well as to parents. This informed my own approach to programme-making. [11]

After this, he took over as producer at *Record Breakers* (1972–2001) in 1988 and then became a web producer, establishing the BBC's first website dedicated to children's content.

Greg took his online unit in BBC Children's into exciting new areas as they formulated a bi-media approach to all content for children and young people on BBC Choice and BBC Knowledge, the BBC's new digital channels: 'We began to develop the synergies between online content, interactivity, and the broadcast programming; effectively this was an early form of transmedia, perhaps the first on the BBC.' This was further progressed when Greg became Head of Children's Digital in BBC Broadcast and culminated in the launch of two digital channels devoted to children's content: CBeebies, for the pre-school audience, and CBBC for older children. He devised the schedules for the new channels, along with the presentation and marketing proposition, and steered them through internal and external consultations. This included their passage through the political process with the Department of Culture, Media and Sport. He also commissioned the first new programmes for CBeebies.

Leaving the BBC, Greg became a freelance advisor on children's television, helping to set up ITV's digital service for children, CITV: 'There was always the potential in the way that CITV was set up that it would become a heavy user of the existing library of materials. There has been little commissioning of new work.' His next job was to advise Al Jazeera on their children's broadcasting:

> I had to work within the strict guidelines provided by the Qatar Education Foundation which funded the enterprise. The Al Jazeera Children's Channel had an approach which combined educational values with entertainment elements. Working in these different environments was of immense benefit in thinking about the context of children's media in the UK.

When Greg joined the CMF his first task was to clarify its purpose:

> The Foundation grew partly out of the Save Kids' TV campaign whose remit was to identify those who seemed intent on cutting the funding to children's television and draw public attention to this, so as to stop it. The CMF always intended to have a wider remit. There was some discussion initially between the board and the executive on how best to resolve the identity of the Foundation. The board didn't want to be an industry body, although they wanted to take a positive stance towards the industry and engage with it. We needed the distance and independence to take a critical view if needed. We want to bring together three sectors crucial to children's media: the audience; the industry; and the researchers, whether commercial, institutional or academic. The job of the CMF is to change the public discourse regarding children's media into something more informed, reasoned and constructive. Research will be crucial to this process.

Evidence of the importance of research to the CMF can be found on its website. In 2014 it developed a resource for parents called 'Parent Portal', which addresses concerns raised by parents, answering frequently asked questions arising from observations of their children's media use, with reference to information digested from the latest and most respected research on the topic. Six topics are currently addressed and more will follow. Also launched in 2014 was the 'Research Blog', which provides a forum for academics interested in children's media from all perspectives including policy, business, media literacy, affects, security, rights, play etc. This is currently proving popular amongst the academic community.

The CMF also decided to involve politicians. Greg explains:

> This met with some initial indifference in Westminster. The view of politicians has often been that children can't vote, so why prioritise this. The CMF's view is that children are the voters of the future and that it's crucial to involve them in democratic discourses. By involving them at an early stage of their development, you plant the seeds of future civic engagement. This is crucial in light of the poor voting figures among young people currently in the UK. This feeds into the wider debate on media literacy. Media literacy can be seen as being directly linked to social and civic engagement.

Greg believes this was something that some politicians were ignorant of:

> Their view was basically that the car industry had been allowed to go to the wall, so why should anyone protect anything as esoteric and ephemeral as children's media. This is clearly a view that it was vitally important to correct. The 2014 announcement of the introduction of a tax incentive for children's television by Chancellor George Osborne is something of a triumph for the turnaround in thinking by politicians of all parties, achieved after three years of lobbying by CMF.

A major part of the Foundation's remit is to support production of British children's media in all its forms:

> Television can play a tremendous role in reflecting and building a sense of national culture. It is essential to have British-made content if we are to achieve this as only British creative talent have the knowledge and sensibility to make material which accurately reflects our shared culture. Another benefit is obviously commercial in that a vibrant production base provides jobs and circulates wealth. Therefore the Foundation backs British-made programmes in the face of massive overseas competition, particularly from America. An example would be the UK animation tax break campaign. The industry wanted the CMF to support this as they felt it would lead to more jobs being based in the UK. We feel that the Foundation always needs to view things from the angle of the indigenous audience. Contemporary animation is always a product of international co-production, therefore many of the producers might not be working in Britain or producing British content. However, on balance, the CMF decided to support the campaign because it would lead to more animation being made in Britain than is currently the case, leading to better health in the animation and children's programming sectors in the UK, with long-term benefits for the audience. We don't always necessarily follow the lead of the industry but will always keep the end user, the child, uppermost in our minds.[12]

A further aspect of the Foundation's activities has been the publication of a yearbook. The first edition appeared in 2013 and covers a wide remit. It is divided into three key areas: industry views; policy and regulation; and research. As its editor, Lynn

Whitaker, puts it in her introduction, the intention is to provide 'a snapshot of the policy, production and research issues' around children's media.[13] The first edition draws in a number of high-profile contributors including Joe Godwin, Director of BBC Children's, and Michael Carrington, chief content officer for the Cartoon Network Europe. The public sector versus commerce debate is evident in their contrasting articles. Joe Godwin defends the BBC and its commitment to the '90 year old tradition of making their [sic] mark on children's minds'[14], while Michael Carrington points to the positive opportunities brought about by deregulation. Their conception of their audience is strikingly different, with Godwin talking of children as 'citizens' and of seeking to inspire them, while the commercial perspective tends to see the audience as paying subscribers whose desires need to be met. Two other pieces point to the role the CMF can play. Jayne Kirkham makes a case for the All Party Parliamentary Group, while David Buckingham looks to the potential for academic researchers to work with the CMF. As he puts it: 'A body such as the Children's Media Foundation – which brings together researchers, media producers, parents, policy makers and other interested parties – might be uniquely placed to make a difference to the situation.'[15] Most notable is a piece by Jeanette Steemers from the University of Westminster, who echoes the central concerns of the CMF, identifying to such trends as the failure of commercial content producers to reflect UK culture in their output, leaving public service broadcasters to fill the gap. The result being that little children's television broadcast in the UK is actually made in the UK, and most of that comes from the BBC.[16] The picture she paints is a bleak one but throws into relief the importance of the Foundation's work.

The second edition of the yearbook, published in 2014, demonstrates the consolidation of the CMF as an organisation and its tone is more celebratory, with many articles from content producers in both the public and private sectors pointing to the quality of children's media in the UK. Other positive developments, such as the BFI's decision to instigate a report into children's film production in the UK, are highlighted. A number of research pieces illustrate the growing involvement of academia in debates in children's media and a new section showcases the CMF's role in facilitating different voices who have contributed to this discussion. Anna Home focuses on the importance of the BBC to the future of children's media in the UK at a time when the Corporation is coming under increasing scrutiny and criticism in some quarters. One area still, perhaps, insufficiently addressed is the view of children themselves on the media they use.

I asked Greg Childs to summarise where the CMF is now:

> This can be boiled down to the following key themes: to change the public discourse regarding children's media so that it is better informed; to provide research relevant to parents; to provide research which is useful for the industry; to bring parents and the industry together in a constructive dialogue; and to present the outcomes to politicians. The CMF is looking now to build groups to help achieve this. For example, it now has a research group whose job is to build the database of relevant findings which can be

> made publicly accessible. The All Party Parliamentary Group is another way to further the Foundation's aims. There are currently three meetings a year and around seventy-five Parliamentarians are members. The group benefits enormously from the leadership of Baroness Benjamin.
>
> Funding does remain a challenging issue for the Foundation. We decided not to become a members' organisation or to seek direct funding from the industry. The main source of funding comes from our founding patrons, and some patrons and supporters. We have started to take on corporate sponsors but we're keen to maintain our independence so they'll be a wide-ranging group with no particular interest served.

Nonetheless, he remains positive about what the Foundation can achieve:

> I am concerned that the CMF should play its part in the public arena. We need to address issues beyond TV and traditional media – such as the digital rights agenda for children and young people. In that context, media literacy is so important. We need to trust children – it's a little like teaching them to cross the road or to ride a bike; you show them the basics but then they have to do it for themselves. There is a great deal of overreaction in the press, whereas what is needed is greater knowledge and understanding.
>
> The CMF are often asked to comment on topical issues in our area and we need to be able to point to the research to develop a clear-sighted public debate. For example, one concern is the commercial exploitation of children, although, again, I feel that children are actually aware of what is good quality and what isn't, as are parents. I don't believe the answer lies in regulation but in making sure parents and children have the information they need, and then leaving them to decide for themselves. There can be tensions between a public service ethos and the commercial sector. This is where the Foundation can play its part in helping to make sure that there is always a corner of the marketplace where public service values can survive. The CMF needs to keep a weather-eye open for exploitation, for questions of taste and decency, for choice, for ensuring that there is sensitivity to race, gender and other issues of diversity. In this way, the CMF will be the vigilant eyes of the public.

Despite the demise of the CFTF as a producer of children's films and television programmes, its legacy is alive and well in the form of the CMF. This body continues to campaign for the creation of indigenous children's media in the UK, with output that responds to and reflects the lives of young people. If such provision is genuinely under threat, its existence is all the more important.

Notes

1. Iain Smith interviewed by the author, 29 January 2013.
2. Anna Home interviewed by the author, 22 December 2014.
3. See the Save Kids' TV archived website at <www.savekidstv.org.uk>.

4. *The Future of Children's Television Programming*, a discussion paper published by Ofcom, 3 October 2007.
5. SKTV's response to the Ofcom discussion paper, 17 December 2007.
6. *A Future for Children's Media: A Model Supporting SKTV's Innovative Proposal for an Alternative Public Service Content Provider for Britain's Children*, 30 April 2009.
7. Anna Home, *Into the Box of Delights: A History of Children's Television* (London: BBC Books, 1993), p. 9.
8. Ibid., p. 14.
9. Ibid., pp. 84–5.
10. Ibid., p. 167.
11. Greg Childs interviewed by the author, 10 January 2015.
12. See the Animation UK website at <animationuk.org>.
13. Lynn Whitaker, 'Editorial', *The Children's Media Yearbook 2013* (London: The Children's Media Foundation, 2013), p. 5.
14. Joe Godwin, 'BBC Children's', in ibid., p. 19.
15. David Buckingham, 'Speaking Out: Research, Public Debate and Policy', in ibid., p. 112.
16. Jeanette Steemers, 'Children's TV and the Rise and Fall of the Preschool Content Specialist', in ibid.

Conclusion

The outlook for children's media in Britain appears unsettled. If a key objective of the CMF is increased levels of indigenous production, then it is swimming against the tide of an increasingly globalised marketplace where competition is intense and the big players are largely American. An article in *Sight & Sound* by Ben Roberts, currently director of the British Film Institute's Film Fund, responded to the call for greater investment in British children's films by suggesting that there was a gap between those lobbying for action and the mood of the industry itself.[1] In a thinly veiled reference to groups like the CMF, he writes that when he attended the annual Children's Media Festival in Sheffield:

> What I discovered was less 'a sector' than a collection of those lobbyists. The strength of voices and opinions was palpable; what was less evident was any sign of an actual 'industry' – of producers, film-makers, financiers, commissioners, who were pressuring us to do more.

In other words, the CMF can call for more British children's media but, in his view, the industry itself isn't that interested. Of course, the job of the Foundation is to represent the audience, the children themselves, rather than officialdom or the film business. He offers as further evidence the idea that it can be difficult to define what a family-friendly film is any more; might it include, he suggests, a British art house film like *The Selfish Giant* (2013), which was granted a '15' certificate and was backed by the BFI. Most children know well enough what appeals to them and it seems unlikely that it would include this title, however impressive a film it might seem to adults. The views expressed here seem to echo the assessment of Anna Home that children's media is often seen as the Cinderella of the industry. The CMF is undoubtedly in for a hard time; state funding is limited and commercial imperatives dominate the children's media marketplace. However, this can only make its task all the more important.

Even if the CMF were successful and the government provided funding for a new body to commission a range of children's media, presumably to be made available via the internet, what standards of 'quality' would apply that would differentiate it from the commercial sector? Over the course of its history the Children's Film Foundation wrestled with the idea of producing films that would be good for children to see. Its very creation in 1951 came as a response to public concerns about the material children could access at their local cinema. This is, of course, a notoriously contentious area. As theorists like Ian Wojcik-Andrews have shown, decisions on what is appropriate viewing for children are invariably made by adults, who impose their own standards on a young audience, usually with little consultation with children themselves.[2] This area is probably where the CMF believes more empirical research is most needed. For Mary Field and Henry Geddes these matters were often self-evident; they believed that children needed to see reassuring images on screen that reinforced the status quo. They should not be shocked or alarmed. The world should be portrayed as a place where honesty, fairness and courage are rewarded, where cheats never prosper, villains are inept and where tenacity and determination win through in the end. Inadvertently, the world they portrayed was also one where boys take the lead and girls prefer to help out behind the scenes, where multiculturalism barely exists and where everyone would prefer to be middle class. From the 1970s onwards the CFF and its successor the CFTF became increasingly self-aware and started to address these issues. In films like *Hide and Seek*, *Friend or Foe* and *Terry on the Fence* the world is a complex place where moral decisions need to be carefully considered and where there can be more than one way of looking at things. These films demonstrated that 'quality' children's films could be challenging, as well as comforting. They showed a respect for young audiences in crediting them with the sophistication and intelligence to deal with, and even enjoy, such stories. If film cannot provide moral instruction, perhaps it can at least reflect the dilemmas children face in their daily lives in an unpatronising manner.

These debates will continue, but the CFF and the CFTF back-catalogue still stands as an invaluable social record of changing times and altering values. Britain unfolds before our eyes, moving from black and white into colour, and the lives of the nation's children are played out for us, even if they sometimes reflect the views of the adults who made the films as much as they do the children who were expected to watch them. For nearly forty years the Foundation supported one of the most significant social activities available to children in the second half of the twentieth century, at least in the UK, one that influenced successive generations: the Saturday film club. It may not have succeeded in modelling future citizens but it certainly showed them ways to make friends, test the boundaries and, above all, have fun. The Foundation started literally hundreds of acting careers, kept legions of technicians in work and helped many small independent production companies to survive. Major directors like Michael Powell were afforded the opportunity to address a very different audience from their habitual one, with fascinating results. Films as varied as *Johnny on the Run*, *The Salvage Gang*, *Go Kart Go*, *The Boy Who Turned Yellow*, *The Battle of Billy's Pond*, *The Man from Nowhere*, *The Glitterball*, *Sammy's Super T-Shirt*, *Black Island* and *Out of the Darkness* are all testament to the Foundation's ability to awaken and entertain. As one of the respondents to my survey told me: 'Saturday mornings were the best part of the week, just waiting for the CFF logo to appear and the show to begin. Happy days!'

Notes

1. Ben Roberts, 'Doing it For the Kids', *Sight & Sound* vol. 23 no. 12 (December 2013), p. 18.
2. Ian Wojcik-Andrews, *Children's Films: History, Ideology, Pedagogy, Theory* (New York and London: Garland, 2000). See also Allison James, Chris Jenks and Alan Prout, *Theorizing Childhood* (Cambridge: Polity, 1998) for an overview on the conceptualisation of children and childhood by adults.

Appendix 1
Production Chronology

The following is a list of work either produced or distributed in the UK by the Children's Film Foundation and the Children's Film and Television Foundation. It is drawn from two main sources: the CFTF catalogue; and the records held by the British Film Institute. This has also been cross-checked with other available sources such as the online Internet Movie Database to produce as accurate and complete a list as possible. The task was far from straightforward as there are discrepancies between all the existing sources. The CFTF catalogue itself was intended as a resource for the use of cinema managers when ordering items for their Saturday screenings and therefore contained only titles for which there were available prints. This meant that some titles were missing. The BFI list is more complete although even this misses a number of titles. Release dates quoted on IMDb are for the US; the original British production dates have been used here with preference given to those quoted by the BFI. The list of items imported from abroad by the Foundation for distribution in the UK is incomplete as no definitive records exist for this. Screenwriting credits are given, along with the author of the original story idea if appropriate, but literary sources for adaptations have not been included. The running time of some early productions was trimmed at a later date by the Foundation for reissue; the later timing is used. By using the available key sources and cross-checking, I have tried to compile as complete and accurate a list as currently possible but apologise for any omissions or errors that subsequently become evident.

AS THE CHILDREN'S FILM FOUNDATION (CFF)

1952 *John of the Fair*
49 minute feature produced by Merton Park Studios. Director and Script: Michael McCarthy. Producer: Frank A. Hoare. Featuring: John Charlesworth, Carol Wolveridge, David Garth, Arthur Young and Glenda Davies.

Rover Makes Good
16 minute short produced by Plymouth Films. Director, Producer and Script: John Dooley. Featuring: Unknown.

Stable Rivals
16 minute short produced by Anglo-Scottish Pictures. Director, Producer and Script: Leonard Reeve. Featuring: Unknown.

The Stolen Plans
57 minute feature produced by Gaumont-British. Director and Script: James Hill. Producer: Frank Wells. Featuring: Mavis Sage, Lance Secretan, Peter Burton, Geoffrey Goodheart and Ludmila Tchakalova.

Swift Water
16 minute short produced by the Documentary Technicians Alliance. Director: Tony Thompson. Producer: Unknown. Script: Wolfgang Wilhelm. Featuring: Guthrie Mason, Jasper Jewitt, Dorothy Hannaford, George Passmore and Sally Sanderson.

To the Rescue
21 minute short produced by Massingham Productions. Director: Ronald Weyman. Producer: Richard Massingham. Script: Ronald Weyman and Richard Massingham. Featuring: Richard Massingham, Jacques Brunius, Fella Edmonds, Adam Massingham, Betty Massingham, John Ruddock and John Stuart.

1953 *Bouncer Breaks Up*
Short with animation produced by S.A.D.F.A.S. (running time unknown). Director: Don Chaffey. Producer: Unknown. Script: Winifred Holmes. Featuring: Bunny May, Mavis Sage and Hilda Fenemore.

The Clue of the Missing Ape
58 minute feature produced by Gaumont British. Director: James Hill. Producer: Frank Wells: Script: James Hill from an original story by Frank Wells, Donald Carter and Commander Gilbert Hackforth-Jones. Featuring: Roy Savage, Nati Banda, Patrick Boxill, William Patrick and George Cole.

The Dog and the Diamonds
49 minute feature produced by London Independent Producers. Director: Ralph Thomas. Producer: Peter Rogers. Script: Pat Latham from an original story by Mary Cathcart Borer. Featuring: Michael Maguire, Robert Sandford, Robert Scroggins, Barbara Brown, Molly Osborn, Kathleen Harrison and George Coulouris.

A Good Pull Up
17 minute short produced by Grendon Films. Director: Don Chaffey. Producer: Frank Cadman. Script: Pat Latham. Featuring: Peter Butterworth, John Levitt, Humphrey Kent and Kurt Wagener.

Heights of Danger
60 minute feature produced by Associated British-Pathé. Director: Peter Bradford. Producer: Howard Thomas. Script: Betty Davies. Featuring: Annette Cabot, Wilfred Downing, Christopher Cabot and Richard Goolden.

Johnny on the Run
68 minute feature produced by International Realist. Director and Producer: Lewis Gilbert. Script: Pat Latham. Featuring: Eugeniusz Chylek, Sydney Tafler, Michael Balfour, John Laurie and Mona Washbourne.

Juno Helps Out
19 minute short produced by British Films. Director and Script: William Hammond. Producer: William Weedon. Featuring: Unknown.

A Letter from East Anglia
Short produced by Clarke and Hornby Films (running time unknown). Director: Cynthia Whitby. Other details unknown.

A Letter from the Isle of Wight
11 minute short produced by Rayant Pictures. Director: Brian Salt. Producer: Anthony Gilkison. Script: Unknown. Featuring: Robin Doyer and Joy Ray.

A Letter from Wales
14 minute short produced by Brunner Lloyd Productions. Director: George Lloyd. Producer: Unknown. Script: John Gwilym Jones. Featuring: Evie Wyn Jones, Katie Wyn Jones, Vera Jones and Sam Jones.

Mardi and the Monkey
19 minute short produced by Peregrine Film Productions. Director and Script: Kay Mander. Producer: Deborah Chesshire. Featuring: Wasmin.

The Secret Cave
49 minute feature produced by Merton Park Studios. Director: John Durst. Producer: Frank A. Hoare. Script: Joe Mendoza. Featuring: David Coote, Nicky Edmett, Trevor Hill, Susan Ford and Johnny Morris.

Skid Kids
49 minute feature produced by Gilbert Church Productions. Director: Don Chaffey. Producer: Gilbert Church. Script: Jack Howells. Featuring: David Coote, Barry MacGregor, Anthony Lang and Angela Monk.

Watch Out
18 minute short produced by Grendon Films. Director: Don Chaffey. Producer: Frank Cadman. Script: Pat Latham. Featuring: Peter Butterworth, Humphrey Kent, Harry Lane and John Levitt.

1954 *Adventure in the Hopfields*
59 minute feature produced by Vandyke Picture Corporation. Director: John Guillermin. Producer: Roger Proudlock. Script: John Cresswell. Featuring: Mandy Miller, Melvyn Hayes, Dandy Nichols, Mona Washbourne, Jane Asher and Anthony Valentine.

Black in the Face
15 minute short produced by Grendon Films. Director: John Irwin. Producer: John Croydon. Script: J. B. Boothroyd and John Croydon. Featuring: Peter Butterworth, Humphrey Kent, Lloyd Pearson and Cecilia Cavendish.

Five o'Clock Finish
19 minute short produced by Grendon Films. Director: John Irwin. Producer: John Croydon. Script: J. B. Boothroyd and John Croydon. Featuring: Peter Butterworth, Humphrey Kent and Lloyd Pearson.

A Letter from Ayrshire
Short produced by Wallace Productions (running time unknown). Director: J. E. Ewins. Other details unknown.

Mystery on Bird Island
57 minute feature produced by Rayant Pictures. Director: John Haggerty. Producer: Anthony Gilkison. Script: Mary Cathcart Borer and John Haggerty. Featuring: Mavis Sage, Jennifer Beach and Vernon Morris.

Tim Driscoll's Donkey
56 minute feature produced by Gilbert Church Productions. Director: Terry Bishop. Producer: Gilbert Church. Script: Pat Latham and Terry Bishop from an original story by Mary Cathcart Borer. Featuring: David Coote, John Kelly, Carole Lorimer and Anthony Green.

1955 *The Flying Eye*
47 minute feature produced by British Films. Director: William Hammond. Producer: William Weedon. Script: Darrell Catling, William Hammond and Ken Hughes. Featuring: David Hannaford, Julia Lockwood, Geoffrey Sumner and Harcourt Williams.

Playground Express
17 minute short produced by Grendon Films. Director: John Irwin. Producer: John Croydon. Script: John Croydon and J. B. Boothroyd. Featuring: Peter Butterworth and Humphrey Kent.

Raiders of the River
Eight-part serial totalling 147 minutes produced by Merton Park Studios. Director: John Haggarty. Producer: Frank A. Hoare. Script: Robert Martin. Featuring: Richard O'Sullivan, Jenny Jones, Jack MacGowran and John Longden.

The Secret of the Forest
61 minute feature produced by Rayant Pictures. Director: Darcy Conyers. Producer: Anthony Gilkison. Script: Darcy Conyers and Gerard Bryant. Featuring: Kit Terrington, Jacqueline Cox, Barry Knight, Diana Day and Michael Balfour.

The Stolen Airliner
59 minute feature produced by Associated British-Pathé. Director and Script: Don Sharp. Producer: Howard Thomas. Featuring: Diana Day, Fella Edmunds, Michael Maguire, Peter Dyneley and Nicola Braithwaite.

That's an Order
18 minute short produced by Grendon Films. Director: John Irwin. Producer: John Croydon. Script: J. B. Boothroyd and John Croydon. Featuring: Peter Butterworth.

1956 *Five Clues to Fortune*
Eight-part serial totalling 120 minutes produced by Merton Park Studios. Director and Script: Joe Mendoza. Producer: Frank A. Hoare. Featuring: John Rogers, Roberta Patterson, Peter Godsell and David Hemmings.

One Wish Too Many
55 minute feature produced by Realist Films. Director: John Durst. Producer: Basil Wright. Script: Mary Cathcart Borer and John Eldridge. Featuring: Anthony Richmond, Rosalind Gourgey, John Pike, Gladys Young and Sam Costa.

Peril for the Guy
55 minute feature produced by World Wide Pictures. Director and Script: James Hill. Producer: Hindle Edgar. Featuring: Frazer Hines, Amanda Coxell, Chris Warbey, Ali Alleney, Kathryn Kath and Peter Copley.

Supersonic Saucer
50 minute feature produced by Gaumont-British. Director: Guy Ferguson. Producer: Frank Wells. Script: Dallas Bower from an original story by Frank Wells. Featuring:

Marcia Monolescue, Fella Edmunds, Gillian Harrison, Donald Gray, Hilda Fenemore and Patrick Boxill.

1957 *The Adventures of HAL 5*
59 minute feature produced by Gilbert Church Productions. Director and Script: Don Sharp. Producer: Gilbert Church. Featuring: William Russell, John Glyn-Jones, Edwin Richfield, Peter Godsell and John Charlesworth.

Circus Friends
63 minute feature produced by London Independent Producers. Director: Gerald Thomas. Producer and Script: Peter Rogers. Featuring: Alan Coleshill, Carol White, David Tilley, Pat Belcher, Meredith Edwards, Mona Washbourne and Sam Kydd.

Five on a Treasure Island
Eight-part serial totalling 126 minutes produced by Rank Screen Services. Director: Gerald Landau. Producer: Frank Wells. Script: Michael Barnes. Featuring: Richard Palmer, Rel Grainer, Gillian Harrison and John Baily.

The Kid from Canada
39 minute feature produced by Anvil Films. Director: Kay Mander. Producer: Ralph May. Script: John Eldridge. Featuring: Christopher Braden, Bobby Stevenson, Eleanor Laing, David Caldwell and Bernard Braden.

Soapbox Derby
51 minute feature produced by Rayant Pictures. Director and Script: Darcy Conyers. Producer: Anthony Gilkison. Featuring: Michael Crawford, Keith Davis, Roy Townshend and Alan Coleshill.

Toto and the Poachers
50 minute feature produced by World Safari. Director: Brian Salt. Producer: Henry Geddes. Script: John Coquillon and Brian Salt from an original story by Henry Geddes. Featuring: John Aloisi, Mpigano, David Betts and Obago.

Treasure at the Mill
51 minute feature produced by Wallace Productions. Director: Max Anderson. Producer: A. V. Curtice. Script: Mary Cathcart Borer. Featuring: Richard Palmer, John Ruddock, Hilda Fenemore, Harry Pettit, Merrilyn Pettit, Hilary Pettit and Harry Pettit Jr.

1958 *Blow Your Own Trumpet*
41 minute feature produced by the Film Producers' Guild. Director and Producer: Cecil Musk. Script: Mary Cathcart Borer. Featuring: Michael Crawford, Martyn Shields, Gillian Harrison and Peter Butterworth.

The Carringford School Mystery
Eight-part serial totalling 134 minutes produced by British Films. Director: William Hammond. Producer and Script: John Haggerty. Featuring: Richard James, Jenny Jones and Anthony Richmond.

The Cat Gang
50 minute feature produced by Realist Films. Director: Darrell Catling. Producer: Arthur T. Villesid. Script: John Eldridge. Featuring: Francesca Annis, John Pike and Jeremy Bulloch.

The Salvage Gang
52 minute feature produced by World Wide Pictures. Director: John Krish. Producer: Hindle Edgar. Script: John Krish from an original story by Mary Cathcart Borer. Featuring: Ali Allen, Amanda Coxell, Frazer Hines, Christopher Warbey and Wilfrid Brambell.

1959 *The Adventures of Rex*
Five-part series totalling 70 minutes produced by Anglo-Scottish Pictures. Director and Producer: Leonard Reeve. Script: Tom Twigge and Leonard Reeve. Featuring: John Pike and Shirley Joy.

Caught in the Net
55 minute feature produced by Wallace Productions. Director: John Haggerty. Producer: A. Frank Bundy. Script: Max Anderson from an original story by Sutherland Ross. Featuring: Jeremy Bulloch, Johanna Horlock, James Luck and Anthony Parker.

The Dawn Killer
Eight-part serial totalling 197 minutes produced by Associated British-Pathé. Director and Producer: Donald Taylor. Script: Vivian Milroy from an original story by Monica Edwards. Featuring: Jeremy Bulloch, Sally Bulloch and Suzan Farmer.

Mystery in the Mine
Eight-part serial totalling 128 minutes produced by Merton Park Productions. Director: James Hill. Producer: Frank A. Hoare. Script: James Hill and Dallas Bower. Featuring: Ingrid Garden, Stewart Guidotti, Peter Copley, Elwyn Brook-Jones and Howard Greene.

The Young Jacobites
Eight-part serial totalling 139 minutes produced by Rayant Pictures. Director: John Reeve. Producer: Anthony Gilkison. Script: Paul Tabori and Gordon Wellesley. Featuring: Francesca Annis, Jeremy Bulloch, Frazer Hines, John Pike and Gareth Tandy.

1960 *Ali and the Camel*
Eight-part serial totalling 135 minutes produced by World Safari. Director, Producer and Script: Henry Geddes. Featuring: Mohamed Rifai, Maurice Denham (voice) and Dennis Waterman (voice).

Hunted in Holland
61 minute feature produced by Wessex Film Productions. Director and Producer: Derek Williams. Script: Derek Williams and Ian Dalrymple. Featuring: Sean Scully, Jacques Verbrugge, Sandra Spurr, Tom Kelling and Walter Randall.

Rockets in the Dunes
57 minute feature produced by Anvil Films. Director: William Hammond. Producer: Ralph May. Script: Gerard Bryant. Featuring: Gena Yates, Heather Lyons, Richard Adam, Peter Wood and Christopher Witty.

1961 *Bungala Boys*
61 minute feature produced by Jimar Pictures. Director and Script: Jim Jeffreys. Producer: Otto Plaschkes. Featuring: Peter Couldwell, Alan Dearth, Terry Bentley, John Dennis and Julie Youatt.

A Film for Maria
17 minute short produced by the CFF. Devised and performed by the children from a Saturday morning film club. Director and Script: Jack Smith. Producer: Fred Murray.

Four Winds Island
Eight-part serial totalling 110 minutes produced by Merton Park Productions. Director and Script: David Villiers. Producer: Frank A. Hoare. Featuring: Amanda Coxell, Annette Robertson, John Pike, Iain Gregory, Robert Langley and Tom Bowman.

The Last Rhino
55 minute feature produced by World Safari Productions. Director, Producer and Script: Henry Geddes. Featuring: David Ellis and Susan Miller-Smith.

The Missing Note
56 minute feature produced by Walton Studios. Director: Michael Brandt. Producer: Henry Passmore. Script: Mary Cathcart Borer from an original story by Frank Wells. Featuring: Heather Bennett, Hennie Scott, John Moulder-Brown and Toke Townley.

The Monster of Highgate Ponds
59 minute feature produced by Halas and Batchelor Cartoon Films. Director: Alberto Cavalcanti. Producer: John Halas. Script: Mary Cathcart Borer from an original story by Joy Batchelor. Featuring: Rachel Clay, Michael Wade, Ronald Howard and Michael Balfour.

The Piper's Tune
62 minute feature produced by A.C.T. Films. Director: Muriel Box. Producer: Robert Dunbar. Script: Michael Barnes from an original story by Frank Wells. Featuring: Mavis Ranson, Roberta Tovey, Angela White, Malcolm Ranson, Brian Wills, Graham Wills and Delene Scott.

1962 *Masters of Venus*
Eight-part serial totalling 128 minutes produced by Wallace Productions. Director: Ernest Morris. Producer: A. Frank Bundy. Script: Michael Barnes and Mary Cathcart Borer. Featuring: Amanda Coxell, Robin Stewart, Robin Hunter and Norman Wooland.

Night Cargoes
Eight-part serial totalling 125 minutes produced by the Film Producers Guild. Director: Ernest Morris. Producer: Cecil Musk. Script: David Villiers. Featuring: Waveney Lee, Hugh James, Stephen Marriott, Ian Curry, Pauline Letts and Neil Wilson.

1963 *Beware of the Dog*
Six-part series totalling 96 minutes produced by Mandarin Films. Director: Philip Ford. Producer: Donald Wynne. Scripts: Paul Tabori and Gordon Wellesley. Featuring: Charles Tingwell, Jane Barratt, Maurice Headley and Mary Merrall.

The Flood
45 minute feature produced by Associated British-Pathé. Director: Frederic Goode. Producers: Lionel Hoare and Terry Ashwood. Script: Jean Scott Rogers from an original story by Frank Wells. Featuring: Waveney Lee, Christopher Ellis, Ian Ellis, Frank Knight and Leslie Hart.

Go Kart Go
55 minute feature produced by Fanfare Films. Director: Jan Darnley-Smith. Producer: George H. Brown. Script: Michael Barnes from an original story by Frank Wells. Featuring: Dennis Waterman, Jimmy Capehorn, Frazer Hines, John Moulder-Brown, Graham Stark, Cardew Robinson, Wilfrid Brambell.

The Rescue Squad
54 minute feature produced by World Wide Pictures. Director: Colin Bell. Producer: Hindle Edgar. Script: Malcolm Stewart and Mary Cathcart Borer from an original story by Frank Wells. Featuring: Christopher Brett, Shirley Joy, Malcolm Knight, Gareth Tandy, Linda Leo, Danny Grove, Michael Balfour and Peter Butterworth.

Seventy Deadly Pills
55 minute feature produced by Derick Williams Productions. Director: Pat Jackson. Producer: Derick Williams. Script: Pat Jackson from an original story by Frank Wells.

Featuring: Leslie Dwyer, Robert Ferguson, Linda Hansen, Gareth Robinson, Sally Thomsett, Warren Mitchell and Len Jones.

Wings of Mystery
55 minute feature produced by Rayant Pictures. Director and Script: Gilbert Gunn. Producer: Anthony Gilkison. Featuring: Judy Geeson, Hennie Scott, Francesca Bertorelli, Graham Aza and Arnold Ridley.

1964 *Daylight Robbery*
57 minute feature produced by Viewfinder Films. Director: Michael Truman. Producer: John Davis. Script: Derry Quinn from an original story by Frank Wells. Featuring Trudy Moors, Darryl Read, Janet Hannington, Kirk Martin, Janet Munro, Ronald Fraser, Gordon Jackson and Norman Rossington.

Eagle Rock
62 minute feature produced by World Safari Productions. Director and Producer: Henry Geddes. Script: Henry Geddes from an original story by Mary Cathcart Borer. Featuring: Pip Rolls, Christine Thomas, Stephen Morris and John Laurie (voice).

Five Have a Mystery to Solve
Six-part serial totalling 96 minutes produced by Rayant Pictures. Director: Ernest Morris. Producer: John Durst. Script: Michael Barnes. Featuring: David Palmer, Darryl Read, Amanda Coxell, Paula Boyd, Michael Wennick, Michael Balfour, Robin Hunter and Keith Pyott.

Treasure in Malta
Six-part serial totalling 92 minutes produced by Anvil Films. Director: Derek Williams. Producer: Ralph May. Script: Anne Barrett and Mary Cathcart Borer. Featuring: Mario Debono, Aidan Mompalaode Piro and Mary Lu Ripard.

Valley of the Kings
Six-part serial totalling 111 minutes produced by Associated British-Pathé. Director: Frederic Goode. Producer: Lionel Hoare. Script: Jean Scott Rogers. Featuring: Ray Barrett, Gwen Watford, Kenneth Nash, Peter Graeffe and Elizabeth White.

The Young Detectives
Eight-part serial produced by Littleton Park Film Productions. Director: Gilbert Gunn. Producer: Ronald Spencer. Script: Michael Barnes and Roy Brown. Featuring: Neil McCarthy, Jonathan Collins, Graham Ashley, Darryl Read, Cardew Robinson and Sam Kydd.

1965 *Cup Fever*
63 minute feature produced by Century Film Productions. Director and Script: David

Bracknell. Producer: Roy Simpson. Featuring: Dennis Gilmore, Raymond Davies, Susan George, Olivia Hussey, Bernard Cribbins, David Lodge, Norman Rossington and players from the Manchester United football team including George Best, Bobby Charlton, Denis Law and Nobby Stiles.

Davey Jones' Locker
59 minute feature produced by Associated British-Pathé. Director: Frederic Goode. Producer: Lionel Hoare. Script: Wally Bosco. Featuring: Susan George, Michael Wennink, Stephen Craig, Vanessa Page and Anthony Bate.

Dead End Creek
Six-part serial totalling 94 minutes produced by Anvil Films. Director: Pat Jackson. Producer: Ralph May. Script: Alec Grieve, Pat Jackson and Michael Barnes. Featuring: Len Jones, Sally Thomsett, John Welsh and Robin Chapman.

Runaway Railway
55 minute feature produced by Fanfare Films. Director: Jan Darnley-Smith. Producer: George H. Brown. Script: Michael Barnes from an original story by Henry Geddes. Featuring: John Moulder-Brown, Kevin Bennett, Leonard Brockwell, Roberta Tovey, Sidney Tafler, Graham Stark, Ronnie Barker and Jon Pertwee.

1966 *Ambush at Devil's Gap*
Six-part serial totalling 95 minutes produced by Rayant Pictures. Director: David Eastman. Producer: John Durst. Script: David and Kerry Eastman. Featuring: Chris Barrington, Sue Sylvaine, Stephen Brown, Jacqueline Mitchell and Deane Gardiner.

The Christmas Tree
57 minute feature produced by Augusta Productions. Director: James Clark. Producer: Ed Harper. Script: Michael Barnes and James Clark from an original story by Ed Harper. Featuring: William Burleigh, Anthony Honour, Kate Nicholls and Brian Blessed.

Danny the Dragon
Ten-part serial totalling 175 minutes produced by Ansus Films. Director: C. M. Pennington-Richards. Producer: Frank Godwin. Script: Michael Barnes and C. M. Pennington-Richards from an original story by Henry Geddes. Featuring: Sally Thomsett, Jack Wild, Christopher Cooper, Peter Butterworth, Kenneth Connor (voice) and Frank Thornton.

Flash the Sheepdog
58 minute feature produced by International Film Associates. Director and Script: Laurence Henson. Producer: J. B. Holmes. Featuring: Earl Younger, Ross Campbell, Alex Allan and Victor Carin.

Operation Third Form
57 minute feature produced by World Wide Pictures. Director: David Eady. Producer: Hindle Edgar. Script: Michael Barnes from an original story by Hindle Edgar and David Eady. Featuring: John Moulder-Brown, Kevin Bennett, Sydney Bromley, Michael Crockett, Ronnie Caryl, Roberta Tovey and Derren Nesbitt.

Son of the Sahara
Eight-part serial totalling 120 minutes produced by Associated British-Pathé. Director: Frederic Goode. Producer: Lionel Hoare. Script: Roger Dunton and Henry Geddes. Featuring: Darryl Read, Ria Mills, Kit Williams and Michael Wennick.

1967 *Calamity the Cow*
55 minute feature produced by Shepperton Studios. Director: David Eastman. Producer: Ian Dalrymple. Script: David and Kerry Eastman. Featuring: John Moulder-Brown, Elizabeth Dear, Stephen Brown, Phil Collins and Josephine Gillick.

Countdown to Danger
63 minute feature produced by Wallace Productions. Director and Script: Peter Seabourne. Producer: A. Frank Bundy. Featuring: David Macalister, Paul Martin, Angela Lee, Penny Spencer, Richard Coleman and Frank Williams.

A Ghost of a Chance
51 minute feature produced by Fanfare Films. Director: Jan Darnley-Smith. Producer: George H. Brown. Script: Pat Latham from an original story by Ed Harper. Featuring: Stephen Brown, Mark Ward, Cheryl Vidgen, Jimmy Edwards, Bernard Cribbins, Graham Stark, Ronnie Barker, John Bluthal and Patricia Hayes.

The Ghost of Monk's Island
Seven-part serial totalling 106 minutes produced by Countrywide Film Producers. Directors: Jeremy Summers and Jan Darnley-Smith. Producer: Michael Fairall. Script: Michael Barnes, Jeremy Summers, Michael Fairall and Anthony Marriott. Featuring: Pierre Bedenes, Peter Bartlett, Robert Bartlett and Lucinda Jackson.

The Hunch
56 minute feature produced by Anvil Films. Director and Script: Sarah Erulkar. Producer: J. B. Holmes. Featuring: Alex Norton, Gordon Robb, Amanda Jones, Ross Campbell and John Bannerman.

River Rivals
Seven-part serial totalling 110 minutes produced by Century Film Productions. Director: Harry Booth. Producer: Roy Simpson. Scripts: Harry Booth and Michael Barnes. Featuring: Darryl Read, Cordel Leigh, Sally Thomsett, Philip Meredith, Rufus Frampton, Julie Booth and Dick Emery.

The Sky Bike
62 minute feature produced by Eyeline Films. Director and Script: Charles Frend. Producer: Harold Orton. Featuring: Spencer Shires, Ian Ellis, Liam Redmond, John Howard, Bill Shine and David Lodge.

1968 *The Big Catch*
55 minute feature produced by International Film Associates. Director: Laurence Henson. Producers: Laurence Henson and Edward McConnell. Script: Charles Gormley and Laurence Henson. Featuring: Andrew Byatt, David Gallacher, Murray Forbes and Simon Orr.

Cry Wolf
58 minute feature produced by Damor Leaderfilm. Director: John Davis. Producer: Michael Truman. Script: Derry Quinn from an original story by John Davis. Featuring: Anthony Kemp, Mary Burleigh, Martin Beaumont, Judy Cornwell, Wilfred Brambell, Pat Coombes, Adrienne Cori, Ian Hendry and Janet Munroe.

Escape from the Sea
53 minute feature produced by Wallace Productions. Director: Peter Seabourne. Producer: A. Frank Bundy. Script: Peter Seabourne from an original story by Frank Wells. Featuring: Nicky Brockway, Paul Martin, Simon Milton, Alison Glennie and Larry Hamilton.

The Great Pony Raid
58 minute feature produced by Associated British-Pathé. Director: Frederic Goode. Producer: Lionel Hoare. Script: Wally Bosco and Geoffrey Hayes. Featuring: Christian Comber, Tina Paget Brown, Andrew Purcell, Shelley Crowhurst, Edward Underdown and Michael Brennan.

Headline Hunters
60 minute feature produced by Ansus Films. Director Jonathan Ingrams. Producer: Frank Godwin. Script: Wally Bosco, Don Nicholl, Jonathan Ingrams and C. M. Pennington-Richards. Featuring: Leonard Brockwell, Susan Payne, Stephen Garlick, Bill Owen, David Lodge, Glyn Houston and Frank Williams.

Lionheart
57 minute feature produced by Michael Forlong Productions. Producer and Director: Michael Forlong. Script: Michael Forlong and Alexander Fullerton. Featuring: James Forlong, Louise Rush, Ian Jessup, Wilfrid Brambell, Joe Brown, Jimmy Edwards and Irene Handl.

The Magnificent 6½ (Series 1)
Six-part series totalling 102 minutes produced by Century Film Productions.

Director: Harry Booth. Producer: Roy Simpson. Scripts: Harry Booth and Glyn Jones. Featuring: Len Jones, Brinsley Forde, Lionel Hawkes, Ian Ellis, Suzanne Togni, Kim Talmadge, Michael Audreson, Deryck Guyler and George Roderick.

Project Z
Eight-part serial totalling 134 minutes produced by Lion Pacesetter Productions. Director and Producer: Ronald Spencer. Script: Michael Barnes from an original story by Ronald Spencer. Featuring: Anabel Littledale, Michael Howe and Michael Crockett.

Up in the Air
55 minute feature produced by Fanfare Films. Director: Jan Darnley-Smith. Producer: George H. Brown. Script: Wally Bosco. Featuring: Gary Smith, Mark Colleano, Susan Payne, Gary Warren, Julian Close, Felix Felton and Jon Pertwee.

1969 *All at Sea*
60 minute feature produced by Anvil Films. Director: Ken Fairbairn. Producer: Hugh Stewart. Script: Pat Latham. Featuring: Stephen Childs, Gary Smith, Stephen Mallett, Norman Bird and Peter Copley.

The Magnificent 6½ (Series 2)
Six-part series totalling 105 minutes produced by Century Film Productions. Director: Harry Booth. Producer: Roy Simpson. Scripts: Yvonne Richards, Don Nicholl, Wally Basco, Michael Barnes and Glyn Jones. Featuring: Robin Davies, Brinsley Forde, Lionel Hawkes, Ian Ellis, Suzanne Togni, Kim Talmadge, Michael Audreson, Melvyn Hayes, Sheila Hancock, Bill Maynard and George Roderick.

Mischief
57 minute feature produced by Shand Pictures. Director: Ian Shand. Producers: Ian Shand and Jack Grossman. Script: Jack Grossman. Featuring: Paul Fraser, Iain Burton, Adrienne Byrne, Michael Newport and Bill Owen.

On the Run
58 minute feature produced by Derick Williams Productions. Director and Script: Pat Jackson. Producer: Derick Williams. Featuring: Dennis Connolly, Robert Kennedy, Tracy Collins, Bari Jonson and Gordon Jackson.

1970 *Egghead's Robot*
56 minute feature produced by Interfilm. Director: Milo Lewis. Producer: Cecil Musk. Script: Leif Saxon. Featuring: Keith Chegwin, Kathryn Dawe, Jeffrey Chegwin, Roy Kinnear, Richard Wattis and Patricia Routledge.

The Hoverbug
57 minute feature produced by Fanfare Films. Director: Jan Darnley-Smith. Producer: George H. Brown. Script: Michael Barnes. Featuring: Jill Riddick, John Trayhorn, Arthur Howard, Francis Attard and Michael Balfour.

Junket 89
56 minute feature produced by Balfour Films. Director: Peter Plummer. Producer: Carole K. Smith. Script: David Ash. Featuring: Stephen Brasset, Linda Robson, Pauline Quirke, Mario Renzullo, Richard Wilson and Christopher Benjamin. Guest Star: Gary Sobers.

Mr Horatio Knibbles
60 minute feature produced by Anvil Films. Director: Robert Hird. Producer: Hugh Stewart. Script: Peter Blackmore from an original story by Wally Bosco. Featuring: Lesley Roach, Gary Smith, Rachel Brennock, John Ash, Anthony Shepard, Freddie Jones and David Lodge.

Scramble!
61 minute feature produced by Eady-Barnes Productions. Director: David Eady. Producer and Script: Michael Gorell Barnes. Featuring: Ian Ramsey, Stuart Lock, Stephen Mallet, Luci Gorell Barnes, Robin Askwith, David Lodge, Graham Stark and Alfred Marks.

1971 *Blinker's Spy Spotter*
57 minute feature produced by Eyeline Films. Director: Jack Stephens. Producer: Harold Orton. Script: David Ash and Harold Orton. Featuring: David Spooner, Arthur Howard, Sally-Ann Marlowe, Martin Beaumont and Bernard Bresslaw.

Danger Point
56 minute feature produced by Damor Productions. Director and Producer: John Davis. Script: Pat Latham. Featuring: Veronica Purcell, Ian Gibson, Raymond Hoskins, John Hicks, John Poore, Bernard Lee, Sidney Tafler, Nicholas Parsons and Hattie Jacques.

The Johnstown Monster
54 minute feature produced by Sebastian Productions. Director and Script: Olaf Pooley. Producer: Gabrielle Beaumont. Featuring: Connor Brennan, Simon Tully, Rory Bailey and Kim McDonald.

The Magnificent 6½ (Series 3)
Six-part series totalling 89 minutes produced by Lion Pacesetter Productions. Director: Peter Graham Scott. Producer: Pat Green. Script: Pat Latham. Featuring: Paul Griffiths, Kay Skinner, Robert Richardson, Jody Lynn Schaller, Jimmy Baxter, Jane Coster and Steven Wallen.

Raising the Roof
54 minute feature produced by Michael Forlong Productions. Director and Producer: Michael Forlong. Script: Michael Forlong from an original story by Norman Taylor. Featuring: Patricia Davis, Michael Gould, Roy Kinnear, David Lodge and Patricia Hayes.

The Troublesome Double
57 minute feature produced by Interfilm. Director: Milo Lewis. Producer: Cecil Musk. Script: Leif Saxon. Featuring: Keith Chegwin, Richard Wattis, Josephine Tewson, Julie Collins, Tracy Collins, Johnny Vyvyan and Larry Martin.

1972 *Anoop and the Elephant*
55 minute feature produced by Anvil Films. Director: David Eady. Producer: Hugh Stewart. Script: Gerard Bryant and Owen Holder from an original story by Stephen Jenkins. Featuring: Anoop Singh, Linda Robson, Phil Daniels, George Roderick, Julian Orchard and Jimmy Edwards.

The Boy Who Turned Yellow
54 minute feature produced by Roger Cherrill Ltd. Director: Michael Powell. Producer and Script: Emeric Pressburger. Featuring: Mark Dightam, Lem Kitaj, Robert Eddison and Esmond Knight.

Forest Pony
Produced by Gaumont-British Instructional (running time unknown). Director: Philip Leacock. Producer: Edward Grossman. Script: Pat Latham. Featuring: Ivor Bowyer, Jill Gibbs, Michael Caborn and Geoffrey Keen.

Hide and Seek
60 minute feature produced by Eady-Barnes Productions. Director: David Eady. Producer and Script: Michael Gorell Barnes. Featuring: Peter Newby, Gary Kemp, Eileen Fletcher, Terence Morgan, Liz Fraser, Robin Askwith, Roy Dotrice, Alan Lake, David Lodge, Alfred Marks and Graham Stark.

I Had a Hippopotamus
Short animation produced by Dennis Hunt Productions (running time unknown). Director and Producer: Dennis Hunt.

Kadoyng
60 minute feature produced by Shand Pictures. Director: Ian Shand. Producer: Roy Simpson. Script: Leo Maguire. Featuring: Leo Maguire, Teresa Codling, Adrian Hall, Bill Owen and Jack Haig.

Mauro the Gypsy
57 minute feature produced by I.F.A. Director: Laurence Henson. Producers: Laurence Henson and Edward McConnell. Script: Pat Latham. Featuring: Graeme Greenhowe, Fiona Kennedy, Graeme Wilson, Victor Carin and Katie Gardiner.

Rangi's Catch
Eight-part serial totalling 128 minutes produced by Michael Forlong Productions. Director, Producer and Script: Michael Forlong. Featuring: Kate Forlong, Andrew Kerr, Tameura Morrison and Vernon Hill.

The Trouble with 2B
Six-part series totalling 103 minutes produced by Balfour Films. Director: Peter K. Smith. Producer: Carole K. Smith. Script: David Ash. Featuring: Richard Wilson, John Warner, Stephen Brassett, Peter Newby, Linda Robson, Pauline Quirke and John Blundell.

Wreck Raisers
55 minute feature produced by Eyeline Films. Director and Producer: Harold Orton. Script: Michael Gorell Barnes from an original story by Harold Orton. Featuring: Paul Hennen, Sally Anne Marlow, Martin Reynolds, Oswald Lindsay, Robin Baldwin, Ian Ramsey, Anthony Barnett and Michael Balfour.

1973 *Paganini Strikes Again*
59 minute feature produced by Interfilm. Director: Gerry O'Hara. Producer: Cyril Randell. Script: Michael Gorell Barnes. Featuring: Philip Bliss, Andrew Bowen, Julie Dawn Cole and John Arnatt.

The Sea Children
40 minute feature produced by Pan Productions. Director: David Andrews. Producer: Gordon Exelby. Script: Murray Smith. Featuring: Earl Younger, Lesley Dunlop, Stephen Garlick, Simon Turner and Perry Balfour.

The Zoo Robbery
64 minute feature produced by Cine-Lingual Studios. Directors, Producers and Script: John Black and Matt McCarthy. Featuring: Karen Lucas, Paul Gyngell, Denise Gyngell, Walter McKone and Luke Batchelor.

1974 *The Boy with Two Heads*
Seven-part serial totalling 116 minutes produced by Eyeline Films. Director: Jonathan Ingrams. Producer: Frank Godwin. Script: C. M. Pennington-Richards and Frank Godwin. Featuring: Spencer Plumridge, Leslie Ash, Lance Percival, Stanley Meadows, Louis Mansi and Clive Revill (voice).

The Camerons
56 minute feature produced by Roger Cherrill Ltd. Director: Freddie Wilson. Producer: Roger Cherrill. Script: Pat Latham. Featuring: Lois Marshall, Joseph McKenna and Paul Kelly.

The Firefighters
56 minute feature produced by Eyeline Films. Director: Jonathan Ingrams. Producer: Frank Godwin. Script: C. M. Pennington-Richards and Jonathan Ingrams from an original story by Rosamund Davies. Featuring: Simon Gipps-Kent, Sharon Fussey, Vincent Hall, Glyn Owen and Anne Stallybrass.

The Flying Sorcerer
52 minute feature produced by Anvil Films. Director: Harry Booth. Producer: Hugh Stewart. Script: Harry Booth and Leo Maguire. Featuring: Kim Burfield, Debbie Russ, John Bluthal, Bob Todd and Tim Barrett.

Professor Popper's Problems
Six-part serial totalling 90 minutes produced by Mersey Film Productions. Director: Gerry O'Hara. Producer: Roy Simpson. Script: Leo Maguire from an original story by Richard Loncraine. Featuring: Charlie Drake, Adam Richens, Debra Collins, Todd Carty and Milo O'Shea.

Smokey Joe's Revenge
57 minute feature produced by Pacesetter Productions. Director and Producer: Ronnie Spencer. Script: Pat Latham from an original story by Wally Bosco. Featuring: Kay Humblestone, Nicky Cox, Danny Martyne and Gareth Thomas.

What Next?
56 minute feature produced by Kingsgate Films. Director: Peter K. Smith. Producer: Carole K. Smith. Script: Derek Hill from an original story by Carole K. Smith and Derek Hill. Featuring: Peter Robinson, Perry Benson, Lynne White, Allan O'Keefe and Janet Davies.

Where's Johnny?
57 minute feature produced by Eady-Barnes Productions. Director: David Eady. Producer and Script: Michael Gorell Barnes. Featuring: Raymond Boal, Kim Clifford, Perry Benson, Graham Stark, Patrick Newell and George Innes.

1975 *Avalanche*
55 minute feature produced by Telstar Productions. Director: Frederic Goode. Producer: Harry Field. Script: Wally Bosco. Featuring: Michael Portman, David Ronder and David Dundas.

Hijack!
59 minute feature produced by Michael Forlong Productions. Director, Producer and Script: Michael Forlong. Featuring: Richard Morant, James Forlong, Sally Forlong and Tracy Peel.

The Hostages
59 minute feature produced by Eady-Barnes Productions. Director: David Eady. Producer and Script: Michael Gorell Barnes. Featuring: Steven Garlick, Jayne Collins, Luci Gorell Barnes, Peter Marshall, Ray Barrett and Robin Askwith.

Robin Hood Junior
61 minute feature produced by Brocket Productions. Director: Matt McCarthy. Producer: John Black. Script: Matt McCarthy and William Smethurst. Featuring: Keith Chegwin, Mandy Tulloch, Maurice Kaufmann and Andrew Sachs.

1976 *Echo of the Badlands*
56 minute feature produced by Little, King and Partners/Eady-Barnes Productions. Directors: David Eady and Tim King. Producer: Unknown. Script: Pat Latham from an original story by Bob King. Featuring: Clive Saunders, Fiona Saunders and David Nkema.

The Battle of Billy's Pond
56 minute feature produced by Mark Forstater Productions. Director: Harley Cokeliss. Producer: Mark Forstater. Script: Howard Thompson, Michael Abrams and Harley Cokeliss. Featuring: Ben Buckton, Andrew Ashby, Talfryn Thomas, Geoffrey Palmer, Miriam Margolyes and Linda Robson.

The Chiffy Kids (Series 1)
Six-part series totalling 109 minutes produced by Anvil Films. Director: David Bracknell. Producer: Hugh Stewart. Scripts: Pat Latham, Wally Bosco, Leo Maguire, Glyn Jones and Michael Gorell Barnes. Featuring: Luke Batchelor, Lesley Saunders, Philip Sadler, Wayne Kebell, Tracy Strand, Harry H. Corbett, Peggy Mount, Alfie Bass, Kenny Lynch, Irene Handl and Valerie Singleton.

Chimpmates (Series 1)
Six-part series totalling 90 minutes produced by Eyeline Films. Director and Producer: Harold Orton. Scripts: Pat Latham, Frank Godwin and Harold Orton. Featuring: Lynne Morgan, Dexter Fletcher, Philip da Costa, Godfrey James, Veronica Lang and Norman Bird.

Chimpmates (Series 2)
Seven-part series totalling 120 minutes produced by Eyeline Films. Director and Producer: Harold Orton. Scripts: Pat Latham, Frank Godwin and Harold Orton.

Featuring: Lynne Morgan, Marcus Evans, Philip da Costa, Godfrey James, Veronica Lang, Roy Kinnear and Graham Stark.

The 'Copter Kids
57 minute feature produced by Pacesetter Productions. Director and Producer: Ronald Spencer. Script: Pat Latham. Featuring: Sophie Neville, Jonathan Scott-Taylor, Paul Chambers, Kate Dorning, Sophie Ward and Derek Fowlds.

Fern, the Red Deer
58 minute feature produced by De Lane Lea. Director and Script: Jan Darnley-Smith. Producer: Adrian D. Worker. Featuring: Candida Prior, Craig McFarlane, Mark Eden, Diana Eden, John Leyton, Madeline Smith and Neil McCarthy.

The Man from Nowhere
57 minute feature produced by Charles Barker Films. Director: James Hill. Producer: Jean Wadlow. Script: John Tully. Featuring: Sarah Hollis-Andrews, Anthony McCaffery, Ronald Adam, Edmund Thomas and Gabrielle Hamilton.

Night Ferry
60 minute feature produced by Eady-Barnes Productions. Director: David Eady. Producer and Script: Michael Gorell Barnes. Featuring: Graham Fletcher, Engin Ashref, Jayne Tottman, Bernard Cribbins and Aubrey Morris

Nosey Dobson
59 minute feature produced by Pelicula Films. Director and Script: Michael Alexander. Producer: Cyril Randell. Featuring: Joe McKenna, James Morrison, Gary Rankin, Iain Andrew and Charles Kearney.

One Hour to Zero
55 minute feature produced by Charles Barker Films. Director: Jeremy Summers. Producer: Jean Wadlow. Script: John Tully. Featuring: Jayne Collins, Andrew Ashby, Toby Bridge and John Forgeham.

Sky Pirates
60 minute feature produced by Ansus Films. Director and Script: C. M. Pennington-Richards. Producer: Frank Godwin. Featuring: Adam Richens, Michael McVey, Sylvia O'Donnell, Bill Maynard and Jamie Foreman.

The Unbroken Arrow
Six-part serial totalling 122 minutes produced by Brocket Productions. Directors and Producers: Matt McCarthy and John Black. Script: William Smethurst. Featuring: Peter Demin, Sean Barrett, Amanda Jones, Mitchell Horner and Keith Jayne.

1977 *Blind Man's Bluff*

58 minute feature produced by Willis World Wide Productions. Director: Gerry O'Hara. Producer: Cyril Randell. Script: Pat Latham from an original story by Pat Latham and Benjamin Lee. Featuring: Debbie Ash, Chris Ellison, Terry Sue Pat, Patricia Fletcher, Steve Fletcher and Richard Parmentier.

The Glitterball

56 minute feature produced by Mark Forstater Productions. Director: Harley Cokeliss. Producer: Mark Forstater. Script: Howard Thompson from an original story by Howard Thompson and Harley Cokeliss. Featuring: Ben Buckton, Keith Jayne, Ron Pember, Marjorie Yates and Barry Jackson.

Seal Island

55 minute feature produced by Pacesetter Productions. Director and Producer: Ronnie Spencer. Script: Pat Latham from an original story by Henry Geddes. Featuring: Andrew Dove, Lisa Norris, Joey Clarke, Donald Douglas and John Savident.

1978 *Black Island*

57 minute feature produced by Kingsgate Films. Director: Ben Bolt. Producer: Carole K. Smith. Script: Peter K. Smith and William Humble. Featuring: Martin Murphy, Michael Salmon, Allan Surtees and Michael Elphick.

The Chiffy Kids (Series 2)

Six-part series totalling 120 minutes produced by Anvil Films. Director: David Bracknell. Producer: Hugh Stewart. Scripts: Pat Latham, Sheila Hodgson, David Bracknell, Wally Bosco and Michael Gorell Barnes. Featuring: Luke Batchelor, Lesley Saunders, Philip Sadler, Wayne Kebell, Tracy Strand, Naomi Campbell, Kenny Lynch, Eric Barker and Colin Jeavons.

Chimpmates (Series 3)

Six-part series totalling 90 minutes produced by Eyeline Films. Director and Producer: Harold Orton. Scripts: Pat Latham, Frank Godwin and Harold Orton. Featuring: Lynne Morgan, Marcus Evans, Philip da Costa and Lucy Griffiths.

Deep Waters

55 minute feature produced by Eyeline Films. Director: David Eady. Producer and Script: John V. Lemont. Featuring: Virginia Fiol, Luke Batchelor, Raymond Persoud, Paul Hillman and Jonathan Burn.

A Hitch in Time

57 minute feature produced by Eyeline Films. Director: Jan Darnley-Smith. Producer: Harold Orton. Script: T. E. B. Clarke. Featuring: Michael McVey, Pheona McLellan, Patrick Troughton, Jeff Rawle and Sorcha Cusack.

Mr Selkie
52 minute feature produced by Wadlow Grosvenor Productions. Director: Anthony Squire. Producer: Jean Wadlow. Script: John Tully, James Hill and Anthony Squire. Featuring: Peter Bayliss, Samantha Weyson, Clark Flanagan and Michael Mannion.

The Peregrine Hunters
56 minute feature produced by Mark Forstater Productions. Director: Cecil Petty. Producer: Mark Forstater. Script: Cecil Petty and Howard Thompson. Featuring: Julia Gambold, Gary Dundavin, Alex McCrindle, Barrie Cosney, Harvey Ashby and Sonia Fox.

Play Safe
10 minute short produced by Barrier Films. Director: David Eady. Producer: Antony Barrier. Script: Neil Ewart. Featuring: Bernard Cribbins (voice) and Brian Wilde (voice).

Sammy's Super T-Shirt
57 minute feature produced by Monument Films. Director: Jeremy Summers. Producer and Script: Frank Godwin. Featuring: Reggie Winch, Lawrie Mark, Richard Vernon, Julian Holloway and Patsy Rowlands.

1979 *Big Wheels and Sailor*
55 minute feature produced by Jeni Cole and Associates. Director: Doug Aitken. Producer: Jeni Cole. Script: Leo Eaton from an original story by Doug and Annie Aitken. Featuring: Nigel Humphries, Matthew Wright, Julian Curry, Sally Hall and Victoria Gibson.

The Boy Who Never Was
58 minute feature produced by Monument Productions. Director: Frank Godwin. Producers and Script: H. MacLeod Robertson and Frank Godwin. Featuring: Paul Atlantis, Gordon Hagen, Christian Bulloch and Melissa Wilkes.

Electric Eskimo
57 minute feature produced by Monument Productions. Director and Producer: Frank Godwin. Script: Frank Godwin and H. MacLeod Robertson. Featuring: Kris Emmerson, Debby Padbury and Ian Sears.

A Horse Called Jester
55 minute feature produced by Eyeline Films. Director: Ken Fairbairn. Producer: John V. Lemont. Script: Zita Dundas. Featuring: Sadie Frost, Michael Sampson, Mark Deamer and Heidi Smith.

1980 *Danger on Dartmoor*
59 minute feature produced by Eady-Barnes Productions. Director: David Eady. Producer: Michael Gorell Barnes. Script: Audrey Erskine-Lindop and Dudley Leslie. Featuring: Marcus Evans, Simon Henderson, Debby Salter, Sam Kydd, Patricia Hayes, Michael Ripper and Barry Foster.

High Rise Donkey
57 minute feature produced by Anvil Films. Director: Michael Forlong. Producer: Hugh Stewart. Script: T. E. B. Clarke. Featuring: Leigh Gotch, Wendy Cook, Linda Frith, Wilfrid Brambell, Roy Kinnear, Alfie Bass and Keith Chegwin.

The Mine and the Minotaur
59 minute feature produced by Sailorman Films. Director: David Cowling. Producer: Emma Cowling. Script: Christopher Penfold. Featuring: Adam Rhodes, William Sooker, Felicity Harrison, Charlie Cork and Janette Legge.

1981 *4D Special Agents*
60 minute feature produced by Eyeline Films. Director: Harold Orton. Producers: Harold Orton and Caroline Neame. Script: Harold Orton and Peter Frances-Browne. Featuring: Lisa East, Dexter Fletcher, Sarah Jenkins, Paul Medford and Philip Cook.

1982 *Friend or Foe*
70 minute feature produced by Elstree Productions. Director and Script: John Krish. Producer: Gordon Scott. Featuring: John Barden, Stacey Tendetter, John Holmes, Mark Luxford, Jasper Jacob and Robin Hayter.

1983 *Tightrope to Terror*
53 minute feature produced by the CFF. Director and Script: Bob Kellett. Producer: Gordon Scott. Featuring: Richard Owens, Rebecca Lacey, Eloise Ritchie, Stuart Wilde and Mark Jefferis.

AS THE CHILDREN'S FILM AND TELEVISION FOUNDATION (CFTF)

1983 *Break Out*
62 minute feature produced by Eyeline Film and Video. Director: Frank Godwin. Producers: Harold Orton and Frank Godwin. Script: Ranald Graham. Featuring: Simon Nash, Ian Bartholomew, John Hasler, David Jackson and John Bowler.

1984 *Gabrielle and the Doodleman*
55 minute feature produced by Elstree Productions. Director and Script: Francis Essex. Producer: Greg Smith. Featuring: Prudence Oliver, Matthew Kelly, Eric Sykes, Windsor Davies, Gareth Hunt, Lynsey De Paul and Bob Todd.

Haunters of the Deep
60 minute feature produced by Longbow Films. Director: Andrew Bogle. Producer: Gordon Scott. Script: Tony Attard, Andrew Bogle and Terry Barbour. Featuring: Gary Simmons, Amy Taylor, Andrew Keir, Bob Sherman and Peter Lovstrom.

Pop Pirates
58 minute feature produced by Welbeck Films. Director and Script: Jack Grossman. Producer: Ralph Thomas. Featuring: Stephen Bird, Spencer Chandler, P. P. Arnold, Roger Daltrey and Jon Finch.

1985 *Exploits at West Poley*
63 minute feature produced by the CFTF. Director: Diarmuid Lawrence. Producer: Pamela Lonsdale. Script: James Andrew Hall. Featuring: Anthony Bale, Brenda Fricker, Charlie Condou, Jonathan Adams and Sean Bean.

Out of the Darkness
68 minute feature produced by the CFTF. Director and Script: John Krish. Producer: Gordon Scott. Featuring: Gary Halliday, Michael Flowers, Emma Ingham, Anthony Winder, Michael Carter, Eric Mason, Charlotte Mitchell and Jenny Tarren.

Terry on the Fence
70 minute feature produced by Eyeline Films. Director and Script: Frank Godwin. Producer: Harold Orton. Featuring: Jack McNicholl, Neville Watson, Tracey Ann Morris, Jon Croft, Susan Jameson and Martin Fisk.

OTHER OUTPUT

The Foundation produced its own newsreel specifically for children entitled *Our Club Magazine*, with sixteen releases from 1952 to 1956. A number of travelogues were also made in the 1950s.

The Foundation occasionally imported foreign-language features that they redubbed into English. These included *Das Geheimnisvolle Wrack/The Mysterious Wreck* (East Germany 1954), *Dobrodružství na Zlaté zátoce/The Big Fish* (Czechoslovakia 1955), *Négyen az Árban/Danger on the Danube* (Hungary 1961), *Dobro Pozhalovat, ili Postoronnim vkhod Vospreshchyon/No Holiday for Inochkin* (USSR 1964), *Táňa a Dva pistolníci/The Brno Trail* (Czechoslovakia 1967), *Ptitsi Dolitat do Nas/Birds Fly to Nas* (Bulgaria 1971), *Vuk Samotnjak/The Lone Wolf* (Yugoslavia 1972) and *Šest medvědů s Cibulkou/Six Bears and a Clown* (Yugoslavia 1972). There were undoubtedly others but it has not been possible to verify them. *Kekec* (Yugoslavia 1951) was screened with an English-language voiceover narration by Maurice Denham. *Dressura/The Lion Tamer* (1970) was an animated Bulgarian short film distributed by the CFF.

They also imported two Australian films: *They Found a Cave* (1962) – a 61 minute feature produced by Visatone Island Pictures – and *The Intruders* (1969), the only feature film produced as an offshoot from the popular Australian television series *Skippy* (1967–).

The CFF produced regular teaser compilations during the first half of the 1970s where a host would introduce a series of short clips from forthcoming attractions. This included items such as *Ed Stewart Introduces* (1970), *Michael Rodd Introduces* (1975) and *Keith Chegwin Introduces* (1978). Sometimes clips were arranged thematically as with *Crime Doesn't Pay* (1970) introduced by David Lodge and *Don't Make me Laugh* (1970) introduced by Richard Attenborough.

Several basic trailers were made for specific films and to advertise the Foundation's overall output, as well as the Saturday clubs in general, such as *Super Saturday* (1972), *Saturday Lovely Saturday* (1972), *Always on Saturday* (1972), *Happy Days* (1972), *Saturday Special* (1973) and *Summer Holiday* (1973).

In 1972 the CFF re-released two films made much earlier by Rank. These were *The Lone Climber* directed by William Hammond and *The Mysterious Poacher* directed by Don Chaffey. Both were scripted by Pat Latham and produced by Gaumont-British Instructional for Rank's Children's Entertainment Films (CEF) unit run by Mary Field. They were shot on location in Austria with local casts. In a similar vein, it also re-released the first Rank feature film made for children, *Bush Christmas* (1947), which was written, produced and directed by Ralph Smart on location in Australia.

In 1983 the CFF released a 90 minute feature film entitled *Professor Potter's Magic Potions*, which was a re-edit of the 1972 six-part series *The Trouble with 2B* featuring Richard Wilson. The original series ran to 103 minutes.

From 1987 the CFTF was involved in funding the early development and script stage of a number of projects that were then realised by other companies. This resulted in the production of four feature films for cinema release: *Just Ask for Diamond* (1988); *Danny, Champion of the World* (1989); *My Friend Walter* (1992); and *An Angel in May* (2002). It also led to several television series: *The Torch* (1992); *The Borrowers* (1992); *The Queen's Nose* (1995–2003); *The Magician's House* (1999–2000); and *Gypsy Girl* (2001).

I have been unable to verify one title credited to the Foundation in the BFI records; this is *Trapped in the Dungeons* (1957).

Appendix 2
Further Reading

Agajanian, Rowana, 'Just for Kids?: Saturday Morning Cinema and Britain's Children's Film Foundation in the 1960s', *Historical Journal of Film, Radio and Television* vol. 18 no. 3 (1998).

Bazalgette, Cary and David Buckingham (eds), *In Front of the Children: Screen Entertainment for the Young* (London: BFI, 1995).

Buckingham, David, *Moving Images: Understanding Children's Emotional Responses to Television* (Manchester: Manchester University Press, 1996).

Buckingham, David, Hannah Davies, Ken Jones and Peter Kelly, *Children's Television in Britain: History, Discourse and Policy* (London: BFI, 1999).

Eyles, Allen, *ABC: The First Name in Entertainment* (London: BFI, 1993).

Eyles, Allen, *Gaumont British Cinemas* (London: BFI, 1996).

Field, Mary, *Good Company: The Story of the Children's Entertainment Film Movement in Great Britain, 1943–50* (London: Longman, 1952).

Field, Mary, *Children and Films: A Study of Boys and Girls in the Cinema* (Dunfermline: Carnegie UK Trust, 1954).

Field, Mary, 'The Beginnings', *Journal of the Society of Film and Television Arts* vol. 18 (Winter 1964–5).

Geddes, Henry, 'The Present and the Future', *Journal of the Society of Film and Television Arts* vol. 18 (Winter 1964–5).

Goldstein, Ruth M. and Edith Zornow, *The Screen Image of Youth: Movies about Children and Adolescents* (Metuchen, NJ: Scarecrow Press, 1980).

Home, Anna, *Into the Box of Delights: A History of Children's Television* (London: BBC Books, 1993).

James, Allison, Chris Jenks and Alan Prout, *Theorizing Childhood* (Cambridge: Polity, 1998).

Kemp, Gary, *I Know This Much* (London: 4th Estate, 2009).

Lusted, David (ed.), *Kidstuff: Childhood and the Cinema* (London: BFI, 1979).

Macnab, Geoffrey, *J. Arthur Rank and the British Film Industry* (London and New York: Routledge, 1993).

Mayer, J. P., *The Sociology of Film* (London: Faber and Faber, 1946).

Messenger Davies, Máire, 'Dear BBC': *Children, Television Storytelling and the Public Sphere* (Cambridge: Cambridge University Press, 2001).
Miller, Emanuel, *Report on the Bernstein Children's Film Questionnaire* (London: Granada, 1947).
Musgrave, Andrew, *Children in Films* (London: CreateSpace, 2013).
Parnaby, M. and M. Woodhouse, *Children's Cinema Clubs Report* (London: BFI, 1947).
Pecora, Norma, John P. Murray and Ellen Ann Wartella (eds), *Children and Television: Fifty Years of Research* (London: Routledge, 2006).
Powell, Michael, *Million-Dollar Movie* (London: Heinemann, 1992).
Richards, Jeffrey, *The Age of the Dream Palace: Cinema and Society in Britain 1930–1939* (London: Routledge and Kegan Paul, 1984).
Shail, Robert, *British Film Directors: A Critical Guide* (Edinburgh: Edinburgh University Press, 2007).
Sinyard, Neil, *Children in the Movies* (London: B. T. Batsford, 1992).
Staples, Terry, *All Pals Together: The Story of Children's Cinema* (Edinburgh: Edinburgh University Press, 1997).
Trevelyan, John, 'The Censor Looks at Children's Films', *Journal of the Society of Film and Television Arts* vol. 18 (Winter 1964–5).
Wheare, K. C., *Report of the Departmental Committee on Cinema and Children* (London: HMSO, 1950).
Whitaker, Lynn (ed.), *The Children's Media Yearbook 2013* (London: The Children's Media Foundation, 2013).
Whitaker, Lynn (ed.), *The Children's Media Yearbook 2014* (London: The Children's Media Foundation, 2014).
Wojcik-Andrews, Ian, *Children's Films: History, Ideology, Pedagogy, Theory* (New York and London: Garland, 2000).

See also the following publications by the Children's Film Foundation:
Annual Reports 1952, 1953 and *1955*
Report on Work Done 1951–1960
Progress Report: The CFF in the Sixties (1964)
Saturday Morning Cinema: A Report of the CFF in the Sixties with a Full Catalogue of CFF Films (1967)
Twenty-five Years of Children's Films (1969)
Young Cinema (1972 and 1976)

And by the Children's Film and Television Foundation:
Catalogue and Index of Films (1985)

Appendix 3
The Cinemas

During the course of the surveys for Chapter 4 of this study, many of the respondents referred to specific cinemas where they had attended Saturday morning film clubs. The following list of cinemas is drawn from those recollections only and is not a definitive list of all cinemas hosting clubs which would, of course, be enormous. Some information was incomplete as respondents were unable to recall exact geographical locations but I have compiled the data as it stands. It is offered as a reference point for the scholar and student and for the interest, nostalgic or otherwise, of general readers. There is a bias towards Wales as that is where many of the respondents grew up but the list does show the huge geographical coverage achieved by the clubs across the UK. Although the major chains like ABC and Rank (Odeon; Gaumont) are well represented, there are a remarkable number of independent venues too. London cinemas are not grouped together but listed under the specific district or area of London.

Aberdare: Palace, Hirwaun
Ammanford: Palace
Barrow-in-Furnace: ABC Ritz; Astra; Rank Coliseum; Palace
Barry: Theatre Royal
Bath: Odeon
Belfast: Ambassador; Willowfield; Castle; Picturedrome; ABC Strand
Bexleyheath: Regal
Birmingham: Kings Norton Cinema
Bolton: Odeon
Brighton: ABC Astoria
Bristol: Odeon Kingswood; Ritz, Brislington; ABC Vandyck, Fishponds; Gaiety; Picture House, Knowle; Broadway, Filwood Park
Cardiff: Capitol; Monico, Rhiwbina; Gaiety, Roath
Chippenham: Palace
Cleckheaton, West Yorkshire: Palace
Colchester: ABC Playhouse
Cradley Heath, West Midlands: Royal
Doncaster: Gaumont
Ealing, London: Forum
Edinburgh: ABC Ritz, Canonmills
Epsom: Granada
Forest Gate, London: Odeon
Forest Hill, London: ABC Capitol
Glasgow: White Elephant, Embassy & Waverley, all in Shawlands; Seamore & Blythswood, both in Maryhill

Hammersmith, London: ABC
Hampstead, London: Odeon
Hebden Bridge, Yorkshire: Picture House
Hereford: ABC
Heswall, the Wirral: Kings
Hornchurch: Odeon
Huddersfield: ABC
Kingston upon Thames, London: Granada; Odeon; ABC Regal
Leyton, London: Gaumont (formerly the Savoy and latterly the Odeon)
Lewisham, London: Odeon
Liverpool: Regal, Norris Green
Llanelli: Odeon (also known as the Classic, the Classic Entertainment Centre and the Llanelli Entertainment Centre)
Long Eaton, Derbyshire: Palace
Manchester: ABC Ardwick (formerly the Apollo Theatre); ABC Blackley
Manor Park, East London: ABC Coronation
Neath: Circle; Windsor
Newcastle upon Tyne: Apollo, Byker
Newport: Odeon
Newtown: Regent
Northampton: ABC
Norwich: ABC
Nottingham: Essoldo, Beeston; Savoy, Derby Road
Pembroke: Haggar's
Pembroke Dock: Palace
Plymouth: The Drake (Odeon)
Port Talbot: Odeon; Plaza
Richmond upon Thames, London: ABC
Rochester: Odeon
Romford: Odeon
Southsea: Odeon
Spennymoor, County Durham: Tivoli
Swansea: Odeon Kingsway; Odeon Sketty; Carlton; Plaza; Castle; Welfare; Rialto, Wind Street; Lido, Gorseinon (formerly the Palace); Albert Hall; Civic Centre, Bonymaen
Wandsworth, London: Palace
Westcliff-on-Sea: Cannon
Weston-super-Mare: Odeon
Worthing: Odeon

Index

Page numbers in *italic* denote illustrations; those in **bold** indicate detailed analysis; *n* = endnote.